LIFE IS RELIGION

ESSAYS IN HONOUR OF H. EVAN RUNNER

With contributions from Bernard Zylstra, Theodore Plantinga,
Johan van der Hoeven, Albert M. Wolters, Henry Vander Goot,
Robert D. Knudsen, Gordon J. Spykman, *and Others*

cantaroinstitute.org

Life is Religion: Essays in Honour of H. Evan Runner.
Published by Paideia Press, a publishing imprint of the
Cántaro Institute, 3248 Twenty-First St., Jordan
Station, ON L0R 1S0

Book design by Paul Aurich

Library & Archives Canada
ISBN 978-1-998711-08-6

Printed in China

Table of Contents

Acknowledgments

A SPECIAL WORD OF APPRECIATION and thanks is due several persons who contributed significantly to this volume. I wish to mention Gordon Spykman of the Department of Religion and Theology at Calvin College and Peter DeVos, Dean of the Faculty, Calvin College. These two persons joined me in initiating this honorary volume, and have followed through with enthusiasm, support, and consultation during the course of the book's preparation.

A very special word of acknowledgment goes to Glenn Andreas of Pella, Iowa. Glenn Andreas is a close personal friend of Evan Runner, whose association goes back to the years they spent together as students several decades ago at Wheaton College. Glenn Andreas has distinguished himself as a Christian business person with remarkable Reformed instinct. By word, advice, and monetary deed, he has supported Reformed Christian causes wherever he saw them represented. Specifically with respect to this volume, I owe Glenn a word of many thanks for his insightful advice on the format and layout of the manuscript as a whole. Finally, without his generous financial help this book could not have appeared in the fine form in which it finally came from the press.

John Hultink, president and owner of Paideia Press of St. Catharines, Ontario, deserves high praise for the efforts and enthusiasm he has shown for this project. John encouraged my efforts with the same gusto which his friends have noted in whatever John has taken upon himself to do. A dedicated student of Evan Runner, John Hultink has gone out of his way to make this project worthy of the career it is presented to honor. Finally, though marketability factors would move most publishers to steer clear of a project such as this, John Hultink has again displayed the serious, primary intention of Paideia Press to serve the cause of the Reformed faith in North America by the dissemination of literature with specifically Reformed vision.

The skilled professional advice and consultation of Theodore Plantinga deserves notice. On technical aspects having to do with layout and specifications for the volume as well as on providing a copy edited version of the book as a whole, Ted Plantinga's help was indispensable. His generosity with time taken out of a busy schedule bespeaks the deep inner devotion with which he is committed to the work Evan Runner has begun among us. Moreover, the ease and comprehensive accuracy with which Ted Plantinga has described Evan Runner's contribution to Reformed faith and thought in his introductory essay is greatly appreciated.

Finally, a word of thanks to the many contributors is in order. These contributors are not primarily, if at all, Evan Runner's students and followers, but colleagues working in many institutions in North America and Europe. Their contributions are expressions of honor and respect for one at whose side they have worked professionally. It is on the occasion of Evan Runner's retirement from the faculty of Calvin College after 30 years of service that this token of appreciation is offered by these colleagues. In this respect, then, this volume distinguishes itself from *Hearing and Doing: Philosophical Essays dedicated to H. Evan Runner,* a collection of articles presented to him on his 60th birthday exclusively by his students and followers.

By sheer commitment of time and energy to the production of good essays, Evan Runner's colleagues show their deep respect for him. Moreover, by the express mention of his views several essayists have shown how seriously they have taken him in their work, even if sometimes respectfully to disagree. Finally, by the utilization in their

scholarly pursuits of Evan Runner's vision as their own, the majority of authors have enhanced even more its tribute to him. I thank them all for their eagerness to contribute and for the worth of what they have finally produced.

Henry Vander Goot, Editor
Grand Rapids, Michigan
Spring Semester, 1981

H. Evan Runner: An Assessment of His Mission

Introduction

It is too early to assess the full significance of the work of H. Evan Runner. However, the contours of the significance of his mission can today be sketched in broad outline. In this preface I will present my personal sketch.

The heart of Runner's mission consists of an attempt to contribute to the spiritual reformation of evangelical Protestantism in the United States and Canada in the conviction that wholehearted obedience to the Word of God on the part of a significant segment of God's people is an indispensable condition not only for the continued presence of Biblical religion in these lands but also for the renewal of North American culture, which is disintegrating under the impact of humanist materialism in its liberal, pragmatic form. Runner's work at reformation—his reformational mission—was directed primarily toward three major interrelated concerns.

In the first place, Evan Runner wanted to contribute to a new consciousness of the relation between the revelation of the Scriptures and the civilization of the West, specifically in the context of the culture of the United States. In the second place, he pressed for a distinctly new way in which Christians should attempt to help shape the culture and the society which they share with humanists in the modern age. This new way consists of organized communal witness and action on the part of Christians outside the realm of the institutional church. Finally, Runner attempted to develop a new Christian mind which he considered essential for radical Christian leadership in the culturally decisive spheres of modern society. I will comment briefly on each facet of this mission. Then I will turn to the context within which Runner attempted to realize his mission. In conclusion, I will state what I think his work means for our common future. It should be kept in mind that what I am writing here is based on my close association with Runner since the early 1950s.

Biblical Religion and the Culture of the West

The overriding concern which Runner addressed is the relation between Biblical religion and the civilization of the West. Human life, he argued, in its individual, societal, cultural, and civilizational scope, is obedient or disobedient response to God's revelation in creation, in Christ, and in the Holy Scriptures. Obedience to that revelation leads to blessing in human life; disobedience leads to disintegration. The magnitude of this concern led Runner again and again to focus on critical junctures in the history of the West: the introduction of the Christian religion in the Mediterranean basin at the beginning of our era; the synthesis of Graeco-Roman culture and Christianity; the arrested sixteenth-century Reformation; and the efforts at a new reformation in the post-Enlightenment period, notably the efforts of Guillaume Groen van Prinsterer, historian and political reformer, Abraham Kuyper, church reformer and shaper of modern Dutch society, and Herman Dooyeweerd, legal thinker and Christian philosopher.

Runner viewed Christianity and Greek culture as the two main spiritual forces in the birth and early development of western civilization. His interpretation here runs parallel to the views of neoclassical philosophers like Eric Voegelin and George Grant, for whom the synthesis of Greek thought and the revelation of the Bible is the single sustaining foundation for human life in the West. For Runner, this initial synthesis, intellectually shaped in the theology of the early Church Fathers and societally embodied in the symbiosis of the Roman Empire and the Roman Church, constitutes the fundamental error in the history of early Christendom, the negative consequences of which have never been overcome. In Runner's view this synthesis was an attempt to fuse two incompatible elements—the worldview and philosophy of the Greeks with the revelation of the Scriptures—which would inevitably lead to the destruction of the integral, all-encompassing nature of Biblical religion. The disintegrating impact of this synthesis evidenced itself quickly in the way human nature was viewed in the early church and in the Middle Ages as a composite of a material body and a spiritual soul; in the way human society was structured in terms of a natural element organized by the temporal state and a spiritual element embodied in the Roman Church; and in the way human theoretical activity was allocated to two distinct domains, that of philosophy, where natural reason is the guide, and that of theology, where divine revelation is the guide. Any effort at the reformation of Christianity, in Runner's view, will have to come to grips with this initial synthesis.

The dialectical synthesis of the major forms of Greek thought with Biblical revelation ultimately led to the split in human existence between "the natural life" and "the spiritual life" in the late Middle Ages. This split gave birth to three new spiritual forces in the West: the Renaissance, which declared the independence of natural life from divine revelation; the Reformation, which was an attempt to return to the radical and all-encompassing authority of divine revelation but which quickly lost its cultural and societal impact because of the revival of rationalism in Protestant scholasticism; and the Counter-reformation, which was the answer of the Roman Church to both Renaissance and Reformation and which contributed to the preeminence of the Roman Church in the new nation-states of southern Europe and the colonial regimes in South and Central America. Runner interprets the history of the modern age as the history of the gradual victory of the spirit of the Renaissance, which unveils itself as the permanent revolution, that is, the revolt of autonomous man against the divine order for human existence. For two centuries the spiritual forces of the Reformation and the Counter-reformation contained the impact of the new Renaissance religion of the autonomy of human personality upon the culture and the society of the West. But after the eighteenth-century Enlightenment, the new religion gradually began to shape both the cultural and material aspirations of western man and the societal structures needed to realize those aspirations. The historical turning point here was the French Revolution. In the nineteenth-century the new religion of autonomous human personality persistently eroded the Christian ethic which had guided ordinary men and women in their concrete daily life. The Christian churches increasingly lost their hold on the mass populations, especially in the industrialized metropolitan centers of western Europe and North America.

Runner's interpretation of the history of the West led him to struggle with a second major concern: is it possible to recover the integrality of the religion of the Bible in the modern age? Can western Christianity experience a new reformation? Can we move from a new consciousness of the spiritual predicament of the West to new forms of authentically Biblical witness and cultural action in a society whose structures reflect the autonomy of man and channel the acquisition of material abundance? Or, is the West, once set upon a path determined by Renaissance humanism, beyond responsible human intervention? Are not Jacques Ellul and George Grant correct in their diagnosis that the West is subject to a technological fate which we cannot change? And even if one rejects the notion of fate, isn't Marx correct in his indictment that the Christian church cannot assume the role of historical change in advanced capitalist societies

4

because only the proletariat, which operates the technological means of production, can effectuate radical change?

Runner's answer to questions like these has always been simple. The Word of the gospel is a power that can change the direction in the lives of individual persons but also the direction in the existence of nations, cultures, societies, and civilizations. It is this belief in the power of the Word of God to give shape to our individual and collective lives that made Runner the kind of person he is. The Word of God, which is the sword of the Spirit, transcends every human situation, subjects every situation to the authority of the risen Lord, and thus can change every situation. Subjection to the Word of God is thus the first requisite for personal and communal reformation.

The fundamental weakness of Christianity in the modern age is, according to Runner, its acceptance of the confinement of religion to the so-called spiritual domains of the church, family, and private morality. This acceptance implies an acquiescence in the religious neutrality of the remaining spheres of life, notably the public realm. Concretely, however, it means that Christians accept the dominance of humanism in these realms and their accommodation to one of the above-mentioned ideologies, the particular choice often being dependent upon their place in the socioeconomic constellation. But Christians have largely surrendered the agenda—the set of priorities of things to be done—in politics, culture, the media, production, and the schools to the secular modernizers, hurrying along at one speed or another.

Runner's model for a new strategy was based on an analysis of the turnabout in Holland since the 1870s, when the concerted political action of the Calvinists and the Roman Catholics led to the demise of the conservative political party, the diminution of the impact of the liberal party, the stemming of the tide of radical socialism, and the constructive reordering of the public realm so that both humanists and Christians were accorded an equal opportunity in the shaping of

Dutch society subject to the rules of the democratic process. This turnabout led to the establishment of Christian political parties, national Christian school systems, and social welfare institutions paid out of public funds, Christian trade union movements, vigorous involvements of Christians in journalism, etc.

The third facet of Runner's mission flows immediately out of the foregoing. Integral Christian cultural witness and action requires the formation of new leadership cadres on the basis of a Biblically based worldview and philosophy. Runner knew that at this point the conflict with the dominant mind in the West would probably be the most acute since the dogma of the religious neutrality of philosophy and science lies at the foundation of the whole of western civilization. On this point traditional Christianity, in both its Roman Catholic and Protestant forms, and humanism had achieved agreement. The early synthesis between Greek thought and Christian theology had accorded philosophy a relative autonomy with respect to revelation. The dissolution of this synthesis gave birth to modern philosophy and science, in which any connection with the authority of revelation was viewed as a remnant of the dark ages. In the Enlightenment such connections were entirely severed, and the very progress of the human race was considered dependent upon the radical secularization of the scientific enterprise and its application in technological innovation and industrial modernization.

The relation of faith and reason, Biblical worldview and modern science, theology and philosophy, occupied Runner's attention from the first year of his undergraduate studies at Wheaton College in the early thirties. His pursuit of a more adequate account of the relation between revelation and the academic enterprise led him to study with Cornelius Van Til at Westminster Theological Seminary in Philadelphia, Klaas Schilder at the Reformed Theological School in Kampen, and finally, after a stint with Werner Jaeger at Harvard, to Vollenhoven and Dooyeweerd at the Free University in Amsterdam.

The five years of study under Vollenhoven's tutelage leading to the completion in 1951 of a dissertation on the development of Aristotle's thought were decisive in Runner's life. This period of study forced him not only to surrender the dogma of the religious neutrality of philosophy and science, but also to come to grips with the two prior issues which I have discussed: the much broader question of the relation between Biblical religion and the civilization of the West, and the possibility of a recovery of integrally Biblical witness and action in a culture dominated by humanism. Runner had gradually come to the realization that the efforts of Vollenhoven and Dooyeweerd to bring the Word of God to bear upon the philosophic enterprise itself was part of a much more encompassing endeavor at reformation. He began to see that the theoretical problems which had occupied his attention for nearly two decades could only be resolved satisfactorily in terms of a greater drama: the salvation which the gospel brings about in the lives of ordinary men and women, caught up in the concrete struggle for meaningful existence in the cultures and societies on both sides of the Atlantic Ocean.

The Strategy of Christian Organizations

It is one thing to establish goals aimed at reforming a segment of the Christian church. It is quite another to accomplish them. Numerous factors play a role here, such as the willingness of God's people to listen to His Word, the clarity of the message preached, the abilities and personality of the reformer, his base of operation, and the possibilities for change in the culture and the society within which the church lives.

Runner's base of operation for thirty years has been the department of philosophy at Calvin College and Seminary in Grand Rapids, Michigan, which, in 1951, was the only post-secondary educational institution in the Christian Reformed Church. I believe that this was probably the only base which Runner could have used to

7

accomplish what he did achieve. But I am also of the conviction that this base was far too narrow for his mission to contribute to the spiritual reformation of evangelical Protestantism in the United States and Canada.

In order to understand the potentials as well as the limits of Runner's base of operation, it is necessary to have a look at the Christian Reformed Church. This denomination has its origin in the second major migration of Dutch Calvinists to North America. The first migration took place in the seventeenth-century; this wave resulted in what today is called the Reformed Church of America. The second one began in the 1840s, as a result of both religious and economic factors. The Dutch government had taken repressive measures against the Secession from the State Church in 1834, and many Seceders, under the leadership of pastors Van Raalte and Scholte, settled in western Michigan and Iowa to seek religious freedom. Upon arrival, they first joined the older Reformed Church but, finding this denomination spiritually lax, a number of them went on their own in 1857 to form the Christian Reformed Church. The third major migration of Dutch Calvinists took place between 1947 and 1960, primarily to Canada, but also to the United States, Australia and New Zealand. It is important to take note of the fact that the Christian Reformed Church became the home of three distinct groups: the Seceders of 1834, whose spirituality was largely pietist; the emigrants who entered the United States (and, in small numbers, Canada) between 1880 and 1930, and whose worldview was highly influenced by the reformed vision of Abraham Kuyper; and the thousands who settled in Canada after the Second World War, and who were also still mainly Kuyperian in outlook.

The migration of Calvinists from Holland to the United States finds its cultural and societal parallels in the migration of Scandinavian Lutherans, German Anabaptists, Polish and Russian Jews, Italian and Irish Catholics, etc. Most of these groups were able to maintain a kind of identity, but nonetheless an identity shaped and delimited by the overarching liberal humanism that dominated American culture.

America has always had its own version of the left-center-right dialectic of humanism, but the extremes of Edmund Burke's conservatism and Rousseau's radicalism never found many adherents. The centrist option of a "middling" liberalism, first in its laissez-faire Lockean sense and later in its welfare-state Keynesian sense, gave the United States an ideological cohesion that helps explain its remarkable political stability for two centuries.

But it should be clearly kept in mind that the various immigrant groups that entered the United States in ever increasing numbers between 1820 and 1920—nearly thirty-five million—had to make a fundamental adjustment. After initial recalcitrance, they were forced to accept liberalism—or "conservatism" in today's terminology—as the source of their public values. This was true of both Christians and socialists. The two major political parties, the public schools, the labor unions, the newspapers; and later radio and television, were the instruments for the "Americanization" of the new arrivals.

This meant that the distinct forms of spirituality which had shaped the cultural and societal experience of the various religious groups in Europe underwent a fundamental transformation. These forms of spirituality could no longer serve as a source for the norms and values in the public realm; their impact was limited to the private lifestyles of their adherents in home and church. This process of Americanization—"modernization"—is poignantly described in the novels of Bashevis Singer with reference to Polish Jews who had to find their way in New York. Authentic Jewish spirituality cannot exist in America except in the limits of ethnicity.

The same can be said of the Dutch Calvinists who settled in the United States. The best example of their Americanization can be found in the adjustment of the Kuyperians who came around the turn of the century. They introduced the issues which Kuyper had

raised in Holland: the relation between Christianity and modern culture, the relation between church and state, and the channels of
Christian witness outside the realm of the church. Kuyper's Stone
Lectures, presented at Princeton University in 1898, gave them a
clear statement of the issues. Their influence was not negligible. Partly because of their presence, the members of the Christian Reformed
Church became the most active supporters of Christian schools in
the United States outside of the Roman Catholic Church. And again,
partly because of them, Calvin College developed into one of the
most significant intellectual centers of evangelical Protestantism.

But in the long run the Kuyperians were forced to accept the
public ideology of liberalism. By and large, the Christian schools,
still avidly supported by members of the Christian Reformed Church,
are not viewed as a repudiation of the monopoly of liberal humanism
in the public realm but as a spiritually and morally protective ram-
part against the evils of the outside world. Instead of being an expression of Calvinian pluralist democracy in the public realm, they rein-
force the ethnic cohesion of Dutch reformed people in the American
melting pot.

This adjustment to the dominant cultural milieu has had another impact on the Christian Reformed Church. The more outstanding
theological leaders were quickly alienated from the denomination
itself. This is evident not only in the continued tension between the
grassroots membership and the intellectuals in the denomination,
but also in the fact that several of its outstanding thinkers made their
mark *outside of* the denomination: Geerhardus Vos left for Princeton
in the 1890s; Herman Hoeksema was expelled in 1924; and Cornelius Van Til taught at Westminster since its founding in 1929.

The interpreter of Runner's work is clearly confronted with a
number of interesting questions. Runner is of Irish Presbyterian
stock, whose forebears from Ulster settled in rural Pennsylvania
just outside of Philadelphia. Runner grew up in the mainline

northern Presbyterian church until the secession of the Orthodox Presbyterian Church in the 1930s. How could he ever maintain himself as an "outsider" in the intellectual center of the Christian Reformed Church? It is one of the paradoxes of the Christian Reformed Church that it provided Runner with a platform for his work while it had no room for the scholars mentioned above, who grew up within its own bosom.

At the same time, the question must be asked whether the paradox is present on Runner's side as well? Was he able to transcend the limits of the Christian Reformed Church in realizing his goals? What kind of strategies were available to him within this basis of operation: a professorship in philosophy in a small evangelical college owned and operated by a largely ethnically introvert denomination with then just over a hundred thousand members?

The question of a viable strategy was complicated by additional problems. Runner's professorship at Calvin was the first regular position he had held in his life. Though he was already thirty-five years old when he assumed this position, he had spent about half of those years in college and university as a student in classics, theology, and philosophy. He had little organizational experience. Though he later proved to be a good strategist and a keen tactician, he was not particularly tactful, able to handle delicate situations with studied care. And tact was necessary, as is illustrated by the simple fact that his colleagues in the philosophy department had not recommended his appointment. That he was nonetheless given the post was due to a quite courageous and unusual decision on the part of the Calvin Board of Trustees, which felt that someone from the Vollenhoven-Dooyeweerd school of thought should join the faculty. And then there was something distinctly un-American about Runner. He was not adept at things at which Americans are adept, like driving a car. (Ellen, his Dutch wife, served as a help meet in this and many other matters!)

11

In spite of these obstacles, Runner pursued a clear strategy from the outset. I have argued above that Runner, in his attempt to contribute to the spiritual reformation of evangelical Protestantism, considered these matters essential: a new understanding of the relation between Christianity and western civilization; a new way in which Christians should attempt to shape American culture; and the development of a new Christian mind. His strategy was an attempt to meet these essentials within the severe restrictions of his base of operation.

In order to contribute to a new understanding of Christianity and culture, Runner did two things. At carefully chosen moments during his entire career he presented a series of lectures to audiences outside of his classroom where he dealt with the meaning of current issues in the light of the underlying movement of spirits in our culture. The first of these was *"Het roer om!"*—"Rudder Hard Over!"—in 1953; the last one "On Being Anti-Revolutionary and Christian-Historical at the Cutting Edge of History," presented in 1979 at the centennial of the Anti-revolutionary Party in Holland, a year before its fusion with the other major Christian political parties into the Christian Democratic Party. Taken together, these speeches constitute Runner's manifesto to orthodox Christianity.

However, these speeches were isolated clarion calls to reformation which Runner was not able to follow through since he lacked a power base in the church, in politics, or in the media. The only power base he had was his professorship at Calvin. This he used to do something else. He organized the Groen van Prinsterer Society—popularly known as the Groen Club—at Calvin in 1953. Formally, it was simply a student club. Substantively, it was Runner's instrument in molding students into a new consciousness of their task in American and Canadian society. He needed a place where he could systematically introduce students to issues outside of philosophy, such as:

> The question of who the Puritans were, the meaning of the Enlightenment, its influence in America, the basic ideas of the Declaration of Independence and the Constitution, the nature of Scholasticism, particularly as manifested in Reformed theology, the concept of natural law, the religious ground-motives that have successively given order to the experience of Western man, the origins of capitalism, the rise of the labor movement, and so on and so forth. *(Hearing and Doing: Philosophical Essays Dedicated to H. Evan Runner* [Toronto: Wedge, 1979], p. 351.)

The fluctuating membership of the Groen Club consisted largely of the sons—very few daughters!—of immigrant families that had settled in Canada after the last world war. Some represented the earlier Dutch settlements in Canada, like Jim Olthuis who was a link with later social action movements in Edmonton. Most of the Americans were also sons of immigrants, like myself. But there was always a handful of others, indigenous Americans who did not join the club for mainly social reasons but principal ones as well.

The high percentage of Canadian students in his philosophy classes and in the Groen Club was Runner's first significant link with Canada. The controversial reaction to his public pronouncements made him realize quite quickly that a spiritual turnabout in the Christian Reformed Church in the United States, though certainly not out of the question, would take a long time. This led to a change in tactics with a specific focus on Canada. He began to view the settlement of approximately forty thousand Dutch Calvinists in Canada, from Halifax to Vancouver Island, as the base for a reformational effort.

This change in tactics also brought to the fore the second facet of his mission: the advocacy of organized Christian action in society. Runner sensed that if this small but nonetheless substantial group of Christians with a common heritage could maintain its spiritual identity long enough, it might in the future constitute a base for wider cultural witness and action. But this would require that from the outset these Christians not get absorbed into the mainline Protestant denominations, into the public schools, and into the labor unions and political parties.

A number of factors coalesced here. The Christian Reformed Church in the United States had established a very efficient system of absorbing the Canadian immigrants into its denominational structure. Christian schools were established. The Christian Labour Association of Canada was organized in the early fifties and the Christian Action Foundation was set up in Edmonton in the early sixties (later it joined with the Ontario-based Committee for Justice and Liberty). In 1956 the Association for Reformed Scientific Studies was founded in the Toronto area with nothing less as its aim than the founding of a Christian university. Runner saw an opportunity and seized it. In the midst of intense personal and cultural dislocations which immigrations bring with them, Runner took it upon himself to give spiritual direction to the postwar Dutch reformed settlers in Canada.

Radically Christian Leadership and a New Christian Mind
The third facet of Runner's mission concerned the development of a Christian mind and the formation of a group of students educated to give leadership in a wide range of cultural sectors. The avenues were his classroom at Calvin College; the ARSS student conferences in Canada; the publication of the lectures presented there under the titles *The Relation of the Bible to Learning* (1960, 1961) and *Biblical Religion and Political Task* (1962); and the founding of the Institute or Christian Studies in Toronto in 1967. Runner's contribution

to the development of a Christian mind was distinctly shaped by the philosophical school of Vollenhoven and Dooyeweerd. He in effect introduced this philosophy in an existentially relevant way to hundreds of students in the United States and Canada. In the fifties and the sixties he sent these students who wanted to pursue an academic career to the Free University. In recent years the students who have become part of this intellectual movement tend to complete their studies on this side of the ocean. Dozens of them occupy teaching posts, at colleges within the Christian Reformed orbit and elsewhere, in the wider evangelical world, and, occasionally, at public universities.

Runner's mission was the reformation of evangelical Protestantism. Reformation must be distinguished from conversion and revival. A conversion is the work of the Holy Spirit in the heart of a person so that he submits himself to the claims of Christ, the Savior and Lord. A revival is the renewal of faith on the part of a significant number of persons within a particular part of the church at a particular time in history. A reformation is a revival so radical and widespread that it affects the direction of the culture and the structuration of society.

The great sixteenth-century Reformation occurred in the first place because Luther and Calvin heard again the radical message of the Word of the gospel revealed in the Scriptures. This Word they preached, in season and out of season. And this Word proclaimed brought new life in a decadent church in such proportions that its exuberance spilled over in the culture and society of northern Europe. To be sure, there are numerous other "causes" that contributed to the Reformation. But at its heart there was the power of the Word of the gospel preached by men who, with a keen sense of the crisis of the times, made such decisions and established such alliances and institutions that the Word of the Lord could "speed on and triumph" (II Thess. 3:1). Without now commenting on their "theologies," I believe that John and Charles Wesley were reformers in eighteenth-century Great Britain and that Abraham Kuyper was a reformer in nineteenth-century Holland.

In the history of Christianity in North America there have been several revivals—conversions and renewals of faith in large segments of the various denominations. The outstanding leaders of American Christianity have indeed been revivalists, from Jonathan Edwards to Billy Graham. The impact of these revivals has indeed not been confined to the private lives of persons and the churches of which they were members. There was a spillover to the larger context of culture and society, but never to the extent that one can speak of a reformation. The main reason for this absence of a reformation in North America is the fact that the revivalists did not so preach the Word of the gospel that its redeeming power was brought to bear on the entire life of the people of God. This meant that the liberal-conservative ideology of humanism was never challenged at its roots and continued to guide both Christians and non-Christians alike in their cultural and societal life.

Runner was fully aware of this from the beginning of his mission. He came from the heart of typical American culture and received his spiritual nurture precisely in the interplay between evangelical revivalism and the modernism of the mainline churches. But Runner's base of operation within the Christian Reformed Church was outside of the mainstream of American Christendom, in its liberal Protestant, evangelical Protestant, or Roman Catholic forms. His base of operation was located at the periphery of American society.

Moreover, Runner's office was that of professor of philosophy. He used this office as much to preach as to philosophize. But his message was directed to students, not to the church in its grassroots existence. In the fifties and the sixties he spent a great deal of time and energy articulating the *raison d'être* for distinct Christian communal action among the Calvinist immigrants in Canada. Together these two activities on his part led to "the reformational movement," which is significant in its intellectual potential as a prime paradigm in Christian thought today. But this potential is not taken seriously by Christian theologians and philosophers, not even within the resurgent evangelical world, as is evident from the benign indifference of *Christianity Today*. And the Christian action organizations? The Christian Labour Association in Canada? The Committee for Justice and Liberty in Toronto? The Association for Public Justice in the United States? They are signposts to which few pay attention.

Did Runner then fail in his mission? In a very specific sense he did. His efforts did not contribute to a reformation, not even within the limits of the Christian Reformed Church, whose average member does not know who H. Evan Runner is. I think that during the last decade of his career Runner became more and more aware of the limits of his potential accomplishments. This awareness did not affect the direction of his mission, but it did change its embodiment. In 1970, he disbanded the Groen Club, which, at the height of the counterculture, apparently no longer served the reformational purposes for which it was founded. A few years later he declined an appointment to the Institute for Christian Studies in Toronto because he felt that the kind of contribution he wanted to make there would not be wholeheartedly supported by its staff. This meant that the shift in the base of operation from Grand Rapids to Toronto did not occur. From the vantage point of the reformational movement in Canada the loss of Runner's immediate leadership cannot as yet be measured. That it was substantial is without question. But there is another angle to this. The United States is the heartland of Anglo-Saxon civilization. And Calvin College is today the most significant undergraduate institution within the evangelical orbit. Runner's decision to stay at Calvin not only meant that he continued to reach

17

its students but also that a much more positive attitude toward his work developed within the institution as a whole.

But Runner also decided to do something else. With his wife, he prepared a translation, not of any of Vollenhoven's or Dooyeweerd's writings, as one might have expected, but of S. G. De Graaf's *Promise and Deliverance*. This is a four-volume book written to help Sunday school teachers and evangelists explain the Word of the Scriptures to anyone who wants to listen. It is significant to note that Runner, in the light of his intense concern for the future of non-Western cultures, has been highly interested in getting precisely this book translated not only into Spanish but also into Chinese and Japanese. Philosophy does not lead to reformation; hearing and doing the Word does.

We cannot today speak of a reformation in North America. Runner is not a reformer. Nonetheless, he did not fail in his mission. He is a pre-reformational figure in the Christian church, somewhat like John Huss was in Bohemia and John Wycliffe in England towards the end of the Middle Ages. They were precursors of Luther and Calvin and Zwingli. As a pre-reformational figure, Runner's spiritual legacy is phenomenal. The final significance of such precursors depends upon what following generations do with their legacy.

Bernard Zylstra   *Institute for Christian Studies*
                              Toronto

18

The Christian Philosophy of H. Evan Runner

I

THE TEACHING OF H. EVAN Runner[1] can best be grasped as an expression of two central themes which take on their full meaning only in relation to each other. The first is the idea of the Law or the creation order as the inescapable context and condition for all human action and thought. Because of God's all-encompassing creation order, human life in its totality is to be understood as *response*. Life is religion—Runner never tired of stressing this point.

This notion of response to the divine creation order might be confused with a nineteenth-century pantheism or idealism if it were not linked with the second major theme in Runner's thinking—that of the antithesis. Human life as response to God and his creation order is not to be conceived of simply as a groping for truth, a pilgrimage in which some people get farther than others, with all of them traveling toward the same

---

1. Those who would like to know more about the personal side of Professor Runner's life and career would do well to read: "Interview with Dr. H. Evan Runner," prepared by Harry van Dyke and Albert M. Wolters, in *Hearing and Doing: Philosophical Essays Dedicated to H. Evan Runner*, edited by John Kraay and Anthony Tol (Toronto, 1979), pp. 333-61.

destination. No, Runner always stressed the necessity and un-avoidability of choosing *direction*. Either man worships the Creator and turns to Jesus Christ, or he turns his back on the Creator by abasing himself before the creature and worshiping a vain idol. There is no third alternative. Despite all the efforts undertaken in the name of ecumenism and inter-faith dialogue, the gulf between these two religious directions can never be overcome.

It has been Runner's fate to be much misunderstood—by his own students as well as by his critics. Generally speaking, those who have misunderstood him have tended to work with one of the two central themes mentioned above (i.e. the creation order and the antithesis) without the other. In this essay I shall endeavor to lay some of the misconceptions to rest by distinguishing Runner's position from a certain other position (or family of positions) contrary to his own. More specifically, I will argue that the current tendency to defend the notion of a religious input or impulse in science on the basis of an epis-temological pluralism or pluralism of viewpoints departs from Runner's thinking in that it proceeds from a conception of re-ligion as unnormed subjectivity, a conception that owes its in-spiration to historicism and the German intellectual tradition in particular.

Later in the essay I will tackle the much more difficult question of the creation order as the neglected theme for Christian philosophical inquiry. This will involve some reflec-tion on the relation between history and truth. To bring out Runner's own stand on this matter, which has often been mis-understood and even confused with the very historicism he combatted, I will make a detour through the thinking of Ni-etzsche, Dilthey and Heidegger. Runner's concerns as a critic of the Western intellectual tradition parallel Heidegger's in an interesting respect—and also draw criticisms much like the ones aimed at Heidegger.

II

In recent discussions about the relevance of faith and commitment to science and scholarship, we find more and more recognition that there is indeed a link between one's worldview and one's scientific and philosophical work. To the extent that ground has truly been gained here, those who are committed to integrally Christian scholarship will rejoice. Still, a word of caution may be in order. Could it be that the relativism and subjectivism developed especially within the German philosophical tradition is responsible for many of the changes underway? If the new openness to the notion of a link between faith and science is indeed a result of the influence of historicism and subjectivism, Christian thinkers would do well to pause before embracing it as a higher wisdom. Just what does all the emphasis on "viewpoint" and "worldview" considerations mean?

It may well be that some earlier ideals of objectivity are being given up, but the suggestion that no scientific formulation can rise above the stream of history and subjectivity surely does not advance the cause of Christian theorizing. A pluralist emphasis in the sense of a diversity of philosophical outlooks that stand unreconciled over against each other is not what the philosophical tradition of which Runner, Dooyeweerd and Vollenhoven are spokesmen has been pleading for. The pluralism which the Philosophy of the Law-Idea exemplifies is first of all a recognition that the basic institutions in human society enjoy a sovereignty within certain bounds and therefore may not dictate to one another, and secondly an ontological thesis that expands the mind/matter distinction into a series of irreducible levels of being, law and functioning which together enjoy a unity and interrelatedness that seem to elude mind and matter conceived of as entirely separate modes of reality.

Pluralism in the subjectivist sense is really not a defense of Christian theorizing at all; it represents rather a trivialization and relativization of any effort to appeal to the Word of God as the foundation for an adequate understanding of reality. In recent pluralist accounts of Christian theorizing, the appeal to the Word of God (the norm for our theorizing) has all too often been replaced by an appeal to Christian faith (which is really a subjective *response* to the norm for our believing). When such an approach is taken, we do indeed wind up with a connection between faith and science, but our theorizing is then rooted in and based upon the subjectivity of man rather than the everywhere-valid Word of God.

We see, then, that the contemporary "pluralism" that allows faith to inspire science is inadequate. This "pluralism" leaves "religion" too much as an undefined, unnormed concept. Runner's thesis that religion takes in all of life and does not simply represent a certain domain of feeling or intuition or moral sense leaves no room for the uncritical acceptance of human subjectivity and creativity in the "pluralist" outlook. Religion does indeed come to expression in feeling and in ethical awareness, but never in a manner that allows of no application of normative criteria by which it is judged. Human religiosity, as response to God's all-encompassing Word for his creation and creatures, is never a law unto itself. Therefore, the detection of a religious impulse at work in theoretical thought is never enough to qualify the thought in question as Christian, that is, as a faithful response to the Word of the God who made the heavens and the earth.

The Philosophy of the Law-Idea has traditionally sought to circumvent such a subjectivistic misunderstanding of the link between faith and science by emphasizing the necessity of developing a full fledged systematic philosophy as a foundation for integral Christian theorizing, a philosophy in which the nature of saving faith in Jesus Christ could also be dealt with. This emphasis on the importance of a systematic Christian philosophy was fully shared by Runner. A mere "inspirational" link between religious sentiment and a set of philosophical and theoretical ideas does not establish much either for or against those ideas. The motives in the heart of a thinker—however laudable—are not uppermost in our judgment of his thought. Hence it is sometimes necessary to take a markedly negative stance over against the theoretical work of someone known to be a dedicated Christian.

Thinkers in the tradition of the Philosophy of the Law-Idea are sometimes accused of teaching a lifeless system, a set of categories to be applied in wooden fashion. The charge of "scholasticism" is occasionally raised, and people ask what all those categories and distinctions are good for.

Whatever one might say of other philosophers who use the Law-Idea, Runner has always worked with the systematic components of his philosophical position in a vibrant way. Moreover, he has never suggested to his students that one ought to concentrate on the Philosophy of the Law-Idea to the exclusion of other systems of thought or to the neglect of experientially-oriented investigation. On the contrary, Runner has constantly pointed his students to intellectual and cultural developments in the present and the past that seemed worthy of careful consideration. He made it clear in his teaching that genuine progress in Christian philosophizing and theorizing was possible only for those who were willing to go far afield in their search for fresh insights, refinements and applications of the central themes of Christian philosophy.

Runner himself exemplified this enthusiasm for broad-ranging study. His own interests were dazzlingly broad, and he demonstrated an ability to find significance in all sorts of far-flung scholarly discussions. In his own work he liked to trace the history of the thinking about the topic under discussion, and his students were often curious to see just how far back he would go in his approach to the subject.

This commitment to a historical approach gave rise to an interesting misunderstanding. How could a thinker who proceeded from the Philosophy of the Law-Idea concern himself so deeply with historical developments in culture and thought? Perhaps he was not really what he claimed to be. I well remember attending a conference years ago at which Runner presented some material against the customary historical background, only to be accused of "historicism"!

This charge represented a serious misunderstanding of what Runner was trying to say. Yet it is worth reflecting on, for the link between history and truth in Runner's teaching has been misconstrued by various of his critics. Although he was keenly aware of the threat of historicism, Runner did not maintain that the Christian thinker can somehow step outside the historical process in his effort to grasp theoretical truth: the truth with which Christian philosophy and science are concerned is intimately connected with the realm of history and culture. To get the nature of the link between history and truth before us, then, let us make a brief excursion into the thinking of Nietzsche.

III

The historicism charge was formulated eloquently by Nietzsche more than a hundred years ago in an "untimely essay" which he entitled "Vom Nutzen und Nachteil der Historie für das Leben" (On the Usefulness and Disadvantages of History for Life). One might conceivably wonder whether Nietzsche was actually addressing historicism, for he did not make use of the term, which only came into general circulation some time later. But whatever one might say about the broad and narrow varieties of historicism, it is clear that what Nietzsche had in mind as he wrote was the widespread notion that history is somehow the main pathway to wisdom and truth.

It is significant that he issued his warning in the name of "life." Nietzsche's essay is no academic discussion of historical method. He opens by quoting Goethe: "I hate everything that merely instructs me without increasing or directly quickening my activity." Complaining about "jaded idlers in the garden of knowledge," he goes on to argue that the study of history "beyond a certain point mutilates and degrades life." Hence there is a sense in which history must not just be ignored but "hated," as a "costly and su perfluous luxury."[2] Nietzsche tells us that life is a higher power than knowledge. Ever the classicist, he contrasts "esse" with "vivere," and man the "cogital" with man the "animal."[3] European man, all but buried under a mountain of superfluous, useless learning, culture and knowledge, struggles to rise to his feet. If only he can shake off the "malady" which Nietzsche describes as an "excess of history,"[4] there will be room for new life to take root, and from the new life can arise a new culture.

Nietzsche does not paint a flattering picture of the German and European of his day. Mercilessly he exposes the superficiality of the quest for truth in history and culture. In his eagerness to possess what everyone else possesses, modern man "runs through art galleries."[5] Nietzsche scorns such an approach to history and culture and brands it "historical education." He complains that

> ...knowledge of culture is forced into the young mind [of the student] in the form of historical knowledge; which means that his head is filled with an enormous mass of ideas, taken secondhand from past times and peoples, not from immediate contact with life...It is the same mad method that carries our young artists off to picture galleries instead of the studio of a master, and above all the one studio of the

---

2. *The Use and Abuse of History*, second edition, translated by Adrian Collins (Indianapolis and New York, 1957), p. 3.

3. Nietzsche, pp. 70, 69.

4. See Nietzsche, pp. 12, 28, 64, 65, 69, 70, 72.

5. Nietzsche, p. 45.

only master, Nature. As if one could discover by a hasty rush through history the ideas and techniques of past times and their individual outlook on life! For life itself is a kind of handicraft that must be learned thoroughly and industriously, and diligently practiced, if we are not to have mere botchers and babblers as the issue of it all! [6]

The way to remain faithful to Nature and the earth and to recover life is to learn to feel "unhistorically," which is only another way of saying that the power of "forgetting" is very much needed. "Life" is "absolutely impossible without forgetfulness." The preoccupation with history "injures and finally destroys the living thing, be it a man or a people or a system of culture."[7] The power of forgetting is the art of "drawing a limited horizon about oneself."[8] The great "fighters against history" know how this is done, for they

>...troubled themselves very little about the "thus it is," in order that they might follow a 'thus it must be' with greater joy and greater pride. Not to drag their generation to the grave, but to found a new one—that is the motive that ever drives them onward; and even if they are born late, there is a way of living by which they can forget it—and future generations will know them only as the first-comers.[9]

Nietzsche was concerned about cultural revitalization—and rightly so. Hence he compared historical culture to the "grayness" of old age,[10] calling upon his fellows to set aside "secondhand thought,

---

6.   Nietzsche, p. 67.

7.   Nietzsche, p. 7; see also p. 6.

8.   Nietzsche, p. 69.

9.   Nietzsche, p. 54.

10. Nietzsche, p. 48; see also pp. 64, 70.

secondhand learning, secondhand action"[11] and reminding them that they could not have the "flower" of genuine culture without the root or the stalk.[12] Life, knowledge and culture are nourished by Nature and the earth, and not solely by preserved products of previous lives—subjectivity objectified and cut off from its ground. History and culture are useful only to the extent that they serve to bring us into living contact with the source of culture. Because of the excess of history, man must "dig himself out," as it were, in order to breathe freely again.

Among the contemporaries of Nietzsche who felt the sting of his criticism was Wilhelm Dilthey, who perhaps epitomized the reverential attitude toward history that Nietzsche made light of. Dilthey commented on Nietzsche at various points, arguing that Nietzsche failed to circumvent or get behind history in his effort to establish a direct relation with the soil from which culture springs: "In vain did Nietzsche seek his original nature, his a-historical essence, in solitary self-observation. He peeled off one skin after another. And what was left? Still only something historically conditioned: the features of the Renaissance man of power."[13]

The question that must be raised in connection with Dilthey and his tradition is how, and under what circumstances, we are able to transcend or rise above the stream of human subjectivity which finds expression in a history or culture. Because Dilthey was at bottom a

---

11. Nietzsche, p. 72; see also p. 67.

12. Nietzsche, p. 68.

13. "Traum," *Gesammelte Schriften*, Vol. 8, edited by Bernhard Groethuysen (Stuttgart, 1931), 226. On the relation between Dilthey and Nietzsche, see J. Kamerbeek, "Dilthey versus Nietzsche," *Studia Philosophica: Jahrbuch der Schweizerischen Philosophischen Gesellschaft*, Vol. 10 (1950), 52-84; and Georg Misch's reply, also entitled "Dilthey versus Nietzsche," *Die Sammlung: Zeitschrift für Kultur und Erziehung*, Vol. 8 (1952), 378-95.

pantheist, the line of criticism involved in this question did not pose a serious problem for him.[14] Yet, for those who cannot follow Dilthey in his pantheism, there is the very real danger of becoming lost or swallowed up in history. Like Nietzsche, Dilthey professed to be a philosopher of "life," but his concept of "life" was thoroughly historical and cultural (*geistig*). Thus he perceived no genuine opposition between history and culture on the one hand and life on the other. Life presents itself to us as history and culture and then draws us into its sweep.

The standpoints of Nietzsche and Dilthey confront each other unreconciled. The debate has been carried further in the twentieth-century, of course, by such figures as Heidegger and Gadamer. Must Christian philosophy associate itself with Nietzsche in his call for a judicious forgetting? This might seem an attractive route to follow, given the widespread Christian rejection of the excesses of our secular culture. Or should Christian philosophy follow the lead of Dilthey by always seeking to advance by drawing strength from the power of the past? Such an approach would surely appeal to the Christian respect for tradition.

These two alternatives deserve careful consideration. But we must not forget to ask whether there is perhaps a way between them.

IV

For twentieth-century Christians, then, the choice between Nietzsche's appeal to forget the past and Dilthey's effort to retain it might seem attractive. Whereas earlier Christian thinkers might have been inclined to adopt an attitude like Dilthey's, many more recent Christians take a largely negative stance toward the philosophical

---

14. I have dealt with Dilthey and the question of history at some length in my book *Historical Understanding in the Thought of Wilhelm Dilthey* (Toronto, Buffalo and London, 1980). See especially Chapters 7 and 8.

tradition. Don't modern Thomists sometimes leave us with the impression that they regard the entire modern era in philosophy as a wandering in a trackless wasteland?

Before drawing the conclusion that the choice between Nietzsche and Dilthey is an unavoidable fork in the road, we would do well to pause and look at another rebel against the philosophical tradition—Martin Heidegger, whose thinking does not fit the pattern of Nietzsche's "forgetting." It seems to me that Heidegger's approach to the tradition has considerable relevance for the question of history and truth and thus can help us understand the teaching of H. Evan Runner and the philosophical agenda which the Philosophy of the Law-Idea has set for itself.

Heidegger is often perceived as a philosopher who likes to make things needlessly difficult. Like Nietzsche, he sees history and the tradition as a serious obstacle to genuine thought and culture. Yet he does not draw Nietzsche's conclusion that a judicious forgetting is called for. On the other hand, he does not side with Dilthey either and appeal for a treasuring of the great tradition of German and European culture. In fact, he is markedly critical especially of the technological impulse in European (and North American) civilization. Heidegger's thinking has helped to give birth to a new approach in hermeneutics articulated mainly by H. G. Gadamer, and in this new approach Dilthey comes in for some telling criticism.[15] Dilthey, it seems, ran aground in history and never managed to get beyond it or transcend it.

Heidegger steers a route of his own between Nietzsche and Dilthey. And in the process he incurs the ire of many a professional philosopher accustomed to a more conventional approach. Richard Rorty notes:

---

15. See Gadamer's *Wahrheit und Methode*, second edition (Tübingen, 1965), especially Part II.

Philosophers who envy scientists think that philosophy should deal only with problems formulatable in neutral terms—terms satisfactory to all those who argue for competing solutions. Without common problems and without argument, it would seem, we have no professional discipline, nor even a method for disciplining our own thoughts. Without discipline, we presumably have mysticism, or poetry, or inspiration—at any rate, something that permits an escape from our intellectual responsibilities. Heidegger is frequently criticized for having avoided these responsibilities.[16]

Heidegger, it appears, will neither explain himself in terms that others can understand nor come out and fight for his position. Rorty comments:

> …Heidegger has done as good a job of putting potential critics on the defensive as any philosopher in history. There is no standard by which one can measure him without begging the question against him. His remarks about the tradition, and his remarks about the limitations the tradition has imposed on the vocabulary and imagination of his contemporaries, are beautifully designed to make one feel foolish when one tries to find a bit of common ground on which to start an argument.[17]

Yet Heidegger does not just stay in his own corner, minding his own business, oblivious to what others think. Despite his rejection of the philosophical (or metaphysical) tradition, he has spent an inordinate amount of time commenting on it. And his comments have provoked great controversy. Many philosophers, operating on the widely accepted premise that a thinker must be explained in terms of his own inten-

---

16. "Overcoming the Tradition: Heidegger and Dewey," in *Heidegger and Modern Philosophy: Critical Essays*, edited by Michael Murray (New Haven and London, 1978), p. 239.

17. Rorty, p. 242.

tions and in such a manner that he would recognize that he has been dealt with fairly, have chided Heidegger for his treatment of the history of philosophy. The most famous quarrel revolves around the book on Kant, entitled *Kant and the Problem of Metaphysics*. Heidegger himself is alleged to have said of this book: "It may not be good Kant, but it's excellent Heidegger."[18] There may be something to this rather cavalier explanation, but in actual fact there is much more that Heidegger can—and does—say in his own defense. When a philosopher deals with a philosophical text, he explains, it is sometimes necessary to "do violence" to the text. One must probe deeper to determine what the philosopher in question really intended to say:

> It is true that in order to wrest from the actual words that which these words "intend to say," every interpretation must necessarily resort to violence. This violence, however, should not be confused with an action that is wholly arbitrary. The interpretation must be animated and guided by the power of an illuminative idea. Only through the power of this idea can an interpretation risk what is always audacious, namely, entrusting itself to the secret élan of a work, in order by this élan to get through to the unsaid and to attempt to find an expression for it. The directive idea itself is confirmed by its own power of illumination.[19]

This approach to Kant drew from Ernst Cassirer the complaint that Heidegger was functioning not as a "commentator" but as a "usurper," using Kant for his own purposes.[20]

---

18. Heidegger to William J. Richardson, as quoted by Bernd Magnus in *Heidegger's Metahistory of Philosophy* (The Hague, 1970), p. 80.

19. *Kant and the Problem of Metaphysics*, translated by James S Churchill (Bloomington and London, 1962), p. 207.

20. "Kant and the Problem of Metaphysics" (originally published in 1931 in German in *Kant-Studien*), in *Kant: Disputed Questions*, edited by Moltke S. Gram (Chicago, 1967), p. 149.

Heidegger has not gone out of his way to defend his treatment of the history of philosophy. But those who are well acquainted with his thought have stressed that there is more to his seemingly high-handed treatment of past philosophers than meets the eye. It is not just a question of accurate interpretation, of finding out what the thinker in question was struggling to say. In the words of William J. Richardson, Heidegger was trying "... to comprehend and express not what another thinker thought/said, but what he did not think/say, could not think/say, and why he could not think/say it." Richardson observes: "It is the unsaid in a thinker which is his true 'doctrine,' his 'supreme gift'...."[21]

Heidegger is reminiscent of Hegel in a number of respects. Both are suspicious of refutation as ordinarily understood. Hegel hoped to include apparent error in an *aufgehoben* version of the truth as formulated from a higher standpoint, whereas for Heidegger refutation simply does not come into the picture in any essential way. It is often the case that when a philosopher is deeply, profoundly, off the track, his error requires careful consideration.

Hegel and Heidegger are also alike in linking truth and history. Despite his critique of the tradition, then, Heidegger cannot join Nietzsche in appealing for a forgetting, a casting off of history. Crisis and conflict in history make room for revelation—a revelation through which Being may perhaps emerge from its hiddenness. Despite the emphasis on "waiting" and "Gelassenheit" as the posture to be taken, we never seek to simply "start over," as though through an act of will we could become youthful, Nietzschean Greeks.

The conclusion suggested by the Heideggerian enterprise is that the question of Being is not to be posed apart from the tradition. The "overcoming" of metaphysics and the "destruction" of ontology are

---

21. *Heidegger: Through Phenomenology to Thought* (The Hague, 1963), pp. 22, 440.

apparently needed to prepare for what Heidegger hopes is to come. How was the question of Being lost from view? It appears that we can find out only if we examine the twists and turns taken by the concept of truth. Hence, we are obliged to trace the route that leads from the Greeks to the modern interpretation of Being as will, with its destructive consequences in technology. To ignore the tradition is to run the risk of perpetuating it.

V

I have dealt with Heidegger's approach to the history of philosophy because it parallels some key themes in Runner's teaching and may help shed light on them. Many of the criticisms directed against Runner are similar to the critiques of Heidegger by disgruntled "outsiders" unable to get their bearings in Heidegger's works. As we saw earlier, some philosophers complain that Heidegger does not allow for "common ground," for a "neutral" formulation of the problems with which philosophy deals, a formulation which would allow different philosophical schools to simply compete in seeking the best solutions. Likewise, Runner has always stressed that the formulation of a philosophical question cannot be separated from one's basic philosophical stance, just as in apologetics the believer and the unbeliever do not jointly set out to answer the (neutral) question whether the evidence presented by reason and the senses entitles us to believe in the God of the Scriptures.[22]

If the *problems* of philosophy cannot be formulated in neutral terms, surely the *material* or *Gegenstand* with which the philosopher

---

22. On the question of method in apologetics, see Robert Knudsen's essay in this volume and also his essay "Progressive and Regressive Tendencies in Christian Apologetics," in *Jerusalem and Athens: Discussions on the Theology and Apologetics of Cornelius Van Til,* edited by E. R. Geehan (Philadelphia, 1971). Also helpful in the Van Til volume are the exchange with Dooyeweerd (pp. 74 ff.) and the two essays discussing Van Til and Edward J. Carnell (pp. 349 ff.).

concerns himself is common to all. This, at least, was the conviction of Dilthey, who also devoted considerable attention to what might be called the "philosophy of the history of philosophy."[23] Dilthey assures us that all philosophers

> ...have before them one and the same world, the reality that appears in consciousness. The sun of Homer shines forever. Plato beheld the same reality as Thales. From this it follows that the unity of all philosophies is grounded ultimately in the identity (*Selbigkeit*) of the outer and inner world. Because of this identity, the same basic relationships are seen again and again.[24]

There is some truth to Dilthey's claim, of course: God's sun has shone on the just and the unjust, on ancient Greeks and contemporary North Americans. But Runner does not regard it as helpful or accurate to declare that all thinkers philosophize about the very same world. As a historical thinker, Runner emphasizes that cultural and historical unfolding must always be taken into account. Hence Plato did not behold the very same reality as Thales two centuries before him, and we do not philosophize about the very same world that Hegel surveyed when he was a professor in Berlin early in the nineteenth-century. The historical dimension of reality may never be left out of the picture.

Like Heidegger, Runner emphasizes that a meaningful encounter with the philosophy of the past requires a grasp of the fundamental issue in philosophy—and not just a grasp of what the thinker in question happened to regard as the fundamental issue. For Heidegger the main question is Being itself—how it has been forgotten and

---

23. See my essay "Dilthey's Philosophy of the History of Philosophy," in *Hearing and Doing* (note 1 above), pp. 199-214.

24. "Zur Philosophie der Philosophie," *Gesammelte Schriften*, Vol. 8 (note 13 above), pp. 207-8.

obscured. Hence Heidegger is interested not just in what a thinker said but also what he left unsaid—or could not say. For Runner the key philosophical issue is that of the Law. When approaching a philosopher in the past, one must always ask what he does about the Law—how he seeks to account for it, or perhaps even tries to ignore it by identifying normativity with subjectivity or objectivity.

The use of such an approach entails that in some cases we will reach conclusions about a certain thinker that will be called into question by proponents of the traditional approach according to which the historian of philosophy must understand and explain past philosophers first and foremost in terms of their own themes and emphases. Runner, well aware of these considerations, has therefore devoted extensive attention to the question of methodology in his own teaching in the area of history of philosophy. His intention, he made it known to the students, was not to somehow "do violence" to the text or to claim past philosophers as grist for his own philosophical mill but to discover what was really going on back there in the mental struggles in which thinkers engaged. Every past philosopher bumped up against the normativity of the creation order, however he might choose to describe it or account for it. How did he respond to the creation order? What room did he leave for the Law in his philosophical system? These were the questions which Runner sought to answer in his own work in history of philosophy.

Runner's recipe for genuine philosophical progress in the twentieth-century, then, is neither to put the past behind us by deliberately forgetting much of it (Nietzsche) nor to absorb and preserve a great deal of it by accepting it on its own terms (Dilthey). The direction pointed out by Runner was rather that we are to pursue the truth by thinking historically in a double sense. We first watch to see how the creation order or Law of God does or does not receive proper recognition in the historical and cultural unfolding process. Then we observe how the creation order—whether generally recognized or not—makes itself felt in theoretical and philosophical reflection on reality, a reflection that cannot help but take cultural and historical unfolding into account.

The Law of God as it impinges on man in all his doings must be the central theme of our philosophizing, Runner stressed. Yet it never presents itself to us in an isolated way for direct inspection; we never study it by itself. It is to be known mainly in its effects. In short, it is like the wind: we never catch sight of it, but we certainly feel its operation.

Here again the parallel with Heidegger comes to mind. Just as Being remains hidden for Heidegger, curiously unaccounted for and conspicuous by its absence, Runner maintains that the creation order is suppressed, distorted and concealed in the thinking of many philosophers. We must recover the (normative) truth of God's Word by bringing the creation order to light again and giving it a central place in our theoretical reflection. This we do by adopting a historical approach to culture and thinking. Such (historical) reflection is an indispensable part of the basis of Christian philosophy and also of Christian theoretical reflection in other disciplines.

Once these philosophical and historical lessons sink in, we see why Runner, as a Christian philosopher, has sent his students out to study a stunning array of cultural phenomena and historical topics. The (normative) truth of reality, he stressed, must be understood in terms of God's creation order. And that creation order becomes familiar especially through the history of its effects on man, thought and culture. It is this recognition that makes the entire realm of culture and history intensely relevant to Christian scholarship. What is called for, then, is an open approach to Christian philosophizing, an approach that does not allow for a narrow scholasticism or a preoccupation with the categories of a certain system of thought embraced as superior to all others. Such is the legacy of Runner's teaching.

Theodore Plantinga   *Calvin College*
                                                            Grand Rapids

Philosophy

"By a scriptural philosophy, then, we do not mean a philoso-phy which is satisfied with Bible study. That would in no sense be philosophy. For we have already said that the field of the philosopher is not the Scripture, but the totality of the cosmos. We mean by a philosophizing in accordance with Scripture a study of the cosmos in the light of Scripture, a philosophical view that in its fundamental aspects continually takes Scrip-ture into consideration by asking, What do the Scriptures have to say about the cosmos as a whole?"

— H. Evan Runner, *The History of Ancient Philosophy*, p. 16.

PETER A. SCHOULS

Descartes' Reformation

Nor is it likewise that the whole body of the sciences... should
be reformed. But as regards all the opinions which up to this
time I had embraced, I thought I could do no better than
endeavour once for all to sweep them completely away, so
that they might later on be replaced, either by others which
were better, or by the same, when I had made them conform
to the uniformity of a rational scheme.... My design has never extended beyond trying to reform my own opinion and
to build on a foundation which is entirely my own
(René Descartes, *Discourse on the Method*).

I cannot forgive Descartes. In all his philosophy he would have
been quite willing to dispense with God. But he could not help
granting him a flick of the forefinger to start the world in
motion; beyond this, he has no further need of God
(Blaise Pascal, *Pensées*).

...declaring ourselves free from the law of God as the Law-struc-
ture of the creation... would be Revolution, pure and simple
(H. Evan Runner, *Christian Perspectives*, 1960).

DESCARTES SAW THE NEED for what he called a "reformation" of
the sciences. Not that he expected himself to be able fully to bring
about such a reformation, but he did expect to be able to make a

beginning, for he believed that in his method he had available the instrument necessary to begin to bring it about.

Although he speaks of the necessity of bringing about a reformation and thus, by implication, of himself as a reformer, it seems to me that Descartes should be seen as one bringing about a *revolution* and should therefore be spoken of as a revolutionary—a revolutionary in anything but a narrow application of that term, for he brought about a totally new outlook in potentially all areas of life. The term *reformation* does not cover so radical an activity. For although reformation may be thought to consist of doing away with the old and replacing it with what is new, it is an activity which takes place within an accepted framework of which at least key aspects are by the reformer himself considered inviolate. Reformation may therefore be thought to consist of improving the old by removing imperfections or faults or errors, in amendment or transformation. And *revolution* may be taken as radical substitution, as removal of a framework itself and therefore of everything within it. If the term *reformation* is restricted to the activity of amending or transforming and the term *revolution* to that of radical substitution, then Descartes' reformation ought to be seen as a revolution, and Descartes himself should be characterized as a revolutionary rather than as a reformer. For he had no sympathy with a reformation which set out merely to transform. Indeed, the only instrument which he considered adequate for the task of bringing about a reformation in the sciences precluded mere transformation. This instrument, the method of the *Rules for the Direction of the Mind* and the *Discourse on the Method*, called for substitution rather than transformation. If revolution consists of two parts, the first being to do away with the old, the second to present the new, then Descartes was sometimes modest with respect to his achievements in the second area but never with respect to his achievements in the first. His doing away with the old he considered fully completed once he had rejected the trustworthiness of both everyday and

scientific knowledge; once he had declared suspect and therefore un-
acceptable as sources of knowledge both the senses and the mind;
once he had pronounced to be non-existent that about which knowledge used to be: things in the world and the relations between and
among themselves as well as their relation to their creator; the world
itself; and the creator himself.

In the *Discourse on the Method*,[1] which is one place in which he
constantly speaks of the need for *reformer le cors des sciences*,[2] Descartes makes it quite clear that he considers himself to have succeed-
ed fully in the task not simply of doing away with much of the old in
the realm of science but of altogether rejecting what was taken to be
science itself. For he writes that "as regards all the opinions which up
to this time I had embraced, I thought I could not do better than
endeavour once for all to sweep them completely away...."[3] Well
before the end of the *Discourse*, he is confident that this endeavor has
been successful. Doing away with the old does not, he here indicates,
prevent one from later on accepting some of it again, or something
much like it. Old opinions are to be swept "completely away, so that
they might later on be replaced, either by others which were better,
or by the same, when I had made them conform to the uniformity of
a rational scheme." Thus what is new may appear similar to, even
identical with, the old. Crucial is that nothing old may be retained
unless it "conforms to the uniformity of a rational scheme." As he

---

1.   Whenever possible my references to Descartes' works will be to the
     edition of Elizabeth S. Haldane and G. R. T. Ross, *The Philosophical
     Works of Descartes*, Vols. I and II, Cambridge University Press (first
     edition 1911; reprinted with corrections 1934; my references are to
     the corrected edition). Passages from the *Principles of Philosophy*
     and the *Passions of the Soul* will be identified by the number of the
     principle or article quoted.

2.   Descartes, *Philosophical Works*, I, 89.

3.   Descartes, *Philosophical Works*, I, 89.

puts it later on in the *Discourse* with respect to doctrines and discoveries to be presented in the *Dioptrics* and the *Meteors*, "I do not even boast of being the first discoverer of any of them, but only state that I have adopted them, not because they have been held by others … but only because Reason has persuaded me of their truth."[4] But before one can be persuaded by reason, the old, regardless of whether it is to reappear as the new, is to be "swept completely away"; that, indeed, is the only condition under which it may legitimately find a place in the new.

Descartes, of course, did not believe that much, if any, of the old would in fact find a place in the new. This is apparent from what he says about the *Principles of Philosophy*. In the final paragraph of the "Author's Letter," which serves as preface to the French edition of the *Principles*, we read "that many centuries may pass until all the truths which may be deduced from these principles are so deduced"; thus, although the new is being presented, it is very far from complete. But we also read that the new is genuinely new rather than the old transformed, for the principles upon which the new are to be founded are themselves new, a "difference which is observable between these principles and those of all other men."[5] The same is clear as well from *The Passions of the Soul*, the last work which Descartes prepared for publication. In the first article of the *Passions* he sounds what might at first be taken as the typically thorough reformer's note: "There is nothing in which the defective nature of the sciences which we have received from the ancients appears more clearly than in what they have written on the passions," for "that which the ancients have taught regarding them is … for the most part so far from credible, that I am unable to entertain any hope of approximating to the truth excepting by shunning the paths which they have followed." Thus a

---

4. Descartes, *Philosophical Works*, I, 129.

5. Descartes, *Philosophical Works*, I, 215.

strategy naturally presents itself: "I shall be ... obliged to write just as though I were treating of a matter which no one had ever touched on before me."[6] Again, the new is clearly presented as new. Speaking of the *Passions'* content as new was, of course, no idle boast, for there existed no precedent of a consistent attempt at an explanation of mental and physiological phenomena entirely by means of simple mechanical processes. What was presented as new did indeed look new and was in fact different from what had gone before. But its newness in appearance should not obscure an important point, which is that whether or not it looked new it would, in Descartes' view, be new simply because it could have been presented only after the old had been completely swept away. Thus, what had the appearance of reformation again turns out to be revolution. That which arises in, as it were, a vacuum or entirely contextlessly cannot fail to be new. If we take seriously Descartes' metaphor that all previous opinions must be swept completely away, then use of the phrases "in a vacuum" and "entirely contextlessly" is legitimate.

Sometimes Descartes speaks as if the *hubris* or, perhaps, the cultural solipsism implicit in the statements of the preceding paragraph is meant to be taken as quite innocent because it is entirely idiosyncratic. In the *Discourse*, for example, we read that "My design has never extended beyond trying to reform my own opinion and to build on a foundation which is entirely my own."[7] In the sentences immediately following this statement, Descartes even seems to warn against following his example. These warnings, however, are stipulated to be for two groups of people. They hold for those who are "precipitate in judgment" and thus simply cannot follow Descartes' example even if they would, for they do not have "sufficient patience to arrange their thoughts in proper order" and therefore cannot reach

---

6.   Descartes, *Philosophical Works*, I, 331.

7.   Descartes, *Philosophical Works*, I, 90.

valid new results. Not paying attention to "order" is attempting to gain truth unmethodically, and the only outcome of that exercise will be opinion and belief, not certainty and knowledge. This outcome comes to be shared by the second group. For the warnings hold as well for those who believe "that they are less capable of distinguishing truth from falsehood than some others from whom instruction might be obtained." Such people "are right in contenting themselves with following the opinions of these others rather than in searching better ones for themselves." These warnings amount to saying that attempts at reformation are for neither the foolish nor the timid. That leaves the wise and the courageous; and as Descartes well knew, men are more apt to classify themselves as wise and courageous than as foolish or timid. Thus, for anyone not satisfied with mere opinion, completely sweeping away all beliefs is a necessary condition for obtaining truth.

Apart from all this Descartes must, of course, say that his design does not extend beyond trying to reform his own opinion and to build on a foundation which is entirely his own. He is forced to say this not out of modesty, or because of political circumspection, or even primarily because he believes many or most of his contemporaries to be either too precipitous or too timid to do scientific work. Instead, he must say this because his position of radical epistemic autonomy forces it upon him: everyone has to do it for himself, can only do it for himself. No one, therefore, can build upon anything which might be called a "primary given," on something given through the senses, or from one's tradition, from education, or from one's contemporaries' thoughts. None of these can provide a solid foundation on which to build a system of knowledge. As the first of the *Principles* puts it, "...in order to examine into the truth it is necessary once in one's life to doubt of all things...." Modest though Descartes' reformation may seem, it is really a thoroughly radical revolution.

It may seem an exaggeration to speak of the radicality of Descartes' revolution if the basic principle of the revolution's manifesto merely forbids the acceptance of a primary given as a foundation on which to build science. It will seem less of an exaggeration once it is remembered that, for Descartes, no action ought to be called truly human unless it can be called rational, and it cannot be called rational unless it is (part of) science or is dictated by (part of) science. Therefore, when it is said that no primary given may be accepted as a foundation on which to build science, this implies that no primary given may be accepted on which to order the practice of any aspect of life, if that practice is to qualify as truly human. That is one reason why in my second paragraph I wrote about Descartes as one who brought about a totally new outlook in potentially all areas of life.

The thorough radicality of Descartes' revolution is closely related to his epistemology and methodology. In terms of epistemology this may be put as follows. The solid foundation must consist of items which are known not in terms of something else, not *per aliud*; instead, it must consist of items which are underived, self-evident, known *per se*. Moreover, such items must be characterized by clarity and distinctness.

In the *Rules for the Direction of the Mind* Descartes refers to the power through which we are to "grasp" such foundational items as "intuition." As a definition of *intuition* he gives:

> By *intuition* I understand, not the fluctuating testimony of the senses, nor the misleading judgment that proceeds from the blundering constructions of imagination, but the conception which an unclouded and attentive mind gives us so readily and distinctly that we are wholly freed from doubt about that which we understand.[8]

---

8.   Descartes, *Philosophical Works*, I, 7.

The mind is there said to consist of the understanding (which is explicated as comprising both "intuition" and "deduction"), imagination, sense, and memory. Memory is never taken to be a source of knowledge, for it can only present that which it has first received from the understanding, imagination, or sense. But if knowledge is to be characterized as certain or indubitable, then, as the definition of intuition states clearly enough through its polemical juxtaposition of "fluctuating," "misleading," and "blundering" to "unclouded," "attentive," and "wholly freed from doubt," we cannot expect to gain knowledge (at least not knowledge which may be called "foundational") from the senses or the imagination, but must depend on the understanding alone. What Descartes wants to bring into dispute for his contemporaries is whether any "givens" ought to be accepted, irrespective of whether their source is sensation or education. For Descartes himself it is beyond dispute that nothing we sense and nothing we learn from others can be accepted as a "given." To put this more precisely: what is thus given may be used as a point of departure for analysis or reduction but must be rejected as a suitable starting point for synthesis, for the construction of systematic knowledge. Those who immediately accept as truth the testimony of their senses may come to believe that cherries are red and sweet or that the sun revolves around the earth. Those who immediately accept as truth the opinions of their teachers may find themselves accepting the dogmas of Aristotle or Aquinas as tenable philosophical positions. This acceptance places such people in the ranks of those who "throughout all their lives perceive nothing so correctly as to be capable of judging of it properly." They have never had anything before their minds with clarity *and* distinctness. For whereas "I term that clear which is present and apparent to an attentive mind... the distinct is that which is so precise and different from all other objects that it contains within itself nothing but what is clear."[9] In other words, in order to be capable of judging properly of anything, it is not sufficient to be merely fully aware of all of that "thing," for such awareness may leave the "thing" intricately enmeshed with many other "things," none of which need themselves be before the mind clearly. In order to be able to judge properly, that of which we judge must be before the mind fully, *and* we must have before the mind nothing but what necessarily pertains to having all of it before the mind.

Items to be known *per se*, if they can be known at all, can only be known clearly and distinctly. Anything known *per aliud* can be known only if that from which it is derived is also before the mind (or, at the least, is remembered as having been before the mind). Thus, anything known *per aliud* ultimately can be known only if it can be seen as following with necessity from the relevant foundation or first principles, from what is known *per se*. Therefore that which the senses give us cannot, as given, be known immediately by the understanding. For what is thus given is concrete, enmeshed in its context, possibly affected as to its "appearance" by the very way in which it is given. For Descartes, its "nature" can be understood only once it has been fitted into the "rational scheme" of a mechanics, medicine, or morals—rational schemes which themselves cannot be developed prior to the development of the "rational schemes" called physics and metaphysics, schemes which in turn rest on the prior knowledge of certain principles known *per se*. Neither can we know immediately that which our education or culture places before us. For neither Euclid's *Elements* nor Aristotle's *Ethics* nor Aquinas' *Summa Theologica* nor Galileo's *Two New Sciences* clearly derives its conclusions from indubitable principles which are known *per se*. None of them, in fact, even went so far as to attempt to state these principles. But even had they stated them, and had they de-

9.   Descartes, *Principles* I, 45.

rived their conclusions from them by uninterrupted chains of arguments, I myself cannot begin at the end, with conclusions. If I am to
understand, I must start where they began, with first principles.

If I am to understand, I must understand for myself, radically so.
To adopt words from the opening paragraph of the *First Meditation*,
someone else's "firm and permanent structure in the sciences" is of
little use to me, for I will not be able to understand it unless I myself
"commence to build anew from the foundation." And no foundation
is given; the foundation is to be established. Whoever wants to under
stand will first have to establish his own foundation. Thus Descartes
speaks for himself and, he believes, for whoever comes to understand, when he writes that "My design has never extended beyond
trying to reform my own opinion and to build on a foundation
which is entirely my own." The need for radical revolution is dictated
by a doctrine of radical epistemic individualism.

That is one way of putting it, looked at primarily in terms of the
"object of knowledge." We come to the same conclusion when we
consider it from the side of the knower or the "subject." For only if
he proceeds methodically can the knower come to establish his foundation and can he develop systematic knowledge upon it. And, as I
said before, Descartes' method is one which calls for substitution
rather than transformation.

Use of the method entails radical revolution. Its very first principle enjoins me "to accept nothing as true which I did not clearly
recognize to be so: that is to say, carefully to avoid precipitation
and prejudice in judgments, and to accept in them nothing more
than what was presented to my mind so clearly and distinctly that
I could have no occasion to doubt it."[10] Avoidance of precipitation
calls for suspension of judgment. That with respect to which judgment has been suspended then needs to be "divided up ... into as

---

10. Descartes, *Philosophical Works*, I, 92.

many parts as possible" (as the second methodological precept has it) so that we may come to see whether it rests on a foundation of items which are self-evident. Both the suspension of judgment and the reduction to simplicity are acts in which the individual asserts his freedom, acts which in turn are to lead to the individual's greater autonomy or self-realization. Through suspension of judgment I am to stay free from prejudice (where a "prejudice" is any belief or item of supposed knowledge which I have not myself constructed upon a foundation of clear and distinct, self-evident knowledge); through reduction I am to reach clear and distinct, self-evident knowledge. Suspension of judgment is motivated by doubt, and reduction of what is experienced as complex is pushed by doubt to its extreme, which is found in utter simplicity or self-evidence. Methodic doubt is a prime manifestation of the individual's autonomy or freedom.

Doubt, therefore, is not a defect. When at the beginning of the Fourth Meditation Descartes writes that "... I doubt, that is to say ...I am an incomplete and dependent being...," this presence of doubt or of method (for the doubt referred to is methodic doubt) does show incompleteness but does not indicate the presence of a "negative quality" like, for example, evil or error. Doubt is to be used, to be pursued; error and evil are to be shunned. Doubt plays a positive role in that it is the road to avoid precipitation and prejudice in judgment, the way in which we stay free from evil and error. Only when doubt is confused with irresolution does it become a defect. For as the *Passions* tell us, irresolution is "a species of fear" which proceeds "from a feebleness of understanding, which, having no clear and distinct conceptions, simply has many confused ones."[11] Doubt, rather than being fear, is firmness of purpose. It proceeds from the state of mind determined not to accept at face

---

11. Descartes, *Passions*, article CLXX.

value whatever may be given to it, but to resolve such givens into a multiplicity of items which are clear and distinct. The practice of doubt is to free reason from prejudice by expelling from the mind all "knowledge" which I have not myself constructed upon my own unshakable foundation.

In his Introduction to *Descartes, Philosophical Writings*,[12] Alexandre Koyré aptly contrasts Descartes and Montaigne. Montaigne "... abandons the external world—uncertain object of uncertain opinion—and tries to fall back upon himself in order to find in himself the foundation of certainty, the firm principles of *judgment*—that is, of a *discriminating discernment between the true and the false*." Montaigne "... looks for a firm foundation" and "finds nothing but perpetual change, instability, void." He "acknowledges his failure" and "fearlessly" faces up to the fact that "We have to accept things as they are," that "we have to renounce the hope with which we started," the hope to find in oneself the foundation of certainty. And so Montaigne's *Essais* are "a treatise of renunciation," a statement that "the last word of wisdom is: We have to abide by doubt."[13] Descartes would align Montaigne's doubt with irresolution, would see it as fear. For Descartes, doubt becomes the first word of wisdom. Doubt, as methodic doubt, becomes the key to the passage beyond renunciation, the passage of hope and self-affirmation, of progress and freedom. Koyré nicely catches this contrast: "... whereas Montaigne stopped the finitude of the human soul, Descartes discovered the fullness of spiritual freedom, the certainty of intellectual truth." And so Koyré labels the *Discourse on the Method* "the Cartesian *Confessions*" or Descartes' *Itinerarium Mentis in Veritatem*, the story of Descartes' "successful break-through," the reply "to the *Essais*." "To the sad story told by Montaigne, the story of a de-

---

12. Alexandre Koyré, "Introduction," *Descartes, Philosophical Writings*, edited by Elizabeth Anscombe and Peter Thomas Geach (London, 1954).

13. Koyré, p. x.

feat, Descartes opposes his own, the story of a decisive victory."[14] Whereas Montaigne "*submits* to doubt as its slave, through weakness... Descartes employs doubt as his tool, or, if one prefers, as his weapon."[15]

Thus, in his juxtaposition of Descartes to Montaigne, Koyré articulates the position I just now presented: doubt and freedom work together for Descartes. Unfortunately, Koyré's analysis stops short of the final truth about both Descartes' doubt and freedom. He does call Descartes a revolutionary[16] but, though a revolutionary, one who accepted the Christian gospels and allowed himself to be taught by St. Augustine.[17] Of course Descartes often professed his adherence to Christianity, but his philosophy was nevertheless quite opposed to it. Koyré has rightly connected method, doubt, and freedom. As he says, Descartes sets himself "the task of re-ordering all our mental activities on a new plan...and it is through freedom that we shall reach the truth, i.e., those clear and distinct ideas which our reason is unable to doubt."[18] That, surely, is the reverse of the gospel's statement that "the truth will make you free." At least in practice, Descartes' revolution in the sciences was accompanied by a revolt against the gospel through a revolt against the Christian view of the place of man. It seems to me that the spirit of Descartes' philosophy is caught better by Vrooman than by Koyré: "Descartes' faith in human reason gave him a non-Christian...conception of man"; "the fundamental principles and method of Descartes" he invokes "in order to restore faith in the human condition and in the possibility of man's being able to govern...his own destiny."[19]

---

14. Koyré, p. xiv.

15. Koyré, pp. xxii-xxiii.

16. Koyré, p. xiii.

17. Koyré, pp. xxiv-xxv.

18. Koyré, p. xxiii.

19. Jack R. Vrooman, *René Descartes: A Biography* (New York, 1970),

Doubt, this prime manifestation of an individual's freedom, is to liberate reason from the bondage of prejudice and in the process is to lead the individual to his fundamental absolute certainty, to the *cogito*. This relation between freedom and the *cogito* has been discussed by many critics. I should like to quote one of these, Hiram Caton, first, to put some of my contentions in somewhat different and perhaps more colorful language, and, second, to indicate some measure of disagreement with Caton on one of the points he makes—a disagreement which leads immediately into my concluding comments.

In *The Origin of Subjectivity* Caton writes:

> The Cogito brings thought to consciousness of its nature... In that moment the mind apprehends an objective limit upon deception, for the Cogito exhibits to thought a limit upon omnipotence circumscribed by thought itself, indeed, *my* thought.

> By bringing reason to consciousness of its inner nature, and embracing that nature...the Cogito emancipates reason from all restraints of piety: it empowers a self-consciously secular reason...An unshakable and immutable will is the basis of the autonomy of reason.... "Self-consciousness constitutes itself in defiance of all omnipotence...here begins in philosophy as such the rebellion against Christianity that we call Enlightenment."[20]

My one misgiving about Caton's statement concerns the word *begins* in the final sentence. For when a "rebellion" "begins," its beginning

---

pp. 260-61.

20. Hiram Caton, *The Origin of Subjectivity: An Essay on Descartes* (New Haven and London, 1973), pp. 124-25. The last two sentences in this quotation Caton takes from Gerhard Krüger, "Die Herkunft des philosophischen selbstbewusstseins,"*Logos*, 22 (1933), 225-72, 246.

may be half-hearted, weak, confused, and therefore easily suppressed. Such a beginning is not Descartes'.

Descartes' beginning is unequivocally reason's unilateral declaration of independence. Descartes, the man, may say—and may possibly mean—what we read in the final paragraph of the *Third Meditation*:

> ...it seems to me right to pause for a while in order to contemplate God Himself, to ponder at leisure His marvellous attributes, to consider, and admire, and adore, the beauty of this light so resplendent, at least as far as the strength of my mind, which is in some measure dazzled by the sight, will allow me to do so.

Nevertheless, there is no doubt whatsoever that Descartes, the philosopher, means it when, recasting the argument of his *Meditations*, he writes:

> But meanwhile whoever turns out to have created us, and even should he be all-powerful and deceitful, we still experience a freedom through which we may abstain from accepting as true and indisputable those things of which we have not certain knowledge, and thus obviate our ever being deceived.[21]

And (if I may continue my use of this artificial distinction for a moment) it is not Descartes the man but Descartes the philosopher who helped shape the modern mind. Pascal's complaint was well-taken: "I cannot forgive Descartes. In all his philosophy he would have been quite willing to dispense with God."[22]

The Third Meditation closes with a statement which invokes the medieval attitude of contemplation. But it opens with a statement to

---

21. Descartes, *Principles* 1, 6.
22. Pascal, *Pensées*, Section 2, p. 77.

the effect that the only ground for doubt of the absolute trustworthiness of reason in all affairs of life is the supposed existence of an Evil Genius.[23] Rejection of that ground for doubt entails the removal of God from philosophy and makes contemplation a matter for the man, not the philosopher. The only ground for doubting reason is the supposed existence of the Evil Genius. For (says Descartes) if God exists, God cannot be a deceiver, for it is contradictory to hold that deception and perfection can coexist in the same being.[24] Therefore, if God exists, there cannot be such doubt, and reason can be taken as trustworthy. But, similarly, if God does not exist, there cannot be an Evil Genius, for the Evil Genius is stipulated to be supremely powerful, that is, must be God, who has been said not to exist. And since the Evil Genius's supposed existence is said to be the only ground for distrusting reason, we can trust reason. Thus, whether God exists or not, we can trust reason.

For all practical purposes, Descartes the Christian gentleman made God irrelevant. Christian gentlemen sometimes have the tendency to do that. But not all of them do. Evan Runner certainly did not. On the contrary, in all his lecturing and writing he constantly stressed the totalitarian nature of "absolute trustworthiness" and the consequences thereof. He always stressed the impossibility of the peaceful coexistence of different faiths in one and the same person, or in one and the same community. With respect to Descartes he would, I am confident, agree that the new faith—the faith of placing total trust in reason as a first and last resort—was robbing the possessors of it from whatever power remained to them as adorers of the Light Resplendent. For as he said:

---

23. Descartes, *Philosophical Works*, I, 159.

24. *Conversation with Burman*, edited by John Cottingham (Oxford, 1976), pp. 2, 6.

If in our search for truth we put our confidence in our 'Reason' and the subjection of all things to the rational inquiry of men, we have changed entirely, as *men*. At first we may *for a time* be able to hold on to some division of our life into what historically have been called the areas of faith and of reason. But life is integral; it's all one piece.... But all faith is totalitarian. And sooner or later the one will destroy the other.[25]

---

25. H. E. Runner, *Christian Perspectives, 1960* (Pella, Iowa, 1960), p. 92.

M. HOWARD RIENSTRA

The Religious Problem of the Renaissance

THAT A CONSIDERATION OF the Renaissance is an appropriate part of a collection of essays dedicated to H. Evan Runner should be evident to anyone acquainted with his writing and teaching. The Renaissance figures prominently in both. Central to Runner's view of life and thought, to his view of history, is the understanding that the Word of God is the driving force (*dynamis*) in the entire order of creation. Everything in life, culture, and history is properly to be seen as a response to this driving force, and all such response is essentially religious. Thus, all of human culture, all of history, is religious. Almost a generation of students has encountered this thesis in his lecture on "Christianity and Humanism."[1] Humanism, as Runner presents it, is that typically modern religion which celebrates the freedom and autonomy of man. It is a religion centered on the *humanum*, man. Humanism originated in the Renaissance. In Runner's view, therefore, the Renaissance is a period of radical religious change that has given direction to all of modern Western civilization. And the secular humanism which is the religion of the Renaissance is theoretically and religiously antithetical to Christianity.[2]

1. H. Evan Runner, "Christianity and Humanism: A Re-thinking of the Supposed Affinity of Their Fundamental Principles" (1968), distributed by the Association for the Advancement of Christian Scholarship, Toronto.

2. For an interpretation similar to Runner's, see Herman Dooyeweerd *Roots of Western Culture: Pagan, Secular, and Christian Options* (Toronto, 1979).

Runner's interpretation of the Renaissance, however, is a product not only of this distinctively Christian vision of the centrality of religion to all of life and thought, but also of a certain stage of scholarship on the concept of the Renaissance. His view of the Renaissance stands in the tradition of Jacob Burckhardt and is sometimes simply called the traditional view. This traditional view sees the Renaissance as a radical break with the Middle Ages and as that movement in history out of which the modern world has emerged. The traditional view emphasizes the pagan and anti-Christian character of Renaissance humanism. The trend of recent studies is to repudiate this traditional view. The trend of recent studies is to emphasize not only the religious, but the essentially Christian, character of Renaissance humanism. This development in scholarship about the Renaissance will be presented as a congenial critique of Runner's interpretation and as an enrichment of his central thesis about the essentially religious character of historical change.

With the appearance of Wallace K. Ferguson's *The Renaissance in Historical Thought*,[3] the historiography of the Renaissance came of age. Ferguson analyzed the varying concepts of the Renaissance that have been held by philosophers and historians from Petrarch down to the mid-twentieth century. Such interpretations have clearly been more a product of the intellectual commitments of their proponents than of the state of scholarship on the period. There have been humanist, rationalist, and romantic views of the Renaissance, and there

---

3. Wallace K. Ferguson, *The Renaissance in Historical Thought: Five Centuries of Interpretation* (New York, 1948). In that same year a Dutch historian, H. Schulte Nordholt, published *Het Beeld der Renaissance: Een Historiografische Studie* (Amsterdam, 1948). His naive adherence to the Burckhardtian tradition was censured in a review by Albert Hyma, *The American Historical Review*, 56 (1949), 870–71. See also the Dutch art historian Herman Baeyens, *Begrip en Probleem van de Renaissance* (Louvain, 1952).

were, and are, distinctively Protestant and Catholic views.[4] The water-
shed of modern Renaissance scholarship, however, was reached with
the publication of Jacob Burckhardt's *The Civilization of the Renaissance in Italy*.[5] The Renaissance is the beginning of the modern world.
It is the era of the discovery of man and nature. Although not everything that is called Burckhardtian can be found in his treatise, there is
a clear sense that culture had become not only secular, but actually
pagan and anti-Christian. A man-centered world had come to be
which, at least by anticipation, was intellectually and spiritually akin to
the Enlightenment and nineteenth-century humanism. This Burckhardtian view has been held both by those who deplore and those who
rejoice in this radical break with the Christian past. One anti-Burck-
hardtian view, characterized by Ferguson as "Medievalist," has argued
that there was no such radical break—rather, there was continuity.
These "Medievalists" generally deplored the secularizing and paganizing tendency Burckhardt saw in the Renaissance, while others of the
same school found the origins of some of the supposed positive inno-
vations of the Renaissance to lie deep within the Middle Ages.[6]

Four years after the appearance of Ferguson's study, an Italian
scholar, Carlo Angeleri, published a similar historiographical
study under the title *The Religious Problem of the Renaissance*.[7]

---

4. Ierbert Weisinger, "The Attack on the Renaissance in Theology Today," *Studies
    in the Renaissance*, 2 (1955), 176–89. Weisinger notes the paradox of
    Protestant theology being so anti-Renaissance that it becomes
    pro-medieval and anti-Reformation.

5. Jacob Burckhardt, *Die Cultur der Renaissance in Italien* (Basel, 1860).
    There are many English editions.

6. The now classic statement of this thesis is by Charles Homer Haskins,
    The Renaissance of the 12th Century (Cambridge, 1927). The best recent
    statement is by Colin Morris, *The Discovery of the Individual:
    1050-1200* (New York, 1972).

7. Carlo Angeleri, *Il Problema Religioso del Rinascimento: Storia della
    Critica e Bibliografia* (Firenze, 1952).

Angeleri correctly saw that the polemic among conflicting interpretations of the Renaissance was a polemic about religion in the Renaissance and that it typically arose out of the religious commitments of the historians. He anticipated both that the polemic would continue to be focused on religion and that research on the period would continue to be concerned with religion. He noted the scant attention which Burckhardt had paid to religion in the sense of *ecclesia*, cult, or piety, but at the same time he noted how crucially religious was the theme of the "discovery of man and nature." In the following we shall be concerned with the religious problem of the Renaissance in both these senses of *religion*.

One note of caution is necessary. Attempting to consider the Renaissance in its entirety requires a level of generalization that only rarely will correspond with the generalizations emerging out of works of detailed scholarship. Scholarship tends to focus on more discrete segments of time and place than the Renaissance as a whole. And this is true also of humanism. At one time it was common to think of humanism as a stage in the development of the Renaissance.[8] For our present purposes the Renaissance is that period in European history that runs from the fourteenth-century through the sixteenth-century, and humanism is a particular movement within that period. Whereas it was once common to speak of a sequence from humanism to Renaissance to Reformation, it is now common to speak of earlier and later Renaissance, with the Reformation incorporated in the later Renaissance.[9] We are thus considering the religious problem of the period from Petrarch to Galileo.

---

8.   The best example of this tradition is Giuseppe Saitta's monumental *Il Pensiero Italiano nell'Umanesimo e nel Rinascimento,* 3 vols. (Bologna, 1949-51).

9.   A general example is the anthology edited by Eric Cochrane, *The Late Italian Renaissance: 1525-1630* (New York, 1970). For a helpful discussion, see William J. Bouwsma, "Changing Assumptions in Later Renaissance Culture," *Viator,* 7 (1976), 421-40.

One of the best known clichés about the Renaissance is that of the Catholic medievalist Étienne Gilson: "The Renaissance is not the Middle Ages plus man, but minus God."[10] Gilson thus simultaneously affirmed and deplored the Renaissance as a break in the continuity of Christian civilization. True, integral, Christian humanism in this contemporary Scholastic view of the matter is thus the humanism of the Middle Ages.[11] A recent example of this perspective is Father Louis Bouyer's contribution to *A History of Christian Spirituality*.

In the fifteenth century and at the beginning of the sixteenth, the inhabitants of a certain world of letters were living on a hollow Christianity, from which the core had been removed. They fed upon the illusion that pagan wisdom in its highest forms…is one with Christian wisdom, provided that the latter silences the demands of dogma and of the Gospel. Ultimately, such wisdom has no use for God or for Christ. Only man remains—whence the term "humanist" that has come to be attached to that Renaissance.[12]

10. Etienne Gilson, *Les Idées et les Lettres* (Paris, 1932), and often republished. "La différence entre la Renaissance et le moyen âge n'est pas une différence par excès, mais par défaut. La Renaissance, telle qu'on nous la décrit, n'est pas le moyen âge plus l'homme, mais le moyen âge moins Dieu, et la tragédie, c'est qu'en perdant Dieu la Renaissance allait perdre l'homme lui-même, mais ce serait une autre et longue histoire à raconter" (p. 192, twelfth edition).

11. See for example, Jacques Maritain, *Integral Humanism* (Notre Dame, 1968). Two valuable studies of twelfth-century humanism are R. W. Southern, "Medieval Humanism," in his *Medieval Humanism and Other Studies* (New York, 1970) and Dom David Knowles, "The Humanism of the 12th Century," in his *The Historian and Character* (Cambridge, 1963).

12. J. Leclercq, F. VandenBroucke, and L. Bouyer, *The Spirituality of the Middle Ages* (New York, 1968), pp. 507-8. (Vol. II of *A History of Christian Spirituality;* original French edition, 1961).

Curiously, however, an almost identical view of the Renaissance is held by modern humanists. Their view is based on diametrically opposed principles. The following is typical:

> The cultural revolution in the West occurred during the Renaissance: it is represented by the movement that is called Humanism.... Against authority and dogma, and for man, is the Humanist position. Since the Renaissance, Humanism has become identified with the attitude emphasizing man's natural powers as against the claims of a supernatural religion.[13]

Contemporary humanists thus affirm and rejoice in the presumed Renaissance break with its Christian antecedents. Such enthusiasm for the Burckhardtian tradition, which, incidentally, would have been offensive to Burckhardt himself, is hardly to be found among Renaissance scholars today. One notable exception is the recent work of H. A. E. Van Gelder. Van Gelder's thesis is that there were two "reformations" in that century, but the Reformation, in both its Protestant and Catholic phases, was actually the minor and less significant "reformation." The major "reformation" as he sees it is that of a new religious movement:

> I shall call it humanistic religion, because it was principally held by those whom we have long been accustomed to call 'Humanists,' and because by shifting attention from God to man, it signified the beginning of the evolution which, via the Enlightenment, finds its most consistent continuation in what in recent years has been called "Humanism" on the continent and 'Ethical Culturalism' in England.[14]

---

13. E. H. Hutten, "Humanism in the Renaissance," *Humanist* (1968), p. 334.

14. H. A. E. Van Gelder, *The Two Reformations of the Sixteenth Century* (The Hague, 1961), p. 8.

This self-confessed "personal appraisal" is generally regarded as an oddity of modern Renaissance scholarship. There are others. For example, the work of Giuseppe Toffanin proposed that Renaissance humanism was in fact a Catholic reaction to late medieval paganism and atheism, especially as represented by the Paduan Aristotelians.[15] The one piece of careful recent scholarship which affirms a Burckhardtian view of Renaissance humanism is that of George Holmes. Holmes notes that there was a certain "indifference or hostility to traditional religion"[16] among early Quattrocento humanists which is very similar to that which occurred again in the Enlightenment of the eighteenth-century. He shows, however, the caution of a disciplined historian.

> The available evidence will probably not allow us to define the humanists' attitude to Christianity much more clearly. They were not atheists or anti-Christians. They were skeptical of some aspects of modern ecclesiastical organization, and about the value of scholasticism. Their philosophical and religious instincts, such as they were, tended towards a simple moral system.[17]

---

15. Giuseppe Toffanin, *Storia della Umanesimo*, 3 vols. (Bologna, 1952). Critical introductions to this and other traditions of Renaissance historiography can be found in the following three studies: William J. Bouwsma, *The Interpretation of Renaissance Humanism*, an American Historical Association pamphlet for teachers of history (Washington, D.C., 1959); the first chapter of Eckhard Kessler, *Das Problem des frühen Humanismus* (Munich, 1968); and the second part of Franco Simone, *Il Rinascimento Francese: Studie e Ricerche* (Torino, 1961).

16. George Holmes, *The Florentine Enlightenment: 1400-1450* (New York, 1969). Holmes' use of the term *Enlightenment* in the context of the Renaissance has been analyzed by C. Behan McCullagh, "Colligation and Classification in History," *History and Theory*, 17 (1978), 267-84.

17. Holmes, p. 123.

His affirmation of Renaissance discontinuity is much more restrained than those Catholic or humanist historians who are looking to the Renaissance for confirmation or disconfirmation of their own religious commitments.

In the same year that Carlo Angeleri's book appeared, 1952, an international conference on the Renaissance was held in Florence. In a paper on "Religion in the Renaissance," Alberto Pincherle asserted, perhaps somewhat prematurely, that the concept of a pagan or irreligious Renaissance could now be considered eliminated.[18] Paul Oscar Kristeller, whose own contributions to an understanding of the Renaissance will be considered subsequently, seemed to agree. In a paper given in 1954 he stated: "…since the religious convictions of Christianity were either retained or transformed, but never really challenged, it seems more appropriate to call the Renaissance a fundamentally Christian age."[19] He further held that "…practically all Renaissance humanists, before and after the Reformation, were Christian humanists, since the alleged cases of openly

---

18. Alberto Pincherle, "La Religione nel Rinascimento," in *Il Rinascimento: Significati e Limiti* (Atti del III Convegno Internazionale sul Rinascimento) (Firenze, 1953), pp. 173-209. "Per quanto riguarda la religione, la concezione di un Rinascimento 'pagano,' o anche irreligioso o indifferente, può ormai—tante correzioni e revisioni ha subíto—considerarsi come eliminate" (p. 175). In a comment to Pincherle's paper, Eugenio Garin observed that even Valla opposed scholastic theology, not Christianity. "Valla è contro la teologia scolastica, non contro la religione cristiana. Il suo *De libero arbitrio* è un tentativo di mostrare l'impossibilità di risolvere con gli strumenti della pura ragione problemi religiosi che la teologia affronta" (p. 209).

19. Paul Oscar Kristeller, "Paganism and Christianity," in *The Classics and Renaissance Thought* (Cambridge, 1955), p. 73. This has recently been reprinted in P. O. Kristeller, *Renaissance Thought and Its Sources,* edited by Michael Mooney (New York, 1979).

pagan or atheistic convictions are rare and dubious."[20] However, returning to the question in 1959, Kristeller seemed to modify this conclusion:

> I strongly disagree with a number of recent attempts to counter the traditional view of pagan humanism by insisting that humanism was basically a Christian and religious movement.... A large body of humanistic literature is neither Christian nor anti-Christian, but simply secular in character.[21]

While still accepting that in a broad sense nearly all humanists were Christian, he importantly acknowledges that "It all depends on how we define religion."[22] To Kristeller, as the context of that almost casual observation reveals, religion is either metaphysical speculation or theological belief. His narrowly circumscribed idea of religion is revealed in another 1959 lecture. In the context of describing the secularism of the Renaissance, he observes, "...it makes as much sense to speak of Christian humanism as of Christian logic or mathematics or physics."[23] His presumption is that

---

20. Kristeller, "Paganism and Christianity," p. 86. See also Kristeller's "The Myth of Renaissance Atheism and the French Tradition of Free Thought," *The Journal of the History of Philosophy* (1968), pp. 233-43.

21. Paul Oscar Kristeller, "Changing Views of the Intellectual History of the Renaissance Since Jacob Burckhardt," in *The Renaissance: A Reconsideration of the Theories and Interpretations of the Age,* edited by Tinsley Helton (Madison, 1961), p. 38.

22. Kristeller, "Changing Views," p. 44.

23. Paul Oscar Kristeller, "Studies on Renaissance Humanism During the Last Twenty Years," *Studies in the Renaissance,* 9 (1962), 19. An almost identical nominalist view of religion can be found in Siro Attilio Nulli, *Erasmo e il Rinascimento* (Torino, 1955). Nulli writes: "Pero parlare di umanesimo cristiano ha lo stesso senso che parlare di geometria cattolica o di chimica cristiana: e una cattiva espressione invece di dire: attivita filologica e culturale esercitata da individui che si professano seguaci del cattolicismo circa argomenti che appartengono alla storia delle Chiese" (p. 445).

such things are in themselves neither Christian nor anti-Christian. Nevertheless, he does concede that it is appropriate to call such Renaissance figures as Erasmus and More "Christian humanists," since they consciously put their humanism to the service of their Christian faith.

The most recent contribution to the historiography of the religious problem of the Renaissance has been made by Charles Trinkaus. Once again, Trinkaus' own major contribution to a new understanding of the relationship between humanism and religion will be considered subsequently. Trinkaus decries what he calls "genetic-modernizing" kinds of history.[24] Historians have too frequently looked to the Renaissance for the roots and ancestors of their own cultural commitments or made it a battleground on which contending forces or spirits raged. He calls for a study of the dynamic relationships, not taxonomic, that subsist between "ideas, purposes, feelings, behavior, beliefs, hopes, and fears."[25] His paper surveys how the study of religion in the Renaissance, in terms of these dynamic relationships, has been unfolding during the past twenty years. He speaks of "transformations...of modes of consciousness" and suggests that such critical change that may have occurred between the Middle Ages and the seventeenth-century occurred only gradually, and later rather than earlier in that period. He does see the Renaissance as central to that process by which religion has

---

24. Charles Trinkaus, "Humanism, Religion, Society: Concepts and Motivations of Some Recent Studies,"*Renaissance Quarterly,* 29 (1976), 676-713. William J. Bouwsma, in his Presidential Address to the American Historical Association, disagrees with Trinkaus on this point, but only slightly. His argument is that if historians don't do this work, others will. See "The Renaissance and the Drama of Western History," *American Historical Review,* 84 (1979), 8.

25. Trinkaus, "Humanism," p. 688.

come to be displaced in the modern world. Secularization of European culture did occur during the Renaissance, but secularization needs careful definition.

> For the secularization of culture and the "deification" of man grew directly out of the movements and attitudes that were present within medieval-Renaissance-Reformation Christianity itself rather than being the program of a secularist opposition movement to 'medieval' Christianity.[26]

A religious transformation took place during the Renaissance, but it is a transformation from some kind of non-secular Christianity to a secular Christianity. Trinkaus' own encapsulating phrase is: "...what was going on was a tendency to secularize the sacred while simultaneously sacralizing the secular."[27] This is no longer the Burckhardtian tradition's paganizing break with the Middle Ages. Christianity was secularized, and that in the long run led to the displacement of religion in the modern world. But Renaissance religion was still essentially and radically Christian.

There are many nuances to this theme of secularization. One of the best known is the Weber-Troeltsch thesis about the secular asceticism of the reformers, particularly John Calvin.[28] The idea that one's religious obligation (*vocatio*) is to be exercised in the activities of one's daily occupation, in business or law, politics or medicine, stands in sharp contrast to the contemplative asceticism of an earlier time. Thomas A. Brady, Jr., has discovered a circumstance in Germany for which the secularizing-sacralizing

---

26. Trinkaus, "Humanism," p. 688.

27. Trinkaus, "Humanism," p. 688.

28. For a challenging discussion of Weber's "innerweltliche Askese," see Benjamin Nelson, *The Idea of Usury* (Princeton, 1949).

theme is fitting.[29] But it has been the work of Hans Baron and Eugenio Garin that has most clearly articulated the meaning of secularization in the context of Renaissance humanism.[30] Humanists such
as Salutati, Bruni, and even Valla celebrated the *vita civile* and the *vita
activa.* Civic humanism is the call to put learning to the service of
man as a citizen of a particular secular community, the Renaissance
city. This humanist celebration of the *vita civile* locates man's religious responsibility among the laity and within the context of the
political and moral circumstances of daily life. It is not, for that, any
less religious than life in the cloister, the contemplative life. It is not,
for being active, less Christian. William J. Bouwsma has succinctly
summarized this point:

Renaissance culture, and notably humanism, were important in the history of Christianity, but in a positive
rather than negative sense. Humanists were allied with
other men of the age in seeking a reformulation of

---

29. Thomas A. Brady, Jr., *Ruling Class, Regime, and Reformation at
Strasbourg: 1520-1555* (Leiden, 1978). "The corporate ideology of the
German cities understandably maintained a more traditional
Christian flavor. The ideal of civic Christianity, however, is almost an
exact analogue to the Italian ideal of civic humanism.... Two solutions
...the Italian solution of secularizing public life (civic humanism); and
the German one of sacralizing it (sacral corporatism)" (p. 17). See also:
Bernd Moeller, *Imperial Cities and the Reformation* (Philadelphia,1972)
and Steven Osment, *The Reformation in the Cities* (New Haven, 1975).

30. For Hans Baron, see his *The Crisis of the Early Italian Renaissance,* 2
vols. (Princeton, 1955) (one-volume revised edition, 1966). For
Eugenio Garin see his *Italian Humanism: Philosophy and Civic
Life in the Renaissance* (London, 1965) (original German edition:
Bern, 1947). Also in English are *Portraits from the Quattrocento*
(New York, 1972) (Italian original: Firenze, 1963) and *Science and
Civic Life in the Italian Renaissance* (New York, 1969).

Christian belief to meet the immediate needs and experience of the individual believer.[31]

Bouwsma's sensitivity to the Christian character of civic humanism is clear when he notes that religious conviction, "... when it properly functions, is not after all a compartmentalized set of beliefs separable from other concerns, but a means of ordering and comprehending every dimension of experience."[32]

Paul Oscar Kristeller's careful studies of Renaissance thought have deeply influenced all current scholarship. His definition of what humanism was, and who the humanists were, in the Renaissance is now almost universally accepted.[33] His is a formal definition, and it is very carefully rooted in the sources. Humanists were essentially those who immersed themselves in the study of grammar and rhetoric. They were poets or, alternatively, rhetoricians. In curricular terms they were committed to the *studia humanitatis*, or the *studia humaniora*. This consisted of grammar, rhetoric, history, poetry, and moral philosophy. Humanists were professionals in these studies who served society by putting these studies into the service of man in both his secular and ecclesiastical institutions and circumstances. Humanism was thus a product of that complex of activities in

31. William J. Bouwsma, a review of Sergio Bertelli, *Ribelli, Libertini e Ortodossi nella Storiografia Barocca* (Firenze, 1973), in *History and Theory,* 13 (1974), 309-10.

32. Bouwsma, "Review of Bertelli," p. 312.

33. Paul Oscar Kristeller, "Humanism and Scholasticism in the Italian Renaissance," *Byzantion,* 17 (1944-45), 346-74. It has been reprinted several times. Citations are from *Studies in Renaissance Thought and Letters* (Rome, 1956), pp. 553-83. For an independent discovery of this original sense of the term *humanist,* see Augusto Compana, "The Origin of the Word 'Humanist,'" *Journal of the Warburg and Courtauld Institute,* 9 (1946), 60-73.

which humanists participated.[34] It was not a philosophy. The humanist polemic against scholasticism was a polemic between enthusiasts for grammar and rhetoric, on the one hand, and enthusiasts for logic and natural philosophy, on the other. Some humanists were philosophers, and some were lawyers and teachers. Some were Platonists, but some also were Aristotelians. Their polemic with philosophers, with Aristotelians, and with Scholastics in general was an argument about utility.[35] Grammar and rhetoric spoke to man in his concrete wholeness, to his heart. Logic and natural philosophy spoke only to his intellect. There may be philosophical and religious commitments which follow from this more modest reconstruction of the terms "humanism" and "humanist" of Kristeller, but he holds them to be characteristics of individual humanists rather than of humanism as such.

For the particular concerns of this paper, however, the work of Charles Trinkaus marks a turning point. While accepting the general thesis of Kristeller, Trinkaus has profoundly enriched our understanding of the religious dimensions of humanist thought.[36] No one, having read Trinkaus's monograph, could ever again think that humanists were indifferent to religion, irreligious, or anti-Christian. It is difficult to summarize a work of this magnitude fairly, but a few lines from the chapter on Lorenzo Valla may illustrate the thesis:

> His [Valla's] was also one of the most powerful assertions of the reality of human experience within a Christian framework in his own age or in any age.... It would be hazardous to suggest that St. Augustine would recognize all the developments out of his ideas, but certainly Valla produced

---

34. Kristeller, "Humanism," p. 582.

35. See also Jerrold E. Seigel, *Rhetoric and Philosophy in Renaissance Humanism: The Union of Eloquence and Wisdom, Petrarch to Valla* (Princeton, 1968).

36. Charles Trinkaus, *In Our Image and Likeness: Humanity and Divinity in Italian Humanist Thought,* 2 vols. (London, 1970).

a version of Christianity solidly based on a rephrasing and transformation of Augustine's own voluntarism, eudemonism and theology of grace.... The precedents for Valla's extraordinary elevation of man (and subordination of the non-human universe to man as the agent and end of divine providence) lay in the humanism of Petrarch and Salutati, in the eroding of the metaphysical and hieratic theology of the thirteenth-century scholastics by their nominalist successors, in the passional life and theology of St. Augustine.[37]

And in a comment on his own work in the previously cited historiographical survey, Trinkaus says:

The discovery of the religious potentialities of rhetoric by the humanists, which I have labeled *theologia rhetorica*, seemed to derive from a dissatisfaction, shared by many of their contemporaries, with abstractness and the metaphysical character of scholastic and canonistic Christian thought, which, for a Petrarch or a Salutati, seemed remote from the Christian feelings and spirituality of the men of their time. Thus humanist religious thought seemed to be an effort to relate in a new way to the social context.[38]

The moral and the spiritual needs of man were now pre-eminent, and humanist thought addressed itself to those needs in all their concreteness and complexity. The response of the Renaissance humanists was both religious and Christian. Trinkaus returned to this theme of a *theologia rhetorica* in 1972 at a conference he convoked at the University of Michigan.[39] In that paper he traces the continuity of the rhetorical

---

37. Trinkaus, *In Our Image,* III, 168-69.

38. Trinkaus, "Humanism," p. 698.

39. Charles Trinkaus, "The Religious Thought of the Italian Humanists and Reformers: Anticipation or Autonomy?" in *The Pursuit of Holiness in Late Medieval and Renaissance Religion,* edited by Charles Trinkaus with Heiko Oberman (Leiden, 1974), hereafter cited as *Pursuit.*

tradition in theology from Petrarch to Calvin.[40] Humanist religion may have been incoherent at times, and unsystematic, but it was Christian.

The papers presented at that 1972 conference are themselves both products of the changes that had already occurred in the study of Renaissance religion and indicators of current trends of research and interpretation.[41] One is almost led to conclude that everything in the life and thought of Europe from the fourteenth-century to the sixteenth-century was religious. It was. Since space prohibits even one-sentence summaries of each paper, the paper of William J. Courtenay will be taken as an example of the others. This paper reviews the changes that have taken place in the interpretation of Nominalism since 1930.[42] According to Courtenay, Heiko Oberman's work has been decisive.[43] Nominalism is no longer seen as a moment in the

---

40. Trinkaus previously considered Calvin in "Renaissance Problems in Calvin's Theology," *Studies in the Renaissance,* 1 (1954), 59–80. Quirinus Breen was among the first to identify Calvin's relationship to Renaissance rhetoric. See his *John Calvin: A Study in French Humanism* (Grand Rapids, 1931) and especially his American Society of Church History presidential address, "John Calvin and the Rhetorical Tradition," *Church History,* 26 (1957), 3-21. It has been reprinted in Quirinus Breen, *Christianity and Humanism: Studies in the History of Ideas* (Grand Rapids, 1968), pp. 107-9.

41. The papers range from studies of popular religion in France to adolescent ritual in Florence, from studies of the Confessional to preaching to the Popes, and studies of nominalism, mysticism, and humanism.

42. William J. Courtenay, "Nominalism and Late Medieval Religion," *Pursuit,* pp. 26-59.

43. Heiko A. Oberman, *The Harvest of Medieval Theology: Gabriel Biel and Late Medieval Nominalism* (Cambridge, 1963). A continuation of his study has now appeared: *Werden und Wertung der Reformation: Vom Wegestreit zum Glaubenskampf* (Tübingen, 1977), reviewed by Hans Hillerbrand in *Renaissance Quarterly,* 33 (1980), 84-86. The direction of Oberman's studies can be found in his "Fourteenth Century Religious Thought," *Speculum,* 53 (1978), 80-93.

demoralization and disintegration of medieval thought. It is no longer seen as primarily a matter of philosophy. Nominalism is a theological stance taken in the context of the synchronic movements of humanism, mysticism, and reform. Nominalism is thus one of several concurrent efforts during the Renaissance to find religious coherence.

Heiko Oberman, in an introductory essay to these conference papers, restated the theme of the Renaissance as a period of changing relationships between the sacred and the secular, especially in its view of man:

> Before the dignity of man went to seed on the European cultural scene and became mere civility of manners, this dignity was based on the awareness that man himself stands on the demarcation line of both worlds, forming the *trait d'union*, the link between the sacred and the secular.[44]

The consensus that emerges from these studies is that the Christian religion of Renaissance humanism was not primarily an anticipation of the Reformation and certainly not an anticipation of the Enlightenment. It was an autonomous moment in the history of Christianity in which the perceived and experienced disjunction between the secular and the sacred was being transformed in the direction of unity.

In 1975, a Kristeller *Festschrift*, on the occasion of his seventieth birthday, was published.[45] It is a truly significant contribution to Renaissance scholarship, far from the usual collection of snippets of research done by one's students. Each essay is a major contribution by an established scholar. The theme is the European "transformations"

---

44. Heiko A. Oberman, "The Shape of Late Medieval Thought: The Birthpangs of the Modern Era," *Pursuit*, p. 18.

45. *Itinerarium Italicum: The Profile of the Italian Renaissance in the Mirror of Its European Transformations*, edited by Heiko A. Oberman with Thomas A. Brady, Jr. (Leiden, 1975), hereafter cited as *Itinerarium*.

of the Italian Renaissance, and thus it provides us with an opportunity for a brief glance at Renaissance religion outside Italy. Religion is a central concern to all the papers. Space permits comment only on two of these six discussions. Sem Dresden, in writing about the humanism and the religion of Lefèvre d'Etaples, Margaret of Navarre, Rabelais, and Montaigne, noted that the search for *humanitas* ties them to each other and to the rest of European humanism.[46] He does also carefully avoid the older polemics of the Burckhardtian tradition when relating the theme of *humanitas* to the Renaissance discussions of the dignity of man.[47] And Jozef Ijsewijn, in a masterful essay which rehabilitates Albert Hyma's interpretation of the role of the *devotio moderna* from the criticism of R. R. Post,[48] reflects very

46. Sem Dresden, "The Profile of the Reception of the Italian Renaissance in France," *Itinerarium,* pp. 119-89.

47. Lucien Febvre's classic, *Le Problème de l'incroyance au XVIe siècle: La Religion de Rabelais* (Paris, 1942), refuted the traditional interpretation of French irreligion, unbelief, and atheism. See also Donald M. Frame's recent study *François Rabelais* (New York, 1977), especially the chapter on "Humanism and Evangelism," for a clear statement of this relationship. On French humanism and its evangelical relations see *L'Humanisme Français au Début de la Renaissance* (Colloque de Tours) (Paris, 1973), *Courants Religieux et Humanisme* (Colloque de Strasbourg) (Paris, 1959), and *Humanism in France: At the End of the Middle Ages and in the Early Renaissance,* edited by A. T. H. Levi (New York, 1970).

48. Jozef Ijsewijn, "The Coming of Humanism to the Low Countries," *Itinerarium,* pp. 193–282. For Albert Hyma, see his *The Christian Renaissance: A History of the "Devotio Moderna"* (Grand Rapids, 1924) and *The Brethren of the Common Life* (Grand Rapids, 1950). For R. R. Post, see his *The Modern Devotion: Confrontation with Reformation and Humanism* (Leiden, 1968). For a more positive view of the "Devotio Moderna," see also Lewis Spitz, "The Course of German Humanism," *Itinerarium,* pp. 371-436, as well as his *The Religious Renaissance of the German Humanists* (Cambridge, 1968), especially p. 268 ff.

carefully on the customary distinction between northern and southern humanism:

> It is better perhaps to speak of humanist Christians than of Christian humanism.... In their eyes [the northern], the fundamental value was not so much a renascence of ancient literature as a renewal of Christian *pietas*, and here lies an abyss between them and the leading Italian *oratores et poetae*.[49]

Although the work of Trinkaus on the Christian religious commitments of Italian humanism refutes the traditional pagan/Christian disjunction between north and south, there is still a difference.

The question which now confronts us is whether a new consensus on the religious problem of the Renaissance has been sufficiently articulated so as to be able to replace the traditional Burckhardtian view. I think the answer is "almost," and that "almost" is best found in the work of William J. Bouwsma. Given the need to understand the unity in the diversity of such elements of Renaissance life and thought as professional humanism, civic humanism, sacral corporatism, nominalism, scholasticism, mysticism, evangelism, dissent, reform, and secularism; and to see all of these as expressive of an unquestionably religious ethos in a society whose practice of personal piety was but dubiously related to either ecclesiastical organization or traditional theology and liturgy; what can be invoked to colligate, classify, or explain such complexity? Bouwsma's maturing studies of Augustinianism may be the key.[50] In his masterful study of Venice,

---

49. Ijsewijn, p. 282.

50. Augustinianism was a part of, but not central to, his first work on Guillaume Postel, *Concordia Mundi: The Career and Thought of Guillaume Postel: 1510–1581* (Cambridge, 1957). It began to assume greater importance in his study of Fra Paolo Sarpi which came to fruition in his *Venice and the Defense of Republican Liberty: Renaissance Values in the Age of the Counter Reformation* (Berkeley,

Augustinianism emerged as the key to understanding the unity of thought, politics, and religion in the Renaissance:

> The correspondence between the Renaissance vision and certain tendencies in Augustine helps to explain the growing attraction, from the 14th century, of a Pauline-Augustinian spirituality. The Renaissance perception of reality was not merely compatible with positive religious values; to men of pious inclinations...it required a restatement of Christianity, a shift of concern within the historic faith.[51]

This Pauline-Augustinian spirituality leads directly to some of the commonplaces of Renaissance life and thought we have previously considered:

> ...salvation itself, on the basis of the Renaissance understanding of essential human nature, had to be conceived as the transformation of a total personality through love, not as intellectual union with eternal wisdom. Thus the Christian life, like civic life, was interpreted as basically active rather than contemplative.[52]

And these religious transformations, these restatements of Christian faith, are not only compatible with, but a force in, the development of Venetian and Florentine republicanism.

Bouwsma returns brilliantly to this theme in his contribution to the Kristeller *Festschrift.*[53] He discerns two motive forces within Renaissance

---

1968), hereafter cited as Venice. It is central to his "The Two Faces of Humanism: Stoicism and Augustinianism in Renaissance Thought," *Itinerarium*, pp. 3-60, hereafter cited as Two Faces.

51. Bouwsma, *Venice*, p. 29.

52. Bouwsma, *Venice*, p. 29.

53. Bouwsma, *Two Faces.*

humanism—Stoicism and Augustinianism. These two forces are in radical opposition to each other; they are antithetical forces or motives:

> The Stoic view of man attributed to him a divine spark or seed, identified with reason, which gave man access to the divine order of the universe, from which the existence, the nature, and the will of God could be known. Stoicism therefore pointed to natural theology, and...virtually required a religious syncretism.[54]

In absolute contrast,

> Augustinianism...did not regard his reason ... as divine and thus naturally capable of knowing God. The primary organ in Augustinian anthropology is not so much that which is highest as that which is central; it is literally the heart (*cor*).[55]

Bouwsma, in concert with Trinkaus, traces the tension between these two religious positions in the Renaissance and the pre-eminence gained by Augustinianism in the thought of not only Petrarch and Calvin, but also Machiavelli and Galileo.[56] The significance of Bouwsma's attempts to find unity in Renaissance life and thought lies not only in his perception of the Stoic-Augustinian tension within humanism which is so helpful to understanding how and why Christianity was

---

54. Bouwsma, *Two Faces,* p. 10.

55. Bouwsma, *Two Faces,* pp. 10-11.

56. Bouwsma, *Two Faces,* p. 45. For a fascinating discussion of how both Augustinianism and Epicureanism are compatible not only in the thought of Lorenzo Valla, but also in French Calvinism, see the following two articles: Jan R. Morrison, "The Dignity of Man and the Followers of Epicurus: The View of the Huguenot François de La Noue," *Bibliothèque d'Humanisme et Renaissance,* 37 (1975), 421-29; and W. H. Huseman, "François de La Noue, la dignité de l'homme et l'institution des enfant nobles,"*Bibliothèque d'Humanisme et Renaissance* 42 (1980), 7-26.

secularized, but also in his uncommon sensitivity to nuances of religious distinctiveness. When discussing the proper use of the term *evangelical* in the context of the Renaissance, he proposes to limit the term "... to those who approached Scripture on the basis of an absolute distinction between the Gospel of Salvation and all secular culture."[57] Christian Augustinianism was the driving force in the secular transformation of Christianity during the Renaissance, but the secular can never be normative. Only the Word of God, the driving force of history and culture, as Evan Runner has so correctly presented the matter, can be normative. Bouwsma is in the process of articulating a new and comprehensive view of life and thought from the fourteenth-century through the sixteenth-century in Europe which builds upon the work of Baron, Garin, Kristeller, Oberman, and Trinkaus. Most importantly, however, it is built on the insight that religious conviction is "a means of ordering and comprehending every dimension of Experience."[58]

---

57. William J. Bouwsma, "Intervention re Father McConica's Application of the Term 'Evangelical' to Erasmus," *Pursuit,* p. 476. Bouwsma also wrote the following: "Renaissance skepticism, with its sense of the limits of the human understanding, its utilitarian conception of the knowledge appropriate to the human condition, and its clear separation between philosophy and religious belief, found expression in the Protestant insistence that the Scriptures alone communicate what is necessary for salvation." In "Renaissance and Reformation: An Essay in Their Affinities and Connections," *Luther and the Dawn of the Modern Era: Papers for the Fourth International Congress for Luther Research,* edited by Heiko A. Oberman (Leiden, 1974), p. 145.

58. Bouwsma, "Review of Bertelli," p. 312.

JOHN VAN DER HOEVEN

History and Truth in Nietzsche and Heidegger

Introduction[1]

IN THE FIRST PART OF this essay, I want to show briefly the significance of the theme "history and truth" in our time. In the second
part I will deal with Nietzsche and Heidegger as exponents of that
significance. Finally, the essay concludes with a few suggestions for a
Christian alternative, highlighting some Biblical key words and directives relevant to the theme.

Significance of the Theme

One observation that can be made regarding the influential currents
of Marxism and Neomarxism in our time is that they appear to be
preoccupied with "history." Most of their questions and problematics converge in that concern.[2] The concern is not altogether new.

---

1. Much of the material in the essay was first presented during
   the final lectures of a course on some key notions of Marxism
   and Neomarxism, given at the Institute for Christian Studies
   in Toronto, 1978. It seems appropriate to present it now as a
   contribution to this *Festschrift* for Evan Runner, the "founding
   father" of the Institute.

2. Concerning Marx, see my book *Karl Marx: The Roots of His
   Thought* (Assen and Amsterdam, 1976), especially pp. 80 ff.
   and 88 ff. About Neomarxism, documentation is hardly needed,
   I believe. Just one relevant quotation: "...the core of truth is historical,

One can show that it was already announced in Kant, especially in his elaboration of the "basic question," "What may I hope for?" and in his attention to the notion of "teleology" as connected with the idea of man as an end-in-himself (*Selbstzweck*).[3] It is only in Hegel, however, that for the first time we see the real breakthrough of that preoccupation. Ever since he defined "the true" as "the whole,"[4] "history" and "truth" have been intertwined in Western thought.

To be sure, the specific way in which Hegel attempted to connect the two elicited several reactions, and new problems appeared through these reactions. But the interconnectedness of the two themes remained. This holds true for Dilthey and his hermeneutic-historical validation of the "humanities" and of cultures and

---

rather than an unchanging constant to be set against the movement of history" (M. Horkheimer and T. W. Adorno, *Dialectic of Enlightenment*, translated by John Cumming, New York, and London, 1972, p. ix).

3. Only "announced." It is easy to show that even in the concept of "end-in-itself," the emphasis remains on the "itself." In other words, the *centrality* of the subject and its position is underscored. Kant's thought keeps gravitating, in a circular way, around that. Moreover, the term *end* primarily connotes a moral *value* ("end" as contrasted with "just a means"). Still, Kant himself contributed to the teleological paradigm, mainly along two lines: First, in Kant's more inclusive model, "nature" becomes more easily connected with "freedom," and even evils in the development of human society seem to be comprehensible from this viewpoint. Second, the paradigm was in keeping with the continuing impact of Renaissance aspiration: man, as being an infinite task for himself (with the tendency to view the classic idea of the "highest good" as the end of a historical process).

4. More fully: "The true is its own becoming, the circle that presupposes its end as its aim and thus has it for its beginning—that which is actual only through its execution and end" (Preface to *The Phenomenology of Spirit*, translated by W. Kaufmann, in *Hegel: Texts and Commentary*, translated and edited by W. Kaufmann, New York, 1965, p. 30).

worldviews as such. Moreover, it also holds true for the whole development of hermeneutical philosophy which Dilthey started and
which in our time resulted in the well-known work of Gadamer
(*Truth and Method*). Furthermore, it holds for Nietzsche, who, in a
sense, played off the preoccupation with "history" against "truth."
Also, it most evidently holds for Heidegger, who in his philosophy of
Being as Time and of Truth as *alētheia* probably represents the most
striking effort to rethink both notions thoroughly and in such a way
that they become completely interdependent. Finally, notwithstanding the difference in context, it seems relevant to mention here as
well the Kuhnian emphasis on history and its connection with the
truth of the scientific method.

I shall have to come back to this at greater length. Now I am
just pointing to the general significance of the theme in our time.
The variations and difference of currents should not be overlooked, but negatively speaking, there seems to be the following
minimal consensus. The new and close connection between "history" and "truth" is felt to be a safeguard against, and a definitive
liberation from, (remnants of) metaphysics, a metaphysics exemplified in the medieval conception of the *verum* (together with
unum and *bonum*) as essentially belonging to, even "transcendentally" constitutive of, "Being"; as such; or as exemplified in a more
modern fashion in Leibniz's *vérités éternelles*, truths entirely necessary and without any trace of contingency because of their
complete logical transparency. But this metaphysics is also felt to
be exemplified in talk of "transcendent norms" or "the supratemporal truth of Christianity."

Remarkably, our time also gives evidence of the experience
of "history" as a burden and of diverse attempts to escape from
it (if only by way of finding islands in the stream). Generally
speaking, such attempts are weak, hesitant, and rather elitist. Yet
they deserve attention.

Some try to become re-motivated by an allegedly pre-meta-physical, even pre-systematic, more reverent, and more open sort of thinking like that of the pre-Socratics, who were still at home in the mysteries of language (as "the house of Being"). Another possibility would be the endeavor to come to terms with the burden and with the concomitant feeling of powerlessness by proclaiming the "end of man" as a center of initiatives and transformations and by explaining that he should be content to see himself as just a "nodal point" in certain "structures" which in some form or other have always been there and which as to their basic set-up are presented to us in "myths."

Anyhow, for a timely reflection on the concern with "history" and "truth," it is important to notice too, a certain fatigue, a certain resignation, and certain efforts to make the best of it. As George Grant puts it: "We have been taught to recognize as illusion the old belief that our purposes are ingrained and sustained in the nature of things. Mastery comes at the same time as the recognition that horizons are only horizons. Most men, when they face that their purposes are not cosmically sustained, find that a darkness falls upon their wills…. What is wisdom when we have been taught by the historical sense the finality of becoming?"[5]

Regarding the significance of Nietzsche for this, he says: "In his twenties Nietzsche saw the crisis with which the conception of time as history presented men. The great writings of his maturity were his attempt to overcome it."[6]

Nietzsche and Heidegger as Exponents
In the setting of this essay both thinkers belong together. One need only witness the intense and elaborate "dialogue" of the latter with

---

5. George Grant, *Time as History* (Toronto, 1974), p. 31.
6. Grant, p. 30.

the former in his two-volume work entitled *Nietzsche*.[7] It is conve-
nient, however, to divide the discussion into two parts.

Nietzsche's View

In the following I shall follow closely George Grant's analysis in the
book to which I already referred. This may be justified by the need
for brevity as well as by a common focus.

The crisis, says Grant, is "authentic, because there is no necessity
about its outcome."[8] He then makes a comparison with Marx:

> For Marx, as for Nietzsche, this is a situation which pro-
> duces widespread and terrible human suffering. But ac-
> cording to Marx, if we have knowledge of the forces now
> at work, we can know that the crisis will inevitably be tran-
> scended. In the midst of the suffering, we have that enor-
> mous consolation and spur to effort. A net of inevitable
> success is put under the performers, so that their actions
> are guaranteed from ultimate anguish. For Nietzsche there
> is no such net.[9]

This may indeed account for the fact that so many different thinkers
nowadays, after having recognized the shallowness and dilapidation
of newly erected shelters against the overpowering force of "history,"
return to Nietzsche once more, to his radicalness, frankness, and dis-
illusioned attitude.

Most features and motives of modern radical historicism are indeed brought out clearly and admirably by him. Grant sums up: "…
the mastery of human and non-human nature in experimental science and technique, the primacy of the will, man as the creator of his
own values, the finality of becoming, the assertion that potentiality is

---

7. M. Heidegger, *Nietzsche*, 2 vols. (P fullingen, 1961).

8. Grant, p. 35.

9. Grant, p. 36.

higher than actuality, that motion is nobler than rest, that dynamism rather than peace is the height...."[10]

Nietzsche also managed to unify all this with the idea of *amor fati*, that is, radically and joyfully to accept time as a unity of past, present, and future that we could not and should not wish to change or "overcome." And on this score, he can once again be compared to Marx.[11]

Let us take a somewhat closer look at Nietzsche's train of thought. First, then, it is important to notice that Nietzsche took over "the inheritance of modern Western man." He made it "explicit."[12] To be sure, the emphasis remains on the radicalization of what "had been implicit," on the full and consistent implementation of the tendency of modern times, on doing away with the remaining hampering inconsistencies. It is precisely these inconsistencies that cause the aforementioned crisis. It is worth noting that in this perspective the term *crisis* itself takes on a medical overtone. It is a grave illness that has reached its crucial stage. Although Nietzsche is merciless in his diagnosis and even repeatedly uses the language of blame, the point is that basically the problems are formulated not in terms of what man does or has done but in terms of a process that has affected him.

This viewpoint also determines the picture of man as he *should* become. Here again, for all of Nietzsche's apodictic, hammering statements, it is not so much a question of conversion, not even of trans- or re-formation, but of *recovery*. The prevailing image for Nietzsche is that of the convalescent, recovering step by step.

Recovery from what, and to what? Briefly stated, in Nietzsche's own language, from the "spirit of revenge," revenge against the *past*, against the "it *was*" of time. This past is seen as something that was

---

10. Grant, p. 44.
11. Grant, p. 46.
12. Grant, p. 25.

not (so) good, not yet perfect. But perfection, then, was itself located in the transcendence of a timeless eternity. This "pretended to be a redemption of time, but it was in fact an expression of revenge against time.[13] Those, however, who are moving "beyond good and evil" learn joyfully to accept history as a whole. According to Nietzsche, they are overcoming the inclination to measure history against something suprahistorical, even if that would occur in the diluted form of playing off the present or the future against the past. In otherwords, they learn joyfully to accept the eternal recurrence of the same.

But in that process, they also display the full will-to-power. For this will cannot fully unfold as long as it manifests itself only, or mainly, in the mastery of nature through the instrument of reason or in the pure resoluteness of the will to mastery for its own sake. The first possibility is exemplified in the last men, the heirs of willful rationalism "in its last and decadent form."[14] The second category is called the nihilists. Though both types are inevitable products of history and there is no real criterion by which to call them wrong or even anti-historical, their appearance provides sufficient reason to talk about a crisis. The nihilists "are unable to use their mastery for joy." It is still too much the negative that prevails in their will-to-the-will: a violent denial of transcendent, suprahistorical truth and values and of an established past. As for the last men, they "simply use the fruits of technique for the bored pursuit of their trivial vision of happiness."[15] And that is enough for Nietzsche at least to raise the question "whether there can be men who transcend the alternatives of being nihilists or last men; who know that they are the creators of their own values, but bring forth from that creation in the face of

---

13. Grant, p. 41.

14. Grant, p. 33.

15. Grant, p. 35.

chaos a joy in their willing which will make them deserving of being masters of the earth."[16]

Now, as we saw, these men are the ones who are recovering from the spirit of revenge and are learning to love history as fate—reminiscent of the Greek tragedies and their "ecstacy of a noble encounter with chaos," though not without indication of the influence of modern voluntaristic rationalism. These people would be the culmination of history. Says Nietzsche: "To transform every 'it was' into 'this is what I wanted'—that alone could I call redemption."[17]

I take it that the above suffices to bring out the significance of Nietzsche for our theme. Now the question must be raised as to what is so instructive about this.

First, it is clear how far we have moved beyond Hegel here. Instead of Absolute Spirit unfolding itself through history and ultimately triumphing over it, it is now Time, Becoming. History as such that is held to as consistently as possible. The polemic point is definitively to overcome false, delusive, will-blocking optimism, an optimism founded on the idea of the "Good" and on the idea of rationality as tuned in to the realm of the "Good." Plato and Christianity ("the Platonism of the people") are the scapegoats, and they survive even in the growing awareness of history as a horizontal sequence of horizons, "manmade perspectives by which the charismatic impose their will to power."[18] They are overcome only in the transition to the group of "real masters" of the earth.

To be sure, this latter group will be a minority, an elite. We may even say that this indicates a certain retreatism on Nietzsche's part, a background of resignation. Nonetheless, this elite is

---

16. Grant, p. 35.

17. From *Also sprach Zarathustra*, in *Werke*, edited by K. Schlechta, II, 394 (see also Grant, p. 41).

18. Grant, p. 29.

put forward as representing and preserving the real truth about history, though it is also emphasized that these men can be what they are in a process of becoming as well, namely, in the process of recovery and convalescence.

This brings us to the second point: Nietzsche's own explicit discussion of the notion of truth is by and large in negative terms. We can almost speak of a willful suppression of this notion.[19] "Truth" is mostly dismissed as something that is directly connected with the attempt to overcome becoming, a sign of weakness. According to Nietzsche, "The very language centering around the word 'truth,' dominated previous western history because it was the most disciplined attempt to sedate consciousness against the terror and pain of becoming."[20] In other words, the real truth about truth is that it is a semblance. As such it is not to be simply disqualified; the historical sense allows for a relative right of this semblance. History moving through shifting horizons and via "man-made perspectives" does have a place for truth in a relative and functional sense. Nietzsche stresses, however, that once the will-to-power, the essential characteristic of history, has become manifest, we can do away with "truth" as an ultimate notion in its own right.

Actually, as we saw in our previous discussion, Nietzsche cannot leave the matter at this. In spite of his largely derogatory account, his own thinking appears to remain haunted by a traditional notion of truth. How else could one explain his preoccupation with the constancy of the will-to-power, culminating in the idea of the "eternal recurrence of the same," (his "greatest discovery," according to himself)? This concern and idea betray, after all, his basic orientation to

---

19. It makes room for the metaphor of illness. Remarkably, this metaphor also prevails in some currents of Neomarxism, especially in Habermas, connected with which there is a new interest in Freud.

20. Grant, p. 27.

some sort of permanence which encompasses "becoming." As he himself once put it: "To give the stamp (*Charakter*) of *Being* to *Becoming*—that would be the highest will-to-power."[21]

Heidegger's Thought
Heidegger's thought is vast, subtle, and complicated. What I want to do in this section is to reproduce his critical reaction to a few key terms that we came across in the brief discussion of Nietzsche, in order to point out how Heidegger wants to move even beyond Nietzsche.

The Issue of Metaphysics
In Heidegger's confrontation with Nietzsche, the issue of metaphysics is central. His claim is that Nietzsche, instead of being successful in overcoming metaphysics, represents its *consummation*; that this, at the same time, is the consummation of *nihilism*; and that this double consummation indicates a real turning point in the sense of a radical reversal as the only historical possibility.

What are "the implications latent" in previous metaphysics that Nietzsche's philosophy 'evolves to their ultimate consequences'?[22] First of all, it is the metaphysics of *modernity*, though, as we will see, this is one special manifestation of a broader and older commitment and tradition. According to Heidegger, the will-to-power as the essence or principle of reality-as-becoming can be traced back already to Descartes. In Descartes we meet with an ontology in which being is conceived primarily as the being of a self-positing subject, that is, a subject that is present and presents itself and that grasps other beings primarily as represented by and in that subject. This self-presentation and representation is already a

---

21. Nietzsche, III, 895 (translation mine).
22. W. J. Richardson, *Through Phenomenology to Thought* (The Hague, 1963), p. 381; see also pp. 373, 363.

willful process. (Indeed, Descartes is as much a voluntarist as a rationalist.) In addition, the idea of 'truth' is basically determined as certitude. Self-presentation is self-certification, and the representation of other beings is true, only if there is an accommodation of these 'objects' to a standard 'imposed by' the pro-posing subject itself, a standard dictated by the nature of the subject, namely, its exigency for clear and distinct ideas.[23]

Heidegger, then, traces this fundamental tendency through Leibniz, Kant, Fichte, Schelling (*Wollen ist Ursein*) and Hegel. If we briefly label this metaphysics as 'subject-ism', then we can say: 'When at last subject-ism in Nietzsche becomes a philosophy of will, *sc.* of Will-unto-Power, the last possibility of metaphysical subject-ism has been exploited. This is the sense in which Heidegger claims that Nietzsche's thought is the 'consummation' (*Vollendung*) of metaphysics in the West."[24]

But how can this consummation at the same time be a consummation of nihilism? To see this, we have to understand that the whole of modern metaphysics remains embedded in a much older metaphysical tradition. That tradition is already nihilistic inasmuch as it is characterized by its forgetfulness of Being, by its having been oblivious to Being-as-Time.

Surely, from the outset metaphysics has been concerned with the "Being of beings." But in what sense and in what manner? What does it mean for that tradition that "there are beings"? According to Heidegger, first and foremost it means that they are present, or presented. The "Being of beings," then, is basically experienced as *presence*. Of course, an experience of "absence," of disappearing, of change, transition, and death was not lacking. However, the exposure of beings-in-their-presence (and of Being as presence) was predominant.

---

23. Richardson, p. 370.
24. Richardson, p. 381.

What this means, according to Heidegger, can be elucidated in three points. First, "Being" itself, in order to be saved from any "contamination" with "finiteness," and "becoming," and to be preserved in its ever-presence, is disconnected from its intrinsic relationship to "beings" ("Being of beings") and elevated to an allegedly "transcendent" realm where, supposedly, it could retain its "high" presence. Second, time itself is understood primarily as a succession of "now" (points, a sequence of present-at-ations. Aristotle already testifies to this conception, but it is reinforced in modern times, when the self-positing subject comes to the fore not only as re-presenting the objects present, but also as the re-presentative, at a higher and more comprehensive level, of a preceding "history." Finally, "Truth," then, is basically conceived of as a *conformity* or *correspondence* between entities that are co-present.

In Nietzsche all of this is brought to its consummation and to its end. (God, the "highest Being," is dead; Truth is "semblance," etc.) Nietzsche deserves, says Heidegger, to be corrected on all these points; only then can we overcome nihilism and re-integrate History and Truth.

The "Being of Beings"

As we observed, Heidegger denounces a certain interpretation of this expression which amounts to a forgetfulness of Being-itself. However, he too wants to take the word *of* seriously. Being is always manifested in and through "beings." Thus, negatively speaking, any attempt to comprehend Being in a straightforward manner is bound to be meaningless and at best illusory. Heidegger even goes so far as to acknowledge that it is "first of all and for the most part (*zunächst und zumeist*) beings that are present in an impressive plurality. In addition, these beings are characterized by a certain availability and a certain urgency. But Heidegger keeps stressing another meaning of *of*—one that in grammar is usually designated the "separative genitive." Being is also *different from* "beings," even when taken in their collectivity; Being is itself always moving-away from beings, is always withdrawal.

This withdrawal on the one hand allows beings to be present, but on the other hand accounts for their passing away. Being as such maintains itself in its very withdrawal. Its "essence" is its absence, so to speak. This way of putting it may serve to emphasize that Heidegger wants not only radically to think Being itself as thoroughly *temporal* (without any haunting reminiscence of something supratemporal), but also fully to reintegrate in that temporal conception the past and the future as dimensions not to be measured against an overexpossed present, but as *co-constitutive* of Being-as-time (co-constitutive in the "negativity" of the "no-more" and "not-yet"). In other words, Heidegger's intention is to rethink Being in such a way that it becomes understandable (and acceptable) as finite, and that without the depreciative undertones of that term.

It follows, for Heidegger, that once we learn to understand this, the need to reintroduce an idea like "the eternal recurrence of the same" is overcome. Furthermore, instead of the quasi-openness of the will-to-power, we may regain a genuine openness of "thought." This is a thought, then, no longer pushed forward by the will to mastery, but a thought open to "Being," a recognition of Being as allowing a plurality of beings to come to be (and to pass) and a recollection of Being in its very withdrawal. In short, by learning this we may eventually indeed overcome nihilism.

We are also dealing with a thought which has overcome the need and urge for a center around which historical movement revolves, for it leaves everything as it is, that is, lets Being be as it has emitted itself in intermittent fashion in different epochs. Yet it is thought, all the same, having the key role of understanding everything in principle.

What does this mean in terms of Heidegger's own "thought"? It is the difference between "Being" and "beings" that is for genuine thought itself fundamental, more so than any pretended and presented "foundation." We may also say that the "ground" itself is an "abyss." But this difference, ground-and-abyss at once, is precisely what makes possible the temporal differentiation that we come across in history. The difference remains a peculiar one, though. Referring once more to the twofold sense *of* (Being *of* beings), we can indicate that peculiarity as follows. At one and the same time there is the fact that Being cannot be disconnected from (and then, elevated above) beings, because it is manifest only in these, and there is the fact that Being is what it is in "absenting itself," in withdrawal.

Here it appears how thoroughly dialectical Heidegger's "historicism" is. Instead of groping somehow to surmount the interplay in the "difference," Heidegger deliberately and ultimately leaves the matter by accepting that interplay as such. This should not prevent us from acknowledging that he shows great philosophical and historical skills in a subtle, sometimes brilliant, and instructive, exploration of that historical interplay. It is also to be admitted that in the development of his own thought the term *dialectical* is virtually lacking. However, neither this nor his preference for terms like *interplay* should lead us astray.

The factual situation can be sketched as follows. On the one hand, there is a primacy of beings in their positivity and presence. With respect to this primacy, "Being" is designated in negative terms (withdrawal, concealment, etc.). On the other hand, at the very same time this negativity of "Being" is turned around into a most positive event which makes possible, and therefore relativizes, the presence of beings. This is where we are after Hegel's "identity of identity and non-identity" and Nietzsche's "eternal recurrence of the same." At the end of his career this concealment and its negative sign are sometimes interpreted as "inexhaustibility," "wealth," "treasure," "hidden fullness." Still, even then the hiddenness, the ineffability of this "fullness," overshadows the fullness as such.

"Truth"

What does the notion of "truth" have to do with what has been said above? After the preceding exposition, we can make a long story short. Heidegger's idea of "truth" turns out to be taken up in the above-mentioned dialectics. It is almost another expression of it. According to Heidegger, truth in the traditional view is considered to be a relation of correspondence between present, or presentable, things. In modern times, Nietzsche, in his confrontation with traditional metaphysics, openly no longer has use for that notion, but implicitly remains bound to is. According to Heidegger, his shortcomings can be put like this: "He has ignored the fact that Being is the process by which things emerge into non-concealment; that this non-concealment is the genuine meaning of truth (*a-lētheia*)."

Indeed, Heidegger wants to revalidate "truth" by returning to that allegedly original Greek meaning and by tying it up intrinsically with the Being-process as just outlined. As to returning to the Greek meaning, this interpretation is widely and strongly contested by philologists. But a possible meaning of the term serves Heidegger's purposes nicely anyway. Notice that the term contains a twofold negation: "*lētheia*," meaning concealment, and "*a-*," a negative, or, as Heidegger sometimes puts it, a privative prefix. However, it is not the negation of negation, which we encounter in Hegel, and which results in a new, superseding positivity; rather, it is an expression and manifestation of the polarity between Being and beings, in which the one can *be* itself only at the expense of the near disappearance of the other, and conversely. There is, again, only a hint of a final center of gravity in that Heidegger, parallel to what we noted about "treasure" and "fullness," sometimes refers to "Lēthe" as a source of truth. But once again this is overshadowed by the intrinsic negativity of the background of concealment, even to such an extent that the thinker does not hesitate to say that the full essence of truth contains within itself its own non-essence. In other words, Being in its negativity includes errance as well. It is this errance—within the "mystery"—that holds a mastery over existent freedom and thereby leads it astray.

The Role of Man in History

Small wonder that Heidegger does not pay much attention anymore to this role of man. Whereas Nietzsche was still concerned with that role and even with the features of the new man (the new elite), Heidegger declares: "Being-as-history is neither the history of men and of humanity, nor the history of man's relationship to beings and Being. Being-as-history is Being itself and nothing else."[25] Heidegger's thinking is an awaiting a new turn, a reversal, for after having exhausted a certain possibility *(in casu*, present-ation) and all the things attendant upon it, Being may be expected to turn to another as yet hidden possibility.

In conclusion, I should say that it is easy to dismiss most of this "thought," if only for its abstruseness. But this might be too easy. For one thing, it seems to be that Heidegger's is the last full-scale exploration and articulation in that important development of Western philosophy that came increasingly to focus upon history and somehow had to save "truth." Despite its abstruseness, Heidegger's thought seems to appeal to many, even outside of Europe. It is also highly instructive in that its very negativity and the thorough dialecticity of its outcome preclude attempts at correction or accommodation.

Just as remarkable is his effort to avoid a closure in some circular model. In other words, Heidegger wishes to keep the movement

---

25. *Nietzsche*, II, 489 (also quoted in Richardson, p. 437). It is fair, however, to mention the next sentence as well: *"Weil jedoch das Sein zur Gründung seiner Wahrheit im Seienden das Menschenwesen in den Anspruch nimmt, bleibt der Mensch in die Geschichte des Seins einbezogen, aber jeweils nur hinsichtlich der Art, wie er aus dem Bezug des Seins zu ihm und gemäss diesem Bezug sein Wesen übernimmt, verliert, übergeht, freigibt, ergründet oder verschwendet."*

open. However, it is kept open as a movement *between* Being and beings, mutually "negating" each other, with man in his existence as the locus where the two meet, only to be related as "different." Finally, the basic attitude with respect to the "mystery" appears to be one of resignation and esoteric retreat, hardly one of real engagement and appeal.

Suggestions for a Christian Alternative

Elsewhere,[26] I have argued that history can hardly be taken seriously enough, but also that this is different from taking it as an incomprehensible, all-embracing power. The preoccupation with history mentioned in the beginning of this essay can almost become an obsession. Nietzsche and especially Heidegger give evidence of that. Perhaps we should speak here of "idolization." An idol is misleading in that, on the one hand, it seeks its force in overdoing and, on the other hand, is bound to show its inner emptiness. It seems to me that precisely this ambivalence has become depressingly clear in Heidegger's thought. I know of no other historicism which is more radical and drastic than his. But in the final analysis a saddening emptiness remains. To be sure, even Heidegger cannot do without at least some structure and meaning in history, but they are outlined in thoroughly dialectical terms. Even then, I think, we have to agree with the Dutch philosopher Mekkes, who with regard to Heidegger once concluded that "history and thought echo each other."[27]

Now, if this evaluation is correct, how do we react? By playing down history in the face of idolization? This would not be appropriate. I believe. Precisely from a Christian standpoint, history can hardly be taken seriously enough. A certain anti-metaphysical tenor should be characteristic of a Christian philosophy. What does de-

---

26. See my *Karl Marx* (Assen and Amsterdam, 1976), pp. 100 ff.

27. J. P. A. Mekkes, *Scheppingsopenbaring en wijsbegeerte* (Kampen, 1961), p. 45 (see also pp. 110 f. on "idols").

serve our special attention is the remarkable and increasing vacillation between an experience of final liberation and an attitude of resignation and various attempts to escape the burden of history. Could it be that the views we have discussed, despite basic intentions, fall short of real openness, dynamic character, and integrality and therefore run stuck in the end? Critically speaking, I am inclined to defend the thesis that historicism is to be opposed not primarily for its relativistic tendencies, but rather for its closedness. But this thesis presupposes a new, authentic openness to revelation. Nothing less will do in view of the appearance and influence of such radicals as Nietzsche and Heidegger. Making that turn, a Christian may learn that both history and truth can and should be taken as all-comprehensive terms, that the range of both terms is nothing less than reality as a whole. The overall relationship of the two means that there is neither an a-historical truth nor an occurrence unrelated to truth. The following is an attempt to begin with a revitalization of our Biblical heritage, in order suggestively to point out its relevance and liberating powers with respect to the problem.

First, when we hear God speaking of himself, telling us about his "being," it is obvious that he does so in a variety of ways. In the last book of the Bible, he does this pre-eminently by saying that he is the Alpha and the Omega, "the One who is and was and comes." This is different from saying that he overarches or transcends history. The linking together of *is*, *was*, and *comes* (as well as the use of comes instead of *will be*) says that he is *involved* in history. We shouldn't miss the sound of thrill and tension. Moreover, this concept also indicates that he himself takes time (past, present, and future) to reveal himself. Let's not lose sensitivity to the striking expression "the coming Kingdom" either. All such expressions and phrases underscore the significance of history, even though the word is lacking.

Second, revelation itself is basically a story told "in varied fashion."[28] This is quite different from the shining of a supratemporal idea in its diverse ramifications. We believe the story to be concluded, to have become a "complete collection of canonical books." But we should not forget, then, that at the very closing of this collection things are recollected and held open: "Do not seal up the words of prophecy in this book, for the hour of fulfillment is near.... Yes, I am coming soon. I am the first and the last...."

Understanding this also makes it possible to acknowledge "concealment," even fully so, and not in a dialectical manner. There is much yet to come. In one breath we are told about "the (as yet) hidden things of the Lord our God" and about the revealed things upon which we should act. Thus, an attitude of fundamental respect and of expectation is the only possibility, together with living by the Word that is very near, in our mouths and in our hearts.[29]

The full awareness of the fact that God himself takes time and history very seriously, to the point of involving himself in it, and that, simultaneously and ultimately, it remains his history which has been set in motion in the primal force of his creation and which has gotten its final destination from him, should liberate us from an obsession with history. Positively speaking, the wisdom of *amor fati* (Nietzsche) and of the "abyss" or inner "controversiality" (*Strittigkeit*) of "Being" (Heidegger) can be replaced by the perspective of a disclosure of meaning. Let me try to point out what I see as some consequences of this liberating openness to history.

Third, one thing that is brought about by openness to history is a wholehearted recognition of history as a process of the increasing interdependence of people. This can be done without getting lost in

---

28   Hebrews 1:1 (New English Bible).

29.   Deuteronomy 29:19; 30:12-14.

the problem of the differences between cultures and periods. This means, for example, that we not only need the past but also that the past needs us, the present generation. The witnesses of the past are still with us but cannot reach the goal without us.

Fourth, no doubt history is a forward movement, involving speed and tension. But the God of history also proves himself to be the God of rest and rhythm, of regular feasts and of celebration. History can be meaningful only if we learn to live by *days*, day after day, not to mention the important regular complement of night and sleep.[30] Philosophers and others who think about history hardly pay attention to this dailiness. Notably, Heidegger is an exception as he introduces and emphasizes the notion of "everydayness" (*Alltäglich-keit*). But the depreciative tone in his use of that notion at the same time indicates a distortion. In order to enter the gate of wisdom, we have to learn to number our days (Ps. 90). Isn't this also a most significant aspect of the creation story? God himself did not simply create the world; he did it day by day. Moreover, the culmination is a day of rest. Even he who is not tempted to rush needed that. Of the patriarchs it is said literally that they died "full of days," and that message is more than a biographical detail. Jesus, too, points to the salutary institution of days when he says that in seeking the coming Kingdom we should not worry about tomorrow, because tomorrow will look after itself.

It is clear enough how important the day of rest, the sabbath, is throughout the Old Testament. It is important precisely in connection with and in opposition to the rush and the lust for a hurried expansion of power that so easily affects history and man's experience of it. The exodus was well-nigh an exodus from bondage to technocratic expansion in Egypt. The subsequent emphatic commandment to remember and observe the sabbath was an eloquent sign against that and a clear

---

30. See also—next to Genesis 1—Psalm 127 and Psalm 4:9.

indication for wholesome historical life. The same applies to the stressing of that sabbath in the later prophecies of Isaiah, though this time it is done to counter the hurriedly expanding power of Babel.

We learn from this that the dynamic of history is not to be transcended, superseded, or checked by an idea of perfection or unchanging meaning, which is untouched by potentiality or change.[31] Rather, the dynamic of history is to be regulated by highlighting certain days, thereby recognizing a rhythm in the course of history itself. When God calls himself the Holy One, this does not so much indicate perfection as his uniqueness with respect to other possible or real powers. Likewise, in the institution of regular holy days, we are called to celebrate what is given and, more specifically, to take time to highlight the ordinary as something very worthwhile.

At this point the question might be raised whether it is all that relevant to mention these things in the context of an essay on history and truth. Or, more pointedly, is that regular alternation and succession of days not simply, or primarily, a matter of "nature," or of the "natural side:" of creation? My answer, then, would be that, as already indicated, the thoroughgoing and at the same time emptying preoccupation with history in contemporary thought requires a serious reorientation to the powerfulness and colorfulness of Biblical revelation. I would agree with the reference to "nature" and to our more or less scientific knowledge of the relationship between the rotation of the earth and the sun (and the practical application of that knowledge in our calendar). However, we must acknowledge the functioning of nature as well *within* history, as co-constitutive of history's full meaning and as wholesome for a full experience of that history. Making its own contribution to that full meaning, nature,

---

31. Grant, pp. 46, 47, who apparently seeks the overcoming of the "crisis" in that direction.

far from being a neutral, impersonal, or independent substratum, is itself taken up into and opened up by history.

Fifth, the foregoing can be elaborated a little if we focus upon "remembering." In contemporary thought, especially among those who have lost belief in progress, this notion has become conspicuous. Already for Hegel, for example, it plays an important role.[32] But in the Scriptures this key word, rather than connoting the deepening of an "inner life" and/or a return-in-thought to the past, let alone the comparison of the present with the past in favor of the present, designates the cooperation of man with God, through prayer and celebration, in the fulfillment and consummation of what has begun. ("Do this in remembrance of me" is certainly not the same as "in memory of me.") Put more philosophically, "remembering" is an activity of men by which the past is brought out in its openness to the present, such that (negatively speaking) the present is prevented from simply "passing (slipping) away" and such that (positively speaking) the present is made to pass over into the future. This does indicate, *n'en deplaise* Heidegger, a pivotal function of the present: remembering as an act is actual, present actuality; still, it differs from a representation motivated either by a will to mastery or by nostalgia.

Its act-character points to the significance of human activity in history, as opposed to an attitude of passive resignation or something similar. Remembering is, however, a kind of activity that does not fit in very well with our traditional and current notions of action and praxis. These are, by and large, oriented to the idea of self-realization and self-expression in an individualistic or a collectivistic fashion. But it is surely a basic act according to the Scriptures. Its import comes out in the fact that it is to be per-

---

32. "Remembrance" (*Er-innerung*) as a final interiorization and integration of what has been "discovered" in the process of "dis-memberment" (alienation).

formed regularly and in a communal and official manner, preferably in the form of a celebration.

Such celebrations in the sign of remembrance may be called "pauses," but then very concentrated pauses—not what we usually call "relaxation," nowadays. It is not a matter of taking a leave from history, of stepping outside of it for a while. The very first feast of Israel, the Passover, was precisely characterized by the vivid awareness of speed, the speed of the liberation from the "old." That is also how Paul picks it up in 1 Corinthians 5. The final great Feast of the Tabernacles indeed underscores the joy of liberation from the self-enslavement of rushing. How inclusive that is appears from the required openness to the abundance of nature: "...you shall take the fruit of citrus trees, palm fronds, and leafy branches, and willows from the riverside, and you shall rejoice before the Lord your God for seven days" (Lev. 23:40). This openness to nature's abundance in the new land is not something separate or merely additional; it is not to be understood in terms of veneration or even contemplation of nature in itself. Fronds and branches had to be cut, and from these the arbors had to be made or built by men. The festival as a whole is significantly named a pilgrim feast ("tabernacles"), a "remembrance" of the journey into which even the dwelling in the new land and its abundance are taken up. Still, that does not in the least detract from the tremendous joy characteristic of the celebration. This becomes amazingly clear when, after the return from the exile, in a situation of utter distress, Nehemiah and Ezra rediscover the Feast of the Tabernacles and venture to tell the mourning and weeping people: "You may go now; refresh yourselves with rich food and sweet drinks and send a share to all who cannot provide for themselves...Let there be no sadness, for joy in the Lord is your strength...." And also: "Go out into the hills and fetch branches...to make arbors...And there was very great rejoicing" (Neh. 8).

The upshot, I suggest, is that it is precisely in the pilgrimage that the creation is opened up in its fullness and richness, not "behind" or "above" it. Didn't that teaching reach its height in the words of him who said: "Foxes have their holes, the birds their roosts; but the Son of Man has nowhere to lay his head"? Certainly this applies to Jesus in a unique manner, but it is in a context where the issue is *following* him, and that not gloomily either, because such a mood would again fall short of what is said in the same context, namely, that " ...Jesus exulted in the Holy Spirit and said: I thank Thee, Father, Lord of heaven and earth, for hiding these things from the learned and wise, and revealing them to the simple." And also: "... turning to his disciples: Everything is entrusted to me." This utterance concludes with the beatitude: "*Happy* the eyes that see what you are seeing" (Luke 9, 10; italics mine).

"Remembering" is not a turn-away from the present and/or the future, but relating oneself, consciously and concretely, to the God who was and is and comes, who has been (and still is) on the way with his creation all the time.

Sixth, another word worth rediscovering is *generation.* In Psalm 146 it even serves to designate the mode of God's presence in history. Right after the words "The Lord shall reign for ever," we hear: "thy God, O Zion, from generation to generation." Here the "biotic" is included and taken up into the "historical." We came to exist, through procreation, within a family, in a certain line, and with a certain name, and this is co-constitutive of our identity and of our role in history. Moreover, it is precisely as a testator, in the transmission of the heritage, that a person who is going to die may preserve his name in and through the heirs. The dead are not left out of history. This is also why, in dealing with and writing on history, we cannot simply deal with products and achievements and problem situations. We cannot do without *names.*

Our predecessors are around us as witnesses and testators, says the Hebrews, while naming a good number of them. As to us ourselves, everyone has to continue the race. The final destination, the full manifestation of the heritage, is not yet laid out before us in detail. We are seekers of the city that is to come (Heb. 13:14). And the course of our race is outside the camp, a course on which Christ suffered. But that is the course along which creation attains its destination. We are not even allowed to save something permanent in an idea of "creation," because the same writer tells us: ". . . now he has promised, 'Once more I will shake not only the earth but also the heavens.' The words 'once more' indicate the removal of what can be shaken, namely created things, so that what cannot be shaken may remain" (Heb. 12:26-27). Yes, this is history in full dynamics and tension, most impressive evidence of the "open-endedness" of created reality throughout.

Seventh, what about the "things"? I think they are taken up and along into history as well, for the sake of men. But how?

We are familiar with the tension or dialectic between "being" and "having," in diverse variations. It is striking in Marx when he talks about production in terms of human self-realization *and* of the appropriation of nature. Marx speaks as if an incorporation into one's selfhood of something that is somehow originally alien. Behind this there is a gnosticism that we have not escaped even when we have "desacralized" things and made them into objects. Gnosticism still shines through in the classic versions of the subject/object scheme. But it is not really overcome either when "things" are taken up as means in a primarily historical process of self-production or as "media" in a historical process of self-expression. (Capitalism and socialism have a common root here.)

I am hoping for a breakthrough that will surmount this basic outlook and attitude. One of the key words, then, seems to be *enjoy-*

ment.[33] It may sound unrealistic, in view of the need for exertion, labor, organization, etc. The primary attribute of the created things as described in the Genesis 1 account is that they were "very good." That is not a synonym of "in order"; rather, the whole story is indicative of divine *pleasure.* Things were made "enjoyable" constitutionally. This is both their nature and destiny.

Moreover, I am struck by the fact that the primary image used in the Bible to depict the relation between things and man involves clothing. After the message that "Adam named his wife Eve, the mother of all the living," it is said that God made *garments* of skin for him and his wife and *clothed* them. This is more than just an emergency measure because of nakedness and shame. At the end of Scripture, the metaphor reappears: the Bride wears fine linen and is dressed up for her husband. But also, Babylon, "the great prostitute," is said to be dressed in fine linen. I am not concerned with a detailed exegesis of these texts. What interests me is that they appear to strike a note different from the one that is dominant in the familiar subject/object scheme as in the means/end scheme.

Surely, man needs clothing, and for the preparation of the "bridal dress" a process of production, even of division of labor, is necessary. But that need is not a need for something external which, then, would require "appropriation." It is a need for something that fits man and is also in the great context of the feast a manifestation of himself, though not to himself but to the bridegroom. The process of production should itself be festive.

One additional observation seems to be in order. In our culture and tradition, enjoyment is easily associated with "privacy." But in the Bible, it is evident that it is not primarily a matter of privacy, not even of family privacy. Enjoyment as such requires sharing and is reinforced by it. It is to be feared that the full meaning of "sharing"

---

33. See also N. Wolterstorff, *Art in Action* (Grand Rapids, 1980), pp. 79 f.

is really no longer understood in our Western society, neither in its individualistic nor in its socialist-communist ideas and practices. There is more at stake here than a proper, efficient functioning of society, let alone a purely external obligation. The point is that sharing is a condition of the enjoyment of the things themselves. John the Baptist lets us know how basic that is when he says to the crowd (not just to the privileged and well-to-do): "The man with two tunics should share with him who has none, and the one who has food should do the same" (Luke 3:11). "Sharing" differs from "giving away"; it is not a matter of concession, nor of scaling down possessions. Economic differences need not simply be done away with, but they have to be made functional in an unusual manner. The best example I can think of is the description of the first Christian community as given in the book of Acts.

Eighth, after this relatively long exposition—sketchy as it remains—of what history involves, it is high time finally to pay attention to truth. As I remarked, truth is to be considered as comprehensive a term as history.

I can't help repeating first of all the most pregnant sentence on truth ever spoken in history: "I am the Truth." That was said by one who came to confer upon history both focus and goal, and it was also said in history. This means that, since that word was spoken, there is no way left somehow to disconnect history and truth or to subsume one under the other, or to play one off against the other.

On the positive side, it is clear that this last word on truth qualifies it at the same time as an announcement of what is yet to come and what now *can* come. It is paralleled by "the Way" and "the Life" so that "the Truth" is connected with the process of carrying creation through death into a new and abundant life. The truth is ahead in the sense in which a first-born or a first fruit is ahead. But as such it is also truly comprehensive: it concerns everything in creation, because "through him God chose to reconcile all things, whether in earth or in heaven, through him alone" (Col. 1:20).

Is this statement about truth understandable? Not if we mean "understandable in terms of some other notion." As the last word on what Truth is, it is intended to relativize and disclose the meaning of all our terms. Basically, it is not a matter of understanding, but of surrender. And "the learned and wise" have a hard time doing that. But if we do learn it, however, we come to perceive something of the full disclosure of meaning. To put it differently, we then perceive something of the "responsiveness" of all things to the Word through which those things came to be and were given a destiny. In this relationship of "responsiveness," things also find their correspondence, their cohesiveness, and their integration, the opposite of which is error (missing the mark) and disintegration (originating in the *diabolos*, the father of disruption and of lies).

It seems to me that in this light, truth should not be primarily related to *premises* leading up to a conclusion. Rather, in the first place it is the truth of a promise, which is to be fulfilled. That's why in Biblical usage a tree can be said to lie when it does not bear and deliver the expected fruits. A tree is "true" when it does fulfill the promise contained in its branches and sustained by its rootedness in the soil. In this dynamic sense "truth" also applies to things and events, and not just to statements. There is a special relationship to human persons, though. That is indicated already in the word *expected*. It is indeed through man, through his *acts* (his statements included), that things and events reach their full truth, their full responsiveness and correspondence or fall short of that.

This brings up the question about *truth* as a criterion by which to judge between *right* and *wrong*. Moreover, what about the status of falsity in this connection?

Here again, I believe, we have to hold on to the central place of the Son of Man. With regard to the consummation of history, the ultimate judgment of creatures has been given to him who fulfilled the law. In fact, he himself *is* the judgment. He has come not to condemn but to redeem and reconcile. But in that very coming and continuation by his Spirit, he is the judgment.

This leaves no room, I think, for an independent existence or power of "untruth," of falsity, nor for an equivalence of any kind between truth and falsity. The latter remains characterized as distortion or, as Paul calls it in Romans 1, a *stifling* of the truth. Falsity is a parasite of the truth. Inevitably such stifling results in error: "Hence all their thinking has ended in futility, and their misguided minds are plunged in darkness," says Paul. Stressing this dependence on the truth does not in the least detract from the distortion, from the perverse character of falsity. Both features—the permanent dependence on truth and the incompatibility of truth and falsity—come together in God's retribution in giving men up to their desires, passions, and depraved reason. It is precisely history that gives full evidence of that: things which as such seem to be normal, such as power or rivalry, almost immediately become entirely distorted.

Did not these two features come most strikingly together in God's own accommodation of himself to the burden of untruth, in order thereby to reopen the way? Henceforth we know about, and are urged to, the most serious battle against the Lie, in ourselves first of all. This battle is entirely worthwhile and full of hope now that the burden has been borne.

ALBERT M. WOLTERS

Notes on the Structure
of *Enneads* II,9[1]

OF THE FIFTY-FOUR so-called "treatises" contained in the collected works of Plotinus, the Enneads, the one numbered II,9 is of special interest. Porphyry, Plotinus' disciple and editor, who organized
the treatises into six groups of nine, gave this unnamed treatise the
title *Pros tous Gnōstikous*, usually translated "Against the Gnostics,"[2]
and informs us that it is thirty-third in the chronological order of the
treatises.[3] Its special interest derives from the fact that it represents an
open confrontation between the Plotinian version of Platonism and
the strange and influential movement of Gnosticism. Moreover,
since the Gnostics whom Plotinus combats are Christian heretics,[4]

---

1. The following abbreviations will be used in this paper: LSJ = Liddell-
    Scott-Jones, *A Greek-English Lexicon* (Oxford, 1940); RE =
    Pauly-Wissowa, *Realen-cyclopädie der classischen Altertumswissenschaft.*

2. Porphyry, *Vita Plotini* 16.11: *biblion hoper "pros tous Gnōstikous"*
    epegrapsamen. All the titles of the Plotinian treatises derive from Porphyry,
    not from Plotinus himself. The title of II, 9 is perhaps better rendered "Reply
    to the Gnostics"; see LSJ s.v. pros C.1.4: "in the titles
    of judicial speeches, *pros tina*, 'in reply to,' less strong than *kata tinos*,
    'against' or 'in accusation.'"

3. *Vita* 5.33.

4. *Vita* 16.1 ff. The Gnostics are there classed by Porphyry as a subgroup
    of "the Christians"; on the grammatical construction of these lines see
    Elsas, Weltablehnung.

the treatise also shows some features of a clash between Plotinus and Christianity. Consequently, it is a central document in the currently revived discussion concerning the relationships between Greek philosophy (specifically Neoplatonism), Gnosticism, and Christianity.

The purpose of the present essay is to examine briefly two points relating to *Enneads* II, 9. They concern the literary composition of the treatise: Is it an integral part of a larger literary unit (as is frequently claimed), and is there a unity of composition discernible within the treatise itself? Though these two questions are largely formal in nature, the answers to them may serve to help "clear the deck" for subsequent investigations.

Our first point might also be designated as an examination of "Harder's thesis" with respect to the unity of *Enneads* III,8-V,8-V,5-II,9. Richard Harder, noted German translator of Plotinus, in 1936 wrote an article under the provocative title '*Eine neue Schrift Plotins*,'[5] in which he sought to demonstrate that the four treatises just mentioned (which are numbers 30, 31, 32, and 33 in Porphyry's chronological order) in fact constitute a single, hitherto unsuspected, literary unit which was arbitrarily dismembered by Porphyry and disposed helter-skelter throughout his edition of Plotinus' works. The overall outline of this reconstituted "new treatise of Plotinus," according to Harder, was as follows:

A. *Prooemium* ([III, 8][30]1-8)B.
B. *Das erste Hauptstück* ([III,8][30]9-11)
C. *Das zweite Hauptstück*
   1. *Der eine Weg* ([V,8][31], minus the last sentence)
   2. *Der andere Weg* ([V,5][32]1-3, plus preceding sentence)
   Recapitulation of B ([V,5][32]4)D.
D. *Das dritte Hauptstück* ([V,5][32]4-II,9[33]3)
Anhang: die Polemik gegen die Gnostiker ([II,9][33]4-18)

---

5. *Hermes* LXXI (1936), pp. 1-10. This is reprinted in Harder's *Kleine Schriften* (Munich, 1960), pp. 303-13.

A glance at this outline shows that, in Harder's view, Porphyry mutilated the original *Gesammtschrift*, not only by dividing it into four scattered treatises, but also by failing to observe the articulation of the overall argument when he did so. Specifically, with reference to II,9 he failed to observe that chapters 1-3 are really part of the preceding section and that chapters 4-18 constitute an appendix to the whole.

Harder's basic thesis has gained wide acceptance in Plotinian scholarship since the publication of his article. It is adopted by such diverse scholars as Becker,[6] Schwyzer,[7] Puech,[8] Henry,[9] Armstrong,[10] Dörrie,[11] Igal,[12] and Wallis.[13] Moreover, it is the unchallenged point of departure of three recent commentaries on the four treatises in-

6. O. Becker, *Plotin und das Problem der geistigen Aneignung* (Berlin, 1940), pp. 88, n. 1. Harder's thesis is here called "recht einleuchtend."

7. H.-R. Schwyzer, "*Plotinos*," RE, 21,1 (1951), cols. 484-85.

8. H.-C. Puech, "*Plotin et les Gnostiques*," *Sources de Plotin* (Geneva, 1960), pp. 161, 183 ("*comme l'a solidement établi* M. Richard Harder").

9. P. Henry, "Introduction" (1962): The Place of Plotinus in the History of Thought," *Plotinus: The Enneads*, translated by Stephen MacKenna, (London, 1969), p. iv.

10. A. H. Armstrong, "Plotinus," *The Cambridge History of Later Greek and Early Medieval Philosophy* (Cambridge, 1967), p. 217.

11. H. Dörrie, "*Der König: Ein platonische Schlüsselwort, von Plotin mit neuem Sinn erfüllt*," *Revue Internationale de Philosophie*, 24 (1970), 228, n. 16 ("*R. Harder hat mit vollem Recht den ursprünglichen Zusammenhang erkannt*").

12. J. Igal, *La cronologia de la Vida de Plotino de Porfirio* (Deusto, 1972), p. 102, n. 32 ("*Harder hizo ver el carácter unitario de estos cuatro tratados*").

13. R. T. Wallis, *Neoplatonism* (London, 1972), pp. 39, 46.

volved: those by Roloff,[14] Cilento,[15] and Elsas.[16] Of recent Plotinus students, only Theiler, to my knowledge, has qualified Harder's thesis, preferring to speak instead of a "cycle" of treatises without a coherent internal structure.[17] With very few exceptions, it seems, there is a scholarly consensus to the effect that *Enneads* II,9 is an integral part of a larger literary whole and must therefore not be interpreted as an independent treatise with its own purpose and structure.

In order to understand and evaluate Harder's 1936 article, it is important to see it in its own polemical context. To a large extent, the purpose of the article is to vindicate Porphyry's chronological order of the Plotinian treatises against the attack on it launched by F. H. Heinemann in his book *Plotin* (Leipzig, 1921). This "unlucky book," as Dodds calls it,[18] had attempted to trace a development in Plotinus' thought by rearranging the treatises in a somewhat arbitrary manner. Harder, in arguing that the treatises numbered 30 through 33 in the Porphyrian order constituted an unbreakable unity, was concerned to show, by independent criteria, that the received chronological order was reliable, and in this way to discredit Heine-

---

14. O. Roloff, *Plotin: Die Gross-schrift III,8-V,8-V,5-II,9* (Berlin, 1970).

15. V. Cilento, *Paideia Antignostica. Ricostruzione d'un unico scritto da Enneadi III, 8, V,8, V,5, II,9* (Florence, 1971). See p. 13: the correspondence of III,8 [30] 9-11 and V,5 [32] 4.1-6 "*fa sí che la ipotesi harderiana di lavoro salga a certezza filologica.*"

16. C. Elsas, *Neuplatonische und gnostiche Weltablehnung in der Schule Plotins* (Berlin, 1975), pp. 12-13, 56-85 and *passim.*

17. W. Theiler, in the introduction to his commentary on II,9: *Plotins Schriften, übersetzt von Richard Harder. Neubearbeitung ... fortgeführt von R. Beutler und W. Theiler.* Band IIIb (Hamburg, 1964), p. 414. ("*Aber die teile des Zyklus sind nicht Glieder eines systematischen Baues*").

18. E. R. Dodds, *Pagan and Christian in an Age of Anxiety* (Cambridge, 1965), pp. 25-26, n. 5.

mann's speculative reconstruction. That is also how his argument was in fact taken by other scholars,[19] who could not fail to notice Harder's rather violent polemic against Heinemann.[20]

Now, Heinemann had accepted that V,8[31] followed III,8[30] and that II,9[33] followed V,5[32], but he had argued that, contrary to Porphyry's testimony, the latter pair preceded the former one, rather than following directly upon it.[21] If Porphyry's order was to be independently verified, Harder had to make a case for the presence of structural links between [30]-[31] and [32]-[33]. He argued that two such links exist: a) the recapitulation found in [32]4.1-6, which appears to refer back to [30]9-11, and b) the last sentence of [31], introducing the argument of [32]. These seem to be the two pillars upon which his whole case rests, and therefore they bear further investigation.

The "recapitulation" at the beginning of [32]4 is a single sentence consisting of two *hoti*-clauses and ending in *eirētai,* "has been said." A schematic and literal translation, leaving out some of the unwieldy elaborations, runs like this:

THAT it is necessary to make the reduction to one and truly one....
and
THAT the intelligible world...is more one than the others ....

has been said.

The verb *eirētai* is here usually translated "we have said," and Harder in effect interprets it to mean "we have said *earlier in our argument,"* taking the sentence to refer back to the last three chapters of [30], which do in fact discuss the ascent from the relatively to the absolutely "one" in very similar terms.

---

19. See Schwyzer and Armstrong as quoted above (notes 6 and 9).

20. It is perhaps not entirely beside the point to observe that Harder was writing in Hitler's Germany and that Heinemann, a Jewish philosopher of some reputation, had recently been forced to flee Germany for Britain.

21. Heinemann, *Plotin,* p. 52.

Let us grant Harder the point that *eirētai* should here be translated "*we* have said" (though this is debatable),[22] and let us also concede the two further points that the sentence accurately summarizes and therefore likely refers to [30]9-11 (though both of these are debatable too).[23] Even so, it does not follow that the chapters alluded to belong to an earlier section of the same literary composition, which is Harder's point.[24] The fact is that Plotinus not infrequently uses the verb *eirētai* in precisely this sense when he is alluding to a specific passage in an undoubtedly independent earlier treatise. So for example at II,1[40]4.26, where *eirētai* refers, according to Henry-Schwyzer, to II,9[33]2.2 and 3.11 ff., and similarly II,5[25]3.36, where Theiler takes the *eirētai* to refer to V,5[23]12.1. In fact, Plotinus quite often explicitly couples the verb form *eirētai* with the phrase *en allois*, "in other

---

22. Plotinus also uses *eirētai* to mean "it has been said *by someone else.*" See V,4[7] 2.8 (Aristotle); II,9[33]6.54 and 7.4 (the ancient Greeks); II,1[40] 6.38 (Plato); VI,2[43]1.14 (Plato and others); VI,3[44]13.2; III,7[45]10.10 (previous philosophers).

23. Can these six lines be said accurately to summarize III,8[30]9-11, when it makes no direct mention of that section's main theme, the mystic's subjective experience of approaching and achieving union with the One?

   Nor need congruence of theme (which is undoubtedly present) necessarily mean explicit reference to this particular section of III,8. Ironically, Roloff follows Harder in seeing [32]4.1-6 as *Rekapitulation*, but not so much of [30]9-11 as of the entire preceding two treatises (*Gross-schrift*, pp. 107-8). Elsas, too, fails to refer specifically to the concluding chapters of [30] in his discussion of [32]4.1-6 (*Weltablehnung*, p. 66). Moreover, as Harder himself says ("*Neue Schrift,*" p. 2), the recapitulation refers to the central tenet of Plotinus's thought and could therefore refer to many places in his earlier writings.

24. "*Neue Schrift,*" p. 2 ("*diese Darlegung* muss also *in dieser Schrift selber stehen*" [emphasis added]).

writings of mine." See, for example, II,3[52]1.3 (where the reference, according to Armstrong and Theiler, is to the fifth chapter
of the much earlier treatise III,1[3]), and II,3[52]8.16 (referring
to the preceding, but definitely distinct, treatise I,8[51]12.5-7).
Our conclusion must be that the reference in [32]4 to [30]9-11,
if it exists at all, does not prove Harder's conclusion that both
passages must belong to the same literary composition.

The second pillar of Harder's argument is the last sentence of
V,8[31]. The printed Greek text of this reads as follows: "*âr' oun
arkei ta eirēmena eis enargē synesin agagein tou noētou topou ē kat'
allēn hodon palin au dei epelthein hôde?*" This may be translated:
"Now is what we have said enough to bring one to a clear understanding of the intelligible realm, or must we once again broach
the matter by another route, as follows?" This is certainly a striking ending for a treatise and undoubtedly looks ahead at the following treatise (V,5), in which the first three chapters approach
the intelligible world from a new angle, quite different from those
tried in V,8.

Harder's case depends upon showing that this last sentence must
clearly be considered a *part* of the ensuing discussion, not simply its
announcement, and this (it seems to me) he fails to do. The fact is
that the sentence is transitional and can be classed as easily with what
precedes as with what follows. Harder adduces the argument that a
question usually indicates the beginning of a new discussion,[25] but
this is at best a very weak argument, and, in any case, it is not at all
sure that the last part of the sentence *is* a question. It would be in
perfect accord with Plotinus' style to punctuate the sentence in
such a way that the question ends after *topou* and to begin a new
sentence with the affirmative *ē* often following questions in Plotinus:
"(Well), we must once again broach the matter by another route, as

---

25. Harder, p. 7, n. 2.

follows."[26] This transitional sentence cannot possibly demonstrate that what we know as V,8[31] and V,5[32] are in fact part of the same original literary unit—though it does fit very well with Porphyry's chronological order.

If Harder's main arguments for his thesis are as weak as we have tried to show they are, then a number of further considerations can serve to invalidate a number of the subsidiary points in his case. Four such considerations come to mind:

1. It is weak and implausible, in Harder's proposed overall outline, to call the first eight chapters of III,8[30] "Proem" and the next three chapters "*Das erste Hauptstück.*" This is disproportionate, especially when the second *Hauptstück is* composed of sixteen chapters, and the third, thirteen.

2. Harder's claim that the last fifteen chapters of II,9 are an *Anhang* is similarly weak and undermines his main thesis. If the four treatises are all part of a single *Gesammtschrift,* then it makes little sense to look upon almost the whole of the fourth component part as an addendum or appendix. II,9 cannot be an integral part and an extraneous addition at one and the same time.

3. III,8 by itself forms a well-rounded literary whole. In his study of this treatise, Deck remarks that "it stands out for its finished literary execution."[27] It also shows a completed progression of thought, moving from *physis* (chaps. 1-4), to *psychē* (5-7), to *nous* (8), to the final ascent to the One

---

26. On this use of ē (reminiscent of Aristotle's style, see H. Bonitz, *Index Aristotelicus* s.v. ē [p. 313a, line 14]: "*post simplecem quaestionem a particula* ē responsio solet ordiri"), see Schwyzer, *RE,* s.v. "*Plotinus,*" col. 519,26-39, and J. Igal, *Emerita* 43 (1975), p. 178: "*Ē sirve para introducir la respuesta, como ocurre frecuentísimamente en Plotino.*"

27. J. N. Deck, *Nature, Contemplation and the One* (Toronto, 1967), p. 3.

(9-11). It would seem to be an independent composition, marked by its own themes (e.g. *theōria*) and internal structure.

4. Harder's proposal, in its commendable intent to confirm Porphyry's reliability in listing the chronological order of the treatises, neglects Porphyry's account in *Vita* 16, which described II,9 as a separate *biblion* with its own occasion and history.

This last point needs some expansion and is at the same time a fitting point at which to move into the second question we proposed to discuss, namely, the internal structure of *Enneads* II,9. We are contending, in fact, that Harder's almost universally accepted thesis with respect to this treatise is ill-founded, for the reasons given above, and that we should try once again to look at it in its own right—not denying its thematic connection with the three preceding treatises in the chronological order (especially the last two), but searching out some of the features which distinguish it from these.

A good way to get a grasp of these features is to analyze the argument of the treatise without reference to an overall plan encompassing three other treatises, but rather with reference to the explicit testimony of Porphyry in *Vita* 16. A tentative sketch of such an analysis has the following shape:

"Reply to the Gnostics"

A. Ontology

1. Negative (chap. 1): No ontological distinctions should be made between "the Good" and "the One," between a potential and an actual first principle; between a resting and a moving, or a non-reflexive and a reflexive Intellect. No *logos* should be distinguished between Intellect and Soul.

2. Positive (chap. 2): There are, however, real distinctions to be made in Soul, to wit: a level always directed upward, a level directed downward, and a level in between.

B. Cosmogony

1. Positive (3.1-15): Reality comes into being in an eternal, timeless process, each superior principle giving rise to its inferior, and none perishing.

2. Negative (3.16 through chap. 4): The hypostases will not be dissolved into matter. The world did not begin at a particular time and by the fall of a forgetful and ambitious world-soul, nor will it ever end by the world-soul's repentance. This world is not of evil origin, but is as good as it can be.

C. Psychology

1. Negative (chap. 5): It is arrogant and false to say that man's soul is superior to the heavenly bodies; it is illogical to speak of "another," material soul, which is composed of the four elements and yet perceives and wills; it is absurd to see the world as an instrument for testing souls. (*Excursus* [chap. 6]: Their ideas are either absurd novelties or plagiarized and misinterpreted doctrines of Plato; in general they lack the proper respect for the ancient Hellenic philosophers).

2. Positive

a) The individual soul and the world-soul (chap. 7): The distinction between the two is important. Only the individual soul is trammeled by the body; the world-soul remains unaffected by its contact with body.

b) The blameless world-government of the world-soul (chap. 8): The cosmos which it produces and rules is the necessary image of the intelligible world, and therefore good.

c) The justice of the world-soul (9.1-26): The inequities of life all fit into the grand harmony.

D. Theology

1. Positive (9:26-43): The gods are to be considered superior to even the most virtuous men.

2. Negative: (9:43-83) It is arrogance to put oneself above the gods.

Conclusion (10.1-17): I will not extend my exposé any longer, out of consideration for those among our friends who hold these views. I have written these things not for them, but for my immediate disciples, as an example to them of how they should critique this false doctrine.

Appendix I: Mythology and Magic

A. The Sophia Myth

1. Negative

a) **Exposition** (10.19-33): One particularly absurd doctrine should still be discussed. They picture the world as a product of the rebellion of their Demiurge against Soul (= Sophia), his mother.

b) **Critique** (chaps. 11 and 12): They entangle themselves in contradictions, especially in that they denigrate the origin and present state of this world, while yet seeing it as derived from the higher world.

2. Positive

(chap. 13): The universe is a harmonious order of succession, which we must accept without murmuring. It is free from horror.

B. Magic (14.1-37): It is absurd to think that we can influence the higher hypostases by magic, or to deal with diseases in terms of evil spirits.

Conclusion (14.37-46): Let the foregoing be an example of how philosophical discussions should be conducted. I will say no more, but leave further investigation to you.

Appendix II: Practical Consequences

A. Ethics (chap. 15): Their doctrine leads to a practical normlessness worse than that of Epicurus. It is significant that they have never written a treatise on ethics.

B. Piety (chap. 16): They are arrogant and impious in despising the gods and their *pronoia*, whereas the whole world plainly demonstrates its divine origin.

C. Aesthetics (chaps. 17 and 18): They should see that there is more to the world than body (which is indeed bad) but that even the corporeal partakes of Beauty. To vindicate the beauty and goodness of the sensible world is not the same as *philōsomatein*, and does not prevent one from striving toward the higher.

A number of points in this outline call for comment. First of all, there does appear to be a definite shift in focus, beginning with the first chapter, to a more directly polemical, or systematically critical, style of writing. This distinguishes it from the preceding treatise V,5[32], where critique is incidental or marginal to the main course of the argument, although there is no denying that the opening lines of II,9 do explicitly pick up where the end of V,5 left off.

In connection with this openly confrontational approach is the strikingly regular alternation, through chapter 14, of predominantly positive and overridingly negative sections. The pattern seems to be a juxtaposition of destructive criticism and thetical alternatives for each major department of philosophical concerns.

Especially noteworthy is the appearance of two "Appendices," each preceded by a conclusion which seems to imply that the treatise is being rounded off. It is particularly instructive to look at the wording of the second "conclusion" (14.36 ff.):

But I leave the rest for you to examine in your reading (*ta d'alla hymin kataleipō anaginōskousin episkopeisthai*)[28] and to consider everywhere the fact that the kind of philosophy pursued in our circles shows integrity of character together with clear thinking.... The kind pursued in the others' circles, however, is constructed throughout on entirely opposed principles. For I should write nothing more, for it is appropriate for us to speak about them in the manner indicated.

This should be compared with *Vita* 16.9 ff.:

Consequently [Plotinus], after himself making many rebuttals in his seminars, and also writing the treatise (*biblion*) which we have entitled "Reply to the Gnostics," left it to us to examine the rest (*hēmin ta loipa kninein kataleloipen*).

The parallels in formulation are quite striking. It seems that Plotinus wrote II,9 as a kind of initial model for his closest disciples to follow in examining and refuting the writings of the Gnostics. Porphyry mentions that both he and Amelius thereupon wrote extensively in critique of Gnostic books, presumably taking II,9 as a paradigm of proper philosophical criticism. At any rate, Plotinus seems to have written the treatise with this in mind.

A similar point comes through in the first "conclusion," though the parallel with the wording in *Vita* is less obvious:

Under detailed investigation (*tis exetazōn*) many other tenets of this school (*polla kai alla*)—indeed we might say all— could be corrected with an abundance of proof.... There is

---

28. The understood object of *anaginōskousi* is not *Enneads* II,9, but the (other) writings of the Gnostics. On this see Schwyzer's critique of his "*Plotinos*" article in *RE Supplementband*, 15 (1978), col. 323,14 ff., where he corrects his earlier view that the verb referred to readers of Plotinus's treatise.

another way in which one might retaliate in writing against those who have the gall to ridicule the eloquent and truthful sayings of the ancient divine men. Let the investigation take place in the former manner (*ekeinōs men oun eateon exetazein*). For it will be possible for those who have accurately grasped what has now been said to make up their minds also concerning all the other points (*peri tōn allōn hapantōn*) (10.1-2; 12-17).

It seems that *ean exetazein* must be understood as a parallel expression to the *kataleipein episkopeisthai* (*krinein*) of the passages quoted above. In each case the reference is to Plotinus's rounding off his initial work of criticism and handing over the task of completing it to his disciples. They are to apply the same principles of critique to the rest (*ta alla, ta loipa*) of the Gnostic teachings.

The first "conclusion" also makes a significant distinction between "friends" (*philoi*) and "disciples" (*gnōrimoi*). Some of the Gnostics are included among the former, and it is out of regard for them that Plotinus does not personally want to continue his critique of the Gnostic position, which is also the reason why his treatise is not addressed to them. Apparently II,9 is a kind of internal memo, meant only for the eyes of close followers like Porphyry and Amelius. This is a further feature which sets this treatise off from its predecessors.

After each of the two "conclusions" there is another section beginning with words to the effect: "There is just one point that I still want to raise." No doubt some time elapsed between the completion of II,9 in its first edition (ending at 10.17), and the addition first of Appendix I (10.17 through 14) and then Appendix II (chaps. 15-18). It seems probable that these Appendices were added during the time that Porphyry and Amelius (together with others, perhaps) were engaged in writing their extensive refutations of the Gnostic treatises

(*Vita* 16.13-19). If this assumption is correct, then a further distinctive of II,9 emerges: unlike Plotinus' other treatises, this one was written in stages.

Curiously enough, the recent studies of the anti-Gnostic *Grossschrift* by Roloff, Cilento, and Elsas make no mention of these "I'll leave it to *you* now" passages in what I have called the two "conclusions,"[29] nor of the parallel wording in *Vita* 16. Consequently, the articulation of the argument escapes them. Cilento does not give an outline of the argument, but Roloff and Elsas do, treating II,9 as a constituent part of the larger whole of the Grossschrift. Roloff's is essentially a repetition of the analysis given by Harder, in which the last fifteen chapters of II,9 (in effect the substance of the treatise) are lumped together as *Epilog* to the presumed larger original. The overall outline given by Elsas is quite different; its main headings are the following:

I. *Theoria: Die Hypostasenreihe und die ihr immanente Bewegung (III,8)*

II. *Eidos: Schönheit und Ganzheit* (V,8)

III. *Der Geist als Stufe wahrer Erkenntnis* (V,5.1-2)

IV. *Der Geist und seine Unterschiedenheit vom Ersten* (V,5.3-13)

V. *Die naturgemässe Stufung der geistigen Welt* (II,9.1-2)

VI. *Kosmologie* (II,9.2-4)

VII. *Persönliche Angriffe* (II,9,5-18)[30]

In this outline, unlike that of Harder and Roloff, the integrity of II,9 (as well as that of the other treatises) is honored, although the heading "personal attacks" to cover its last fourteen chapters

---

29. Interestingly enough, the end of the second "Appendix," which is the conclusion of the whole treatise as it now stands, is not really a "conclusion" in the literary sense. The two announcements of conclusion are both in the body of the treatise itself (as it now stands).

30. Elsas, *Weltablehnung*, pp. x-xi.

seems quite anomalous. Elsas divides this last section into five subsections; what I have called Appendices I and II correspond to his subsections 3/4 and 5, which seems to confirm the point that there is a major break in the argument where the two Appendices begin (10.17/19 and 15.1).[31]

We may conclude, therefore, that Harder's thesis has obscured insight into the internal structure of *Enneads* II,9 and is at least partially responsible for the fact that this treatise has been misunderstood. This is particularly true if our conclusion is correct that II,9 affords a glimpse into the internal communications within Plotinus' circle, concerning the mounting of a massive literary attack on Gnosticism. Understood in this way, this unique treatise increases in both value and interest.

---

31. I first proposed the two-appendices hypothesis in a graduate paper written in 1970, five years before Elsas' book appeared.

PART TWO

Theology

"Underlying all the diversity of the Scriptures as we have them in this temporal life is the unity of the Word of God. It is, after all, the WORD*. How else could this big collection of sixty-six books be properly spoken of as the Word? And whence the 'system' of systematic or dogmatic theology? It is not the mind of the theologian, going to work on the many texts of Scripture, that constructs for the first time out of many passages a unity of meaning. This unity the theologian does not* make*; he* finds *it."*

— H. Evan Runner, *Relation of the Bible to Learning*, pp. 96-7.

HENRY VANDER GOOT

Tota Scriptura: The Old Testament in the Christian Faith and Tradition

Introduction

IT IS NOT OUT of proportion to the reality of the situation to speak today of a crisis in Biblical theology that is owing to the fact that much Christian reflection fails to view the Scriptures as a single narrative whole.[1] Modern Biblical theology seems unable to hold together in a positive, comprehensive, and coherent unity the Old and New Testaments. Much so-called pre-critical theology assumes—as does, for example, the Belgic Confession (Article IV)—that the Word of God is contained in both the New *and Old* Testaments, that New and Old comprise a "pedagogical homogeneity."[2] But under modern pressures the Scriptures have been treated as *disjecta membra*, with grave consequences for the Old Testament in particular. It is not an exaggeration to suggest that in the debate over the Old Testament as an integral part of the Word of God in a comprehensive sense there are at stake two well-nigh mutually exclusive understandings of

---

1. See Brevard Childs, *Biblical Theology in Crisis* (Philadelphia, 1970) and *Introduction to the Old Testament as Scripture* (Philadelphia 1979), pp. 27-61.

2. Heinrich Bornkamm, *Luther and the Old Testament* (Philadelphia, 1969), p. 252.

the Christian religion as such. Though a part of the canon, the Old Testament is widely depreciated or sometimes reconstructed on singularly New Testament bases, with the consequence that a growing number of voices allege that in modern theology especially the Christian religion is being transformed into a Gnostic religion with a Christic fixation.[3]

---

3. This is especially strongly and expressly argued by Arnold van Ruler (*The Christian Church and the Old Testament*, Grand Rapids, 1971), Walter Zimmerli ("Promise and Fulfilment," in *Essays on Old Testament Hermeneutics*, edited by C. Westermann, Richmond, 1969 and *The Old Testament and the World*, Atlanta, 1976), and Gustaf Wingren (*Theology in Conflict*, Philadelphia, 1956; *Creation and Law*, Philadelphia, 1961; and *Flight from Creation*, Minneapolis, 1971). Moreover, Eric Voegelin (*Science, Politics and Gnosticism*, Chicago, 1968 and *The Ecumenic Age, Baton Rouge*, 1978), Hans Jonas (*The Gnostic Religion*, Boston, 1963), and Norman Cohn (*Pursuit of the Millennium*, Fairlawn, N.J., 1957) have done much to disabuse moderns (even modern Christians) of the illusion that secularism has brought with it the final vitiation of other-worldliness and the Gnostic religion. Especially Voegelin and Jonas show that the modern world view harbors Gnosticism, though in metamorphized form. To the extent that "Christian" theology has based its future on "coming to terms with secularism"—which usually means accepting it as an inescapable and unalterable given—this metamorphized Gnosticism too has come to exercise an overwhelming and subtle influence on the development of "Christian" thought. I offer as a prime example of the eclipse of creation and the Old Testament under the guise of its repristination Jürgen Moltmann's recent book, *The Future of Creation* (Philadelphia, 1980). In this work the concept of creation in its classic Christian sense is thoroughly transformed on the basis of Marxist and Hegelian philosophical assumptions about the negativity of antecedent being, the essential fluidity of the present order in the light of human freedom, and the determinative role of the open horizon provided by futurity. Similarly, in his recent book Norman Young (*Creator, Creation and Faith,* London, 1976) errs by uncritically assessing

Failing to appreciate properly the Old Testament and its relationship to the New poses some problems for Christian reflection
which I shall discuss later. But at this point it is necessary to survey
briefly the modern theological landscape to delineate theological positions which tend to rob the Old Testament of its true significance
for the Christian church.

Lutheranism

Historically, the Lutheran tradition is first. Though Lutheranism has
produced Ernst Käsemann's "canon within the canon" theology,
which reduces the Word to the *in loco justificationis* as understood by
Martin Luther,[4] Lutheranism itself is more complex. Rather than reducing the Word (contained in the Old and New Testaments) to a
theme or motif found in the New, Lutheranism has traditionally
placed the divine wrath *alongside of* the divine mercy, law *in sequence*
with the gospel. Thus, in Luther's theology the Old Testament per-

---

secular and liberationist theologies as attempts within Christianity
to reaffirm and take full advantage of the Christian teaching
concerning creation simply because many such theologies advocate
a turn to *this* world as the proper locus of relevance of the
Christian faith.

Voegelin, however, has shown convincingly that in itself this turn
to the secular and immanent order of things by no means indicates the
decline of Gnosticism in the modern period. According to Voegelin,
one can still in good Gnostic fashion rid oneself of the world. But
whereas the ancient aversion to what is given in the world takes on the
form of escape—an upward flight from creation—in the modern
period Gnosticism expresses itself in the advocacy of a *total
transformation* of what is through action based on special knowledge
(*Science, Politics and Gnosticism*, pp. 99 f.). Norman Cohn's
assessment of the social philosophies of spiritualist, Anabaptist,
and millenialist groupings rests upon the same view.

4.   See the argument of John Gibbs, *Creation and Redemption* (Leiden
1971), pp. 67 ff. and 95 ff.

forms a necessary and indispensable function: it precedes and clarifies the New. For the Lutheran tradition gospel cannot be what it is, namely, victory, except that there be forces to overcome. Just as light depends on darkness, so gospel depends on law, and New on Old.

But though Luther at least affirmed the law-gospel sequence (which Käsemann, for example, fails to do), that sequence was from the beginning of the tradition *dialectically* conceived. Since the gospel was proclaimed to have overcome the law, the Old Testament has become merely a preliminary to the New. Specifically, the Old Testament has been interpreted over against the New. For example, viewing the Old Testament quite simply as a Hebrew document, Anders Nygren in his famous work *Agape and Eros* places the so-called Nomos perspective of the Old squarely in antithesis with the Agape perspective of the New. In a section of his work entitled "The Transvaluation of all Ancient Values" Nygren asserts that Agape "is like a blow in the face to Jewish legal piety." "Agape," he continues, "is the opposite of 'Nomos,' and therefore a denial of the foundation on which the entire Jewish scale of values rested."[5]

Moreover, that Nygren regards the Old Testament as the basis of Nomos piety and as therefore an ambiguous revelation at best is also clearly affirmed in his designation of Nomos as the Old Testament's "controlling idea."[6] According to Nygren, in the Old Testament love and grace have their place only within a "legal framework." "The Nomos motif," says Nygren, "stands in the most intimate relation to the Old Testament."[7]

To this Judaistic background, Agape and the New Testament are related negatively. Nygren formulates the tension between the Old Testament Jewish view of love and the New Testament view of love thus: "…love set within the scheme of law—love breaking down the

---

5.   Anders Nygren, *Agape and Eros* (Philadelphia, 1953), pp. 200-1.

6.   Nygren, p. 250.

7.   Nygren, p. 254.

scheme of law." But, even though "the idea of Agape (in Paul) first appeared in opposition to the Jewish ...conception of fellowship with God," the Old Testament Nomos motif has in Nygren's view continued to dominate the understanding of Christianity. Intimating that Old Testament piety represents a lower level of religious experience, Nygren argues that in the apostolic and apologetical periods of the early church "the *Commandment* of love was easier to grasp and (thus) ...led back to the Old Testament level, so that Agape was again brought under the scheme of Nomos."[8]

In line with Luther and his assessment of the Old Testament, the Old Testament law represents to many Lutheran theologians sinful Israel, tormented conscience, guilt, and death.[9] Just as Luther's own medieval experience as a guilt-ridden monk conditioned his view of the Old Testament, so in Lutheranism the Old Testament acquires a predominantly negative significance for the Christian. It is the thesis of this essay that the scope of revelation has been seriously reduced because the Old Testament has become radically misunderstood, being judged and interpreted by contrast to the limited experience of justification by faith.

One of the most influential contemporary examples of the Lutheran view—a view that may in Luther's own personal case be understandable but as a systematic position for today makes the Old Testament content impossible to handle—is the theology of Rudolph Bultmann. According to Bultmann, the Old Testament presents us with a history of miscarriage and failure, specifically the failure of Israel as it sought to assert itself before God on the basis of the law.[10] For Israel the rule of God is thought realizable within the

---

8.   Nygren, p. 251.

9.   Bornkamm, pp. 114 ff.

10. Rudolf Bultmann, "Prophecy and Fulfilment," in *Essays on Old Testament Hermeneutics*, edited by C. Westermann (Richmond, 1969), p. 75 (hereafter this work will be referred to simply as *Essays*).

world. No wonder that Israel had a bad conscience and that Israel really represents our bad conscience. It is, according to Bultmann, this bad conscience, this Israel, that is borne within us as "something which has been overcome." For Bultmann only in this sense does the Old Testament represent prophecy and promise, a hope "reduced to absurdity by the grotesque form of a priestly and legalistic theocracy"[11] and thus "fulfilled in its inner contradiction."[12]

Liberalism

A second theological position which devalues the Old Testament stems from the Enlightenment, Liberal, and historicist tradition. Many factors have contributed to this devaluation, among which anti-Semitism is not the least significant. But the most crucial factor is, I believe, the historicist and Enlightenment idea of progress, according to which human consciousness has undergone a progressive development from primitive fertility religion to ethical moral awareness, or, as the nineteenth-century theologians put it, to ethical monotheism. According to this view, Biblical religion marks a final stage in this evolution of the free human spirit.

But even within the Biblical material a further progressive differentiation of consciousness is noticeable, represented by the advance of the New Testament beyond the Old Testament and its mind. In the fifth of his famous *Speeches on Religion Addressed to its Cultured Despisers*, Schleiermacher strongly sounds an apologetical note, arguing for the superiority of Christianity vis-à-vis all other monotheisms. The Old Testament, Liberal theologians argued, does not really know the distinction between the fulfillment of the moral law, on the one hand, and religion and the infinite worth of the free human spirit, on the other. And, therefore, in this respect, viewed from this important theological aspect, according to Schleiermacher Judaism

11. Bultmann, p. 73.
12. Bultmann, p. 72.

is systematically related to Christianity in essentially no other manner than heathenism. Says Schleiermacher:

> The truth rather is that the relations of Christianity to Judaism and Heathenism are the same, in as much as the transition from either of these to Christianity is a transition to another religion. The leap certainly seems greater in the case of Heathenism, since it had first to become monotheistic: in order to become Christian. At the same time, the two processes were not separated, but Monotheism was given to the heathen directly in the form of Christianity, as it had been previously in the form of Judaism. And the demand made upon the Jews, to give up their reliance upon the law, and to put a different interpretation upon the Abrahamitic promises, was just as large a demand. Accordingly we must assume that Christian piety, in its original form, cannot be explained by means of the Jewish piety of that or of an earlier time, and so, Christianity cannot in any wise be regarded as a re-modelling or a renewal and continuation of Judaism.[13]

For the Liberal school, the New Testament—the consciousness of Jesus—is indicative of an advance to consciousness of human freedom and autonomy. Because, according to Schleiermacher, "a strong inclination to the use of Old Testament texts in expressing pious feeling is almost invariably accompanied by a legalistic style of thought or a slavish worship of the letter,"[14] the Old Testament does not share the normative dignity of the New. Therefore, to Schleiermacher and the entire Liberal school following him, the continued theological use of the Old Testament by the Christian community was viewed—in the words of Adolf von Harnack—as the result of

---

13. Friedrich Schleiermacher, *The Christian Faith* (Edinburgh, 1928), Par. 12.

14. Schleiermacher, Par. 132.

"religious and ecclesiastical paralysis."[15] For Schleiermacher the fact that the church has given instruction from the Old Testament does not warrant its continued use. Moreover, for Schleiermacher the fact that Christ and the apostles themselves refer to the Old Testament does not establish "that for our faith we still need these earlier premonitions." Instead of believing on the ground of the Old Testament witness and authority, which reliance would presuppose Israel's historical experience of God is *sui generis*, Schleiermacher expressly advocates "actual experience... and (the) immediate certainty (men have) through their own perception."[16]

Disturbed by the continued use of the Old Testament in the Christian church after the early period, Schleiermacher concludes that it is only for reason of historical fidelity that we preserve the Old Testament in the canon. From a systematic and theological point of view, it warrants no more place in the canon than as an appendix to the New Testament. As a matter of fact, Schleiermacher goes so far as to suggest that the present arrangement of texts (Old first followed by New) obscures the real connection of the Old Testament and Judaism to Christianity and the New. "The real meaning of the facts," Schleiermacher concludes, "would be clearer if the Old Testament followed the New as an appendix, for the present relative position of the two makes the demand, not obscurely, that we must first work our way through the whole of the Old Testament if we are to approach the New by the right avenue."[17]

Thus, we can see that the major exponents of nineteenth-century Liberalism depreciated the Old Testament by application to the Scriptures of their evolutionary conception of the emergence

---

15. Adolf von Harnack, *Marcion: Das Evangelium vom fremden Gott* (Darmstadt, 1960), p. 217.

16. Schleiermacher, Par. 132.

17. Schleiermacher, Par. 132.

of religious consciousness from ethical awareness to idealized human freedom. Moreover, from the earlier lengthy Schleier-macher quotation it is abundantly clear that the Liberal idea of the normativity of what is given in immediate conscious-ness came thoroughly to relativize the contemporary *theological* significance of Israel's historical experience for the Christian church and for us now. The very ambiance, then, of nine-teenth-century German theology fostered a negative theolog-ical assessment of the Old Testament. Especially the heightened consciousness of freedom as ostensibly exemplified by Jesus and his new community was stressed. But, furthermore, the cultural accommodationism of nineteenth-century German Protestant-ism was firmly grounded upon the assumption that this ideal of freedom had been recapitulated by the German people in its new-ly established and emerging culture. Following the lead of Martin Luther's idea of the gospel ("Free from the Law, oh happy condi-tion!"), the German people had committed itself to the struggle against Jewish legalism, which it must have viewed as the most seri-ous challenge to the ideal of absolute human freedom. It is in this anti-Semitic frame of mind that German theology in general and German higher and historical critical scholarship in particular were first developed into imposing disciplines.[18]

Neo-orthodoxy and Karl Barth

The third Christian position deserving mention is the Neo-orthodox one.[19] Here a more complicated relationship to the Old Testament appears, especially in the theology of Karl Barth. Although Barth neither ignores the Old Testament nor assigns it an indispensable

---

18. See Hans-Joachim Kraus, *Geschichte der Historisch-Kritischen Erforschung des Alten Testaments* (Neukirchen Kreis Moers, 1956), pp. 93 ff. and pp. 160-88.

19. See Appendix

negative function in relationship to the New, he does not allow the Old Testament to stand on its own feet; that is, he accords it no significance in its own right.

For this claim I present as evidence Barth's *redemptocentric* method of Biblical interpretation, of which a revealing example is his exegesis of the Genesis story of creation.[20] It is not only the case for Barth that God creates the world through Christ, that he moves toward the world through his Son in order thereby to establish an orderly disposition and management of things. For Barth this action is very deliberately *not* distinguished from the work of election and reconciliation in Jesus Christ. Barth, then, views Christ's work in creation as a work of *saving* responsiveness, that is, under the aspect of the second article of the Apostolic Creed. According to Barth, right in the very first words of the story of creation we see that in God's act of creation he *protects* the world from the threat of the primordial chaos, from the danger of *nicht sein*, or *das Nichtige*. It is then in this way that Barth rebuilds the Old Testament, especially seriously violating those elements in the Old Testament narrative that seem to fall—as to content—outside of the salvation-historical message, or outside of the immediate consciousness of Israel. Creation becomes for Barth a foil through which the people of Israel gave evidence of their faith in the lordship of Jehovah more comprehensively than they did in any other story in the Old Testament. Instead of coming first in the Bible, the story of creation should, for Barth's tastes, stand much later in the narrative.

Notice in the above that I have not criticized Barth's recasting of the Old Testament and creation into something other than they are as "Christocentric" or "Christomonistic." With Barth (and Calvin, for that matter), I believe that all things (both being and faith) are in Christ and that, therefore, the Old Testament itself calls for a Chris-

---

20. Barth, pp. 349 ff.

tological interpretation of sorts. The work of Christ cannot be restricted to the work of Jesus Christ in the redemption of the world.
Christ the eternal Son of God also has a cosmic, or creational, function. In other words, stressing classic trinitarianism, I follow Calvin's
teaching that God the Father *originates*, but Christ the eternal Son
always reveals on behalf of the Father. "Even if man had remained
free from all stain," says Calvin, "his condition would have been too
lowly for him to reach God without a Mediator."[21] God moves toward the world only in and through the eternal *logos*.

However, in Calvin's theology this primary function of the eternal Son, the *logos asarkos*, is clearly distinguished from the work of
election and reconciliation in Jesus Christ. On this point Calvin and
Barth quite obviously differ, for Calvin never views Christ's activity
in creation as a work of *saving* responsiveness, that is, under the aspect of the second article of the Apostolic Creed. As Calvin argues,
"...we understand first that the name of Mediator applies to Christ
not only because he took flesh or because he took on the office of
reconciling the human race with God. But already from the beginning of creation he was truly Mediator because he was always Head
of the Church and held primacy even over the angels and was the
first born of all creatures (Eph. 1:2; Col. 1:15 ff.; Col. 2:10)."[22]

There is, then, the rule of God over all the world and the angels
through the Son. In Calvinist thought this rulership is called "the
kingdom of God," and its Christological equivalent is called "the
lordship of Christ." These phrases indicate that from the beginning,
before the fall, Christ was present in creation. In creation Christ has
a function logically independent of God's redemptive purpose. Only

21. John Calvin, *Institutes of the Christian Religion* (Philadelphia, 1960),
    II.xii.1.

22. John Calvin, "Responsum ad Fatres Polonos," *Opera Omnia*
    (Braunschscvig, 1863-1900), 9:338.

after the fall, because of sin, did this rule of God through the Son come to special expression in the church, where Christ the lord of history performs his saving, *reconciling* work, drawing the elect into fellowship. Outside of the sphere of the church, Christ always was and is lord over all. But apart from the fellowship of belief there is no salvation and reconciliation.

Thus, Calvin can distinguish the two orders of creation and reconciliation while at the same time viewing all of life as life in Christ the eternal Son. As David Willis has convincingly shown, there is in Calvin's theology a work of the Son that is not restricted to or exhausted by the humanity and flesh of Jesus Christ: the eternal Son has existence "also outside of the flesh" (*etiam extra carnem*). In other words, Calvin subjects "the idea of mediation to two different nuances: mediation as reconciliation and mediation as sustenance." As reconciler, Jesus Christ came into the world because of the fall. But "as sustainer, the Mediator always was the way creation was preserved and ordered."[23] Calvin's principle of unity in Christ thus does not force the trinitarian elements of the Biblical narrative through the single bottleneck of the second article of the Apostolic Creed.[24]

Systematically put, this means that whereas for Barth creation must be viewed in terms of the broader purpose (from all eternity) of redemption (the Old Testament in terms of the vision of the New), for Reformed thought following Calvin (though not for scholastic, decretalist Reformed orthodoxy) redemption must be interpreted in the horizon determined by creation and the multifaceted theocratic vision of life presented in the Old Testament. I agree, then, with van Ruler's judgment that Barth's typological use of the Old Testament "seems...uncritically guided by the...principle that Jesus Christ is

---

23. David Willis, *Calvin's Catholic Christology* (Leiden, 1966), p. 70.

24. For the same view, see also H. Schroten's *Christus, de Middelaar, bij Calvijn* (Utrecht, 1948), pp. 149-54.

the final end of the ways of God with his people Israel."[25] Asking rhetorically whether "in creation ... God (is) really concerned about grace, the covenant, salvation," or whether "rather in salvation (he is) concerned about created reality," van Ruler responds to Barth by affirming that the "incarnation is exclusively motivated by sin," that "we are Christians in order that we might be men," that everything is oriented not to the one who saves, but to the saved and to the Father unto whom Christ restores his kingdom, and, finally, that, therefore, to "put it briefly and sharply, Jesus Christ is an emergency measure that God postponed as long as possible (Cf. Matt. 21:33-46)."[26]

Summary

None of the three positions mentioned so far accords the Old Testament an equal and fully authoritative status with the New. None accepts the Old Testament as a positive, indispensable revelation of the Word of God that is both continuous with the New and its necessary *prolegomenon*. All fail to view the Bible comprehensively and affirmatively from beginning to end. None takes full interpretive advantage of the Christian doctrine of the Trinity when assessing the Bible, thus failing to see that Scripture is a record of the works of God (and of men's responses to those works) from creation to consummation: that is, from the work of the Father to the work of the Son and the Holy Spirit. All fail to see that the Bible is a total vision of reality, comprehending everything about life within the perspective of faith. All fail to see the Bible as universal history in the sense of Augustine's *City of God* and thus are unaware that that history is not itself a *Heilsgeschichte* but has a *Heilsgeschichte* within it. Each position tends to identify a single redemption-oriented element of the whole ongoing narrative with the narrative itself, thereby reduc-

---

25. Van Ruler, p. 67.
26. Van Ruler, pp. 68-69.

ing the narrative structural whole to some putative salvation-historical essence or center within the Bible. None understands that the theme, the fundamental motif, of the Bible is trinitarian, following the pattern "creation-fall-redemption."[27]

It appears that the one current within modern Christianity which overcomes the problems of the three positions I just briefly described is the Reformed, Calvinist tradition. It has granted full-fledged status to the Old Testament alongside of the New as a Word proclaimable today. It regards the Old and New together as constituting an unbreakable positive continuity that loses its meaning if one of its narrative elements is pitted dialectically against the New as *Nomos* versus *Agape*, or is neglected, or is recast in the image of *Heilsgeschichte*.

Calvin and the Old Testament

Calvin himself argued for this positive basic role of the Old Testament in the Christian church. He understood that the one revelation of God is given in the Old-New sequence, emphatically not in either alone. Calvin claims in effect that the Old and New say the same thing in substance and differ only as to form of management and administration. Old and New together present to us the one God who acts, has always acted, and will always act in *Covenant* with us.[28]

---

27. On the distinction between a trinitarian and a Christological interpretation of the Bible, see Amos Wilder, *Kerygma, Eschatology and Social Ethics* (Philadelphia, 1966), pp. 15-16.

28. Calvin, *Institutes*, II.x.1-2. See also Calvin's *Commentary* on II Timothy 3:17 (Grand Rapids, 1948), p. 251, where Calvin says: "Seeing that Paul speaks of the Scriptures, which is the name given to the Old Testament, how does he say that it makes a man thoroughly perfect? for, if it be so, what was afterwards added by the apostles may be thought superfluous. I reply, so far as relates to the substance, nothing has been added; for the writings of the apostles contain nothing else than a simple and natural explanation of the Law and the

Thus, for Calvin the Biblical witness is not a law-gospel dialectic, *Nomos* piety alongside of *Agape* faith, or salvation history; it is, rather, pre-eminently *one covenant history*. Covenant is the overarching concept which holds Old and New Testaments together.[29] Therefore, the common term *testament*, meaning *covenant*, is used to designate both "books." Furthermore, showing the foundational character of the covenant idea, Calvinist theology speaks in particular of a "Covenant of Works" in creation. From the beginning man's relationship to God is a covenantal one. Covenant belongs to the very nature and order of things. Covenant relationship and dependence do not appear on the scene for the first time after the fall into sin. The Bible represents from beginning to end a history of man's obedience and disobedience in the face of God's faithfulness in the covenant. The covenant dynamic is the all-inclusive, dominant concept in terms of which every element of the Biblical narrative—including Jesus—is interpreted by the Reformed, Calvinist theologian.

Moreover, this positive conception of continuity in which Old precedes New and in which the one cannot be without the other (neither Old without New nor New without Old) determines the method of interpretation used in the Reformed tradition.[30] Calvin scorned allegorical interpretation, attending closely to the so-called "plain and simple sense" in exegesis. In this regard

---

Prophets, together with a manifestation of the things expressed in them."

29. Hans Heinrich Wolf, *Die Einheit des Bundes: Das Verhältnis von Altem und Neuem Testament bei Calvin* (Neukirchen Kreis Moers, 1958), pp. 19-66. In the Reformed tradition the covenant theological dimension of Calvin has been developed especially by the line running through Ames, Perkins, Coccejus, and Edwards. For an analysis of Coccejus's prominent role, see G. Schenk, *Gottes Reich und Bund in älteren Protestantismus, Vornehmlich bei J. Coccejus* (Gütersloh, 1923).

30. For an elaborate treatment of this point through acquaintance with *Calvin's Commentaries*, see Wolf, pp. 121-65.

his teacher was John Chrysostom. With his method Calvin replaced allegory with typology.

Typological Interpretation

It must be emphasized immediately in this connection that the typological interpretation of texts is not an arbitrary process, as the common view would have it. In fact, 1) it has its basis in being, 2) rests upon one of the most elementary functions of thinking, 3) has a strictly historical character, and, 4) in the Reformed tradition has been circumscribed by stringent restraints and standards of application.

1) As for its basis in the very constitution of reality itself, mention should be made of the Platonic philosophy, which founds an entire system upon the theory of analogy and correspondence between things present (becoming) and being itself. Another prominent example would be the monadology of Leibniz. Suffice it to say that these philosophies show that everything in the world refers to everything else. In each and every thing there is a little of other things.

There is then a general analogy among beings within the world. Analogy is rooted in being. Present and past experiences, events, and things intimate something of what is not yet present. Analogy assumes that we cannot say that the thing or event intimated is not present but only that it is not *wholly* present yet. Because there is continuity in reality and because things suggest one another, the present and the past lean toward a future which will have a determinate character and which is not totally fluid and characterizable by absolutely freely self-projecting beings. Past and present provide the future with the horizon within which the new and the unique can present themselves.

The Dutch Calvinist philosopher Herman Dooyeweerd has referred to this premonition of the future in the present and the past as "the opening up process" in all historical reality.[31] Moreover, Dooyeweerd has also developed a general ontological theory according to which the various ascending levels of complexity and differentiation in being (the numerical, spatial, physical, organic, psychical, logical, historical, lingual, social, economic, aesthetic, jural, ethical, and pistical) refer, each specifically in its own way, backwards and forwards to the others. For example, the logical law of parsimony—Occam's Razor—refers forward to (anticipates) the essence of the economic order, whose modal meaning is scarcity and maximally efficient productivity. Or, the quality of faith described in classical theology by the term *fiducia* refers retrospectively to the ethical order of troth in marriage and family. Or, again, psychical emotion refers back by analogy to the more primordial reality of physical *motion*, which is the ontic prerequisite of all psychically qualified life. One could go on and on in this manner to show how created reality is an indissoluble coherence of meanings (not being in and for itself), each of which is dependent on and reflective of all other meanings. Truly, reality is a typology of beings.

2) Moreover, because this is so, analogy is a very elementary function of all thought as well, as Gerhard von Rad has rightly pointed out in the context of his discussion of typological interpretation in Old Testament theology.[32] Furthermore, typology as a form of analogy is a specifically *textual* way of understanding. In Scripture, as von Rad has shown, typology is characteristically prototypical and oriented to eschatology; that is, the primordial event is a type of exemplum of the final event.[33] Events and persons as appearing in the

---

31. Herman Dooyeweerd, *A New Critique of Theoretical Thought* (Philadelphia and Amsterdam, 1953-57), Vol. I, pp. 29-30; Vol II, pp. 181-92, 335-65; Vol. III, pp. 66 and 142.

32. Gerhard von Rad, "Typological Interpretation of the Old Testament," *Essays*, p. 17.

33. Von Rad, p. 20.

Biblical record do not represent earthly realities with heavenly meanings. Heaven only knows what the limits of interpretation could be if this were the case. Rather, events and persons in the narrative represent other events and persons in the same narrative, so that the narrative provides its own conditions and limits of interpretation. Events and persons in the narrative stand for types (beginning with Adam and Eve in creation) that will appear again and again in an ongoing, evolving story. Typology, then, is closely related to repetition. The same situations and figures return repeatedly. New persons and events are described in terms of old ones in the Bible (for example, Christ the second Adam) and by the addition of each new event or person so described, a repetition occurs that contains progress and presses on to a higher eschatological plane.[34]

3) Noteworthy especially in this is the point, emphasized by von Rad, that typology is bound strictly to the Bible's *historical* sense.[35] What happens in the below of history does not signal the above but rather the before and the after, *Urzeit* and *Endzeit*, in the ongoing development of Scripture's narrative arc. As Hendrikus Berkhof has also aptly put it: typology differs from allegory because

> ...it does not think in terms of timelessness, but entirely in terms of history. For here the external is not a parable of the internal, but the earlier is a parable of the later, or better, the historical is like the Historical. Allegory looks inward, into the soul. Typology looks ahead, into history. That is, typology looks back into the past and there finds

---

34. See also Walter Eichrodt, "Is Typological Exegesis an Appropriate Method?", *Essays*, pp. 224-29.

35. Von Rad, p. 20.

the key to the present and future in the encounters between God and the world.[36]

4) Finally, with respect to typology as practiced in the Reformed tradition, it should be said that clear restraints have been placed upon its proper use. An old Reformed rule is that we interpret in Scripture as types only those persons, things, and events that are taken to be such by Scripture itself. The narrative is the norm, providing its own best means of interpretation. Representing the common position of the orthodox theologian Heidegger, Heinrich Heppe says:

> In judging of what is typical, we must proceed with the greatest care. Only by Scripture is it established, what must rank as a type. A thing or person is not yet a type because it has actually become a pre-indication of a subsequent thing or person, but because it is recognized as a type by Holy Scripture itself: (Substantiation) "Since Holy Scripture has no mere types, it is not enough for a type, that something should be found in Scripture; but that it should be pronounced a type in Scripture."[37]

Naturally, how the New Testament interprets the Old has been given prominent consideration in the Reformed tradition.

With its notion of covenant and kingdom and with its method of typology, Reformed Calvinist theology thus expresses its commitment to the Old Testament as a good and indispensable part of the Biblical proclamation for today. The Old Testament has full-fledged, authoritative status equal to that of the New. To understand Scripture, the various parts of Scripture—in this case Old and New Testaments—are needed to refer to one another, for Scripture is its own

---

36. Hendrikus Berkhof, *Christ the Meaning of History* (Grand Rapids, 1979), p. 111.

37. Heinrich Heppe, *Reformed Dogmatics* (Grand Rapids, 1978), p. 403.

interpreter.[38] Only when Scripture is allowed to interpret itself in this way can certainty be produced and can analogy to autonomous reason and experience be brought under the just judgment it deserves. Hence Reformed theology, especially Dutch Reformed exegetical theology, is suspicious of and avoids the modern Biblical theological method of dissonance that places things in the Bible *over against* one another. Rather, it prefers and practices the method of consonance, taking full advantage of the analogy of faith in its interpretation of the Bible.

Calvin, the Old Testament, and Systematic Theology

The Reformed tradition thus also bears witness to the systematic theological relevance and necessity of a positive and authoritative use of the Old Testament. For Calvin the Bible is its own interpreter. The Bible provides even the categories, interpretations, and structures whereby its saving message can best become known. In brief, for Calvin this framework of judgments and structures is especially closely related to (1) the revelation concerning creation in the Bible and (2) the dependence of that revelation of creation on the presence of the Old Testament in the canon. The following pages represent an effort to explore the systematic theological interrelationship and significance of these two claims.

Crucial to an elaboration of Calvin's position on the first point is, I believe, Calvin's own deliberate location of the doctrine of Scripture in the first pages of his *Institutes*, which opens with an extremely long book on "The Knowledge of God the Creator."[39] (Few theologians have noticed this peculiarity, and fewer still have bothered to

---

38. As Brevard Childs has recently said: "By reading the Old Testament along with the New as Christian scripture a new theological context is formed for understanding both parts which differs from hearing each in isolation" (*Introduction*, p. 671).

39. Calvin, *Institutes*, I.vi.1-x.

consider its systematic importance.) For Calvin, unlike the scholastic tradition to which much of his theology is a critical response, creation (God's existence as well as origination and determination of being) is emphatically not knowable by unaided reason but belongs (as all things do) to the perspective of revelation and faith. Everything belongs to the Christian faith-perspective. Therefore, right from the outset of the theological enterprise where we discuss creation, the world, experience, man, and what each of these is ought to be as well as how we are to understand their origin and total meaningfulness, Scripture becomes necessary.[40] For Calvin the Bible reveals not only a saving message, Jesus and our salvation, but also, and that "first in the order right teaching requires," creation and law. For a proper knowledge of both God and man, we are, according to Calvin, dependent upon the Biblical revelation. Without it we flounder. Therefore, even when not yet attending to "the proper doctrine of faith whereby men are illumined unto the hope of eternal life,"[41] Calvin introduces Scripture as an indispensable light unto our path and as spectacles through which to see.

Scriptural revelation thus has minimally a twofold purpose, or, better, a twofold content or word. As Calvin himself puts it, Scripture is a *duplex cognitio Dei*, a twofold revelation of the knowledge of God.[42] The Christian faith is not just a way of salvation, not just a religion of emergency. For the Christian revelation also speaks about the framework in terms of which the gospel must be understood and with which alone it is commensurate. For Calvin it is not possible for the

---

40. This fact does not mean—as Barth supposes—that everything is, therefore, purely gracious and in that sense purely Christic, including creation and law. Rather, this fact means that the purely gracious and Christic in God's actions (*das Heil*) belongs as one among many things to the perspective of faith, which encompasses also our understanding of being (*das Sein*) as such.

41. Calvin, *Institutes*, I.vi.1.

42. Calvin, *Institutes*, I.ii.1.

gospel to be explained out of immediate perception, natural reason, and unaided rumination on creation-reality, for such as are prone to do this revel in their own vanity. Furthermore, those that do this depend on themselves for a correct understanding of Christ (nothing could vitiate the Word more) and finally then remake Christ in the image and likeness of corruptible man. In order that an excellent defense be available to man for a correct understanding of Jesus and our salvation, Scripture, specifically the Old Testament, provides us with the proper directives and understanding.[43] For God's Word is not simply a proclamation of salvation from on high, but also a Word about the nature of the world below into which (and in terms of which) the Word from on high is spoken.

The second point in this argument is the assumption that it is exactly on the Old Testament in Scripture that we are dependent for our conception of man and the world.[44] The story of creation—the

---

43. Sounding a most Calvinist note, van Ruler says: "In the Old Testament this original and final element, this faithfulness to the earth and time, is more plainly visible. In my view this means that, in this respect, we have to speak most emphatically of the greater value of the Old Testament as compared with the New. The Old Testament has a more positive concern with creation and the kingdom, with the first things and the last, with the image and the law, with sanctification and humanity, with ethos and culture, with society and marriage, with history and the state. These are precisely the matters at issue in the Old Testament. For this reason the Old Testament neither can nor should be expounded christologically, but only eschatologically, in other words *theocratically*. There is in it a profound confidence in the goodness of the world, the serviceability of man, and the possibility of sanctifying the earth" (pp. 88-89).

44 See for example, the argument of Walter Zimmerli, *The Old Testament and the World*; chapter 3 ("The Necessity of the Old Testament for the Christian Church") of van Ruler's book; and Theodoor Vriezen, *Hoofdlijnen der Theologie van het Oude Testament* (Wageningen, 1949), pp. 147 ff.

story of God's making and governance of all things—is specifically important and foundational. Speaking of Scripture as guide and teacher for anyone who would come to God the Creator, Calvin says:

There is no doubt that Adam, Noah, Abram, and the rest of the patriarchs with this assistance penetrated to the intimate knowledge of him that in a way distinguished them from unbelievers. I am not yet speaking of the proper doctrine of faith whereby they had been illumined unto the hope of eternal life. For, that they might pass from death to life, it was necessary to recognize God not only as Creator but also as Redeemer, for undoubtedly they arrived at both from the Word. First in order came that kind of knowledge by which one is permitted to grasp who that God is who founded and governs the universe. Then that other inner knowledge was added, which alone quickens dead souls, whereby God is known not only as the Founder of the universe and the sole Author and Ruler of all that is made, but also in the person of the Mediator as the Redeemer. But because we have not yet come to the fall of the world and the corruption of nature, I shall now forego discussion of the remedy. My readers therefore should remember that I am not yet going to discuss that covenant by which God adopted to himself the sons of Abraham, or that part of doctrine which has always separated believers from unbelieving folk, for it was founded in Christ. But here I shall discuss only how we can learn from Scripture that God, the Creator of the universe, can by sure marks be distinguished from all the throng of feigned gods. Then, in due order, that series will lead us to the redemption. We shall derive many testimonies also from the Law and the Prophets, where express mention is made of Christ. Nevertheless, all things will tend to this end, that God, the Artificer of the universe, is made manifest to us in Scripture, and that what we ought to think of him is set forth there, lest we seek some uncertain deity by devious paths.[45]

But the story of creation in Genesis isn't the only thing that is important. Its very inclusion in revelation and restriction to the perspective of faith indicates that Scriptural revelation consists not just in the word of salvation (*kerygma*) but also in the Word spoken to us as the Bible all along the way works over, and itself listens to, man's response to the divine direct address. Creation is thus not just present in Genesis 1. It is present throughout the Bible in the fact that the Bible records for us not just what God proclaims but also how—whether rightly or wrongly—men respond in their lives to that proclamation. That, too, belongs to the infallible Word of God, and that, too, is creation, namely, the creation and law of every human experience recorded and every character appearing in Scripture. Scripture works those experiences and characters and human actions over, and from this judgment of curse or promise of blessing—whichever the case may be—we learn about the kingdom, the world, its normative structures, and our proper response to God. As Calvin repeats time and again in one form or another in his works:

For the Holy Spirit did not praise Abraham simply because he was without avarice, spurning silver and gold. But he has held him up before us as an example so that we might see what rule [*Regel*] we should follow in order to accomplish what he accomplished.[46]

---

45. Calvin, *Institutes*, I.vi.1..

46. Calvin, *Johannes Calvin Abraham predigten*, translated into German by E. Bizer (München, 1937), p. 19 (translation into English mine).

Finally, creation is not just the story about the world in the Bible—though that story is the indispensable foundation of every other appearance of "world" and "creation" in the Bible. Neither is creation simply the condition in which all Biblical characters live. It is also the creation reality and worldly history in which we live today, now. Creation is the truly universal element that links our lives with the Word spoken to men and women in the Bible so that finally the Word spoken to them is the Word spoken to men and women *such as we are* and ultimately is the Word spoken *to us*. As Gustaf Wingren has so poignantly argued in *The Living Word*:

> To think of the Bible, and not to think at the same time of Israel and the Church, is to omit from the Bible its character as message. The Bible does not acquire that character because we preach its Word, but already possesses it as a historic fact, and having that character it preaches. Our preaching, then, is just the Bible's own preaching—the passage to be expounded already has that meaning—and as God's people belong to the Bible's preaching, so the congregation belongs to ours.[47]

Without this dimension, that is, without the presence of experience, the world, man, and us ourselves in the Bible, the proper sense of the message of salvation remains ambiguous. The Bible is its own interpreter (*sui ipsius interpres*). The experience relative to which the message of salvation can alone be properly disclosed is not *brought* to the Bible but is envisioned and depicted by the Bible itself, especially in

---

47. Gustaf Wingren, *The Living Word* (Philadelphia, 1960), p. 26. See also Wingren's more systematically formulated articulation of the connection between us as we live under the law now and the Word in the Bible—what Wingren calls "the double phenomenological connection" in *Theology in Conflict*, pp. 161 ff. and "Den springande punkten," *Svensk Teologisk Kvartalskrift*, 3 (1975), 101-7.

the Old Testament. Not only the answers that the Bible offers but also the questions we ask it are finally authored, not partly by us and partly by the Bible, but wholly by the Bible itself.

A Christianity, then, that does not honor as fully as possible the Old Testament as the Word of God (as none of the three positions outlined above does) is in danger of fashioning not only its own vision of reality but also its own message of salvation.[48] Such Christianity runs the risk of imposing on the New Testament an alien structure of concreteness—runs the risk, for example, of interpreting redemption as the undoing of creation, as flight from creation, as the self-correction of creation, or as superordinate to the purpose of creation. In the history of Christianity such mistakes have been made. In fact, the most persistent major problem of Christianity in the West has been its accommodation to prevailing "natural" conceptions of order and experience. The New has been interpreted apart from the Old and has thus become vulnerable to heresy, having been interpreted, for example, spiritualistically in Greek terms as the sal-

---

48. See Gustaf Wingren, *Creation and Law* (Philadelphia, 1961), pp. 16-17, where Wingren says the following: "The main point which I shall make is that it is only on the basis of the Old and New Testaments together, and by commending with the work of Creation, i.e. the order which the trinitarian Creed represents, that it is possible to escape the false alternative of an early Christian faith expressed in a purely theoretical form, or an anthropology derived from philosophy...The Old Testament fulfills the legitimate theological need of an anthropology. ...In isolation from the Old Testament it is in danger of evolving a philosophical anthropology...To read the Bible as a unity, consisting of a single long narrative, is to read the Bible as it was read before the Enlightenment. No modern interpreter reads the Bible in this way, though every congregation does so in public worship, especially if it makes confession of the trinitarian Creed." See also Wingren, "Gamla testamentets teologiske betydelse," *Ny kryklig Tidskrift*, 32 (1963), 104-15. Finally, see Childs, *Introduction*, p. 671.

vation of the immortal soul from the prison house of bodily existence; or, for example, materialistically as the liberation of socio-economically poor classes from the rich; or, again, individualistically and existentialistically as in the case of Bultmann's kerygmatic theology.[49] In the early church the battle over such distortion was fought in principle already against the Gnostics, and it was fought by the construction of an Apostolic Creed with three articles in which the one concerning the Father Creator comes first and by the construction of a canon in which the Old Testament comes first and is given full authoritative status alongside the New.[50] For the early church and for us, confronted, as it was, with syncretisms of many kinds, the Old is the only proper way into the New. Paul and Jesus are continuous with the Hebrew tradition.

Conclusion

I would repeat and emphasize the Reformed claim that the Bible is its own interpreter. For Calvin this means that we know about creation and our condition only by faith. Moreover, *sola scriptura* means that Scripture is a whole whose parts explain each other and that for a proper knowledge of ourselves and the world we are dependent especially upon the Old Testament as the foundation of the Christian faith. It is to this part of the Bible alone that the disclosure of Jesus Christ is appropriate.[51] Apart from it, the entire story of the Bible becomes susceptible of transformation into an alternative and alien story about God, man, and the world. Apart from the Old Testament in the canon, no vindication of the Word of God as it applies to our lives is possible. Upon the foundation of the Old Testament in the canon, the whole house of Christian teaching rests. In conclu-

---

49. Walter Zimmerli, *Essays*, pp. 119-20 and *Old Testament and the World*, pp. 137-50.

50. Wingren, *Creation and Gospel* (Toronto, 1979), pp. 17-26.

51. Van Ruler, p. 84.

sion, we might say that the principle *sola scriptura* fleshed out in accordance with the principle *sui ipsius interpres* finally becomes the principle *tota scriptura*. It is this final implicate or corollary of the two others that the crisis of modern Biblical theology has increasingly forced contemporary theologians to respect.

ROBERT D. KNUDSEN

Apologetics and History[1]

EARLY MODERN PHILOSOPHY WAS not oriented to history. The word was not "history" but the "power of reason," and this reason was thought to be elevated above history. It was understood along mathematical lines and was endowed with creative capabilities. "Give us material," said René Descartes, the father of modern philosophy, "and we shall construct a world from it."[2] Reason, thought Descartes, was sufficient on its own to demolish the world and to build it up again by its own creative power. History did not dominate reason; instead, reason dominated history. Reason was supposed to interpret and guide history by means of its superhistorical ideas.

The attitude of René Descartes toward the relationship of reason and history prevailed in early modern philosophy. A historical manner of thinking was introduced into modern thought by Giambattista Vico only in conscious opposition to the ideas of Descartes.[3]

---

1. This essay is a revised form of a lecture delivered on November 30, 1979, at Trinity Theological College, Bristol, England.

2. As quoted by Herman Dooyeweerd, *The Secularization of Science*, translated with an introduction by Robert D. Knudsen (Memphis, 1979), p. 19.

3. See *The New Science of Giambattista Vico*, translated by Thomas Goddard Bergin and Max Harold Fisch (Ithaca, N. Y., 1948) and

Descriptions have often been given as to how the modern rationalistic spirit came to dominate theology, gradually replacing revelation with reason. This tendency came to expression in the movement called "deism," which is typified by the title of the book of Matthew Tindal (1656-1733), *Christianity as Old as the Creation* (1730). By this title Tindal did not mean to express only that the truths of Christianity were ancient and venerable, reaching back to the creation. For him "creation" and "reason" were virtually synonymous. That Christianity was as old as the creation meant for him that the truths of Christianity were simply a restatement of the truths of reason. According to many with deistic tendencies, Christianity had simply stated, at an earlier time and to a wider audience, the truths that reason of itself was able to discover.[4]

In response to the rationalistic challenge of deism, evangelical Christians attempted to establish a preserve for revelation, where reason could not trespass. Reason was limited, they said, unable to lay claim to the entire territory. It was difficult, however, for the evangelical to make his strategy work, because he had not found a way intrinsically to delimit reason. He was forced to stand by as more and more of his territory was conquered, as more and more truths of revelation were either abandoned altogether or were declared to be at bottom truths of reason.

An influential attempt to countermand the influence of deism was that of Bishop Joseph Butler (1692–1752), who is famous for his *The Analogy of Religion, Natural and Revealed, to the Constitution and Course of Nature* (1736).[5] Butler sought to turn the edge of deistic

---

Robert D. Knudsen, History (Cherry Hill, N. J., 1976), p. 9.

4.   Ernest Campbell Mossner, *Bishop Butler and the Age of Reason* (New York, 1936), pp. 74 ff., 77.

5.   *The Works of the Right Reverend Father in God Joseph Butler* (Oxford, 1874), Vol. I.

criticism by appealing to the deist's own faith in the order of nature, which for the deist was the order of reason. You criticize the truths of revelation, Butler said, but look around you at nature. It has difficulties analogous to those in the sphere of revelation, and yet you daily exercise faith in it.[6] Whatever difficulties there are in revelation, Butler argued, they are not sufficient to render it unreasonable for a rational man to vest his faith in it.[7]

In developing his argument, Butler divided the terrain, as was customary, into two parts, that of nature and that of grace. His reasoning with regard to the sphere of nature was typified by his argument for immortality.[8] During our lives, he reasoned, we observe that we undergo many transformations (childhood, youth, maturity, old age) without losing our identity. This experience establishes a presumption that our personal identity will continue on even beyond that transformation called "death," unless there is sufficient reason to the contrary.[9] Butler claimed that there was no evidence for such a reason. There are indeed difficulties, but these are not such as to render it unreasonable for a rational man to believe in an afterlife. Butler's approach was similar in the realm of grace.[10] You hear of the Christian doctrines concerning the Mediator, the need for grace, etc. These truths lie closer to your experience than you might suppose. There are analogies within our experience to the truths of Christianity. We observe, for instance, an analogy to the Christian doctrine of grace in the fact that one is not always forced to bear the full conse-

6. Butler, p. 5.

7. Butler, pp. 10, 11-12.

8. Butler, part I, chapter I, "Of a Future Life."

9. "There is in every case a probability, that all things will continue as we experience they are, in all respects, except those in which we have some reason to think they will be altered" (Butler, p. 15; see also pp. 16, 21-22).

10. Butler, part II, "Of Revealed Religion"; see also pp. 202-03.

quences of his errors. We find an analogy to the work of the Mediator in that one sometimes gives himself in the place of another. Whatever difficulties there may be with such Christian doctrines, they do not override the force of the analogies to them within our experience. The difficulties are not such as to make it unreasonable for a rational man to vest his faith in them.

It has often been described how David Hume (1711-1776) attacked the Butler-type apologetics.[11] Butler's argument rested on the possibility of forging a link between what lies within and what lies beyond our experience. Working within a sphere of thought obviously dominated by the mechanics of Isaac Newton, he had reasoned that momentum once established could reasonably be assumed to continue, according to the law of inertia, unless there was sufficient reason to the contrary.[12] Once having gotten a good start, one might reasonably expect to jump successfully from the one bank to the other. David Hume brought into question the possibility of forging such a link. There was no way of bridging the gap between what is within and what is beyond our experience, he argued, except by way of the idea of causality; but the idea of causality itself rests upon our customary experience and is valid only within that experience. It cannot serve to establish a link between our experience and what lies beyond it.[13] Furthermore, what truly underlies our attempt to fill in the gaps of our experience and to come up with the kind of world in which a Butler-type apologetics might

---

11. See Mossner, pp. 156-65. A more recent discussion is that of Anders Jeffner, *Butler and Hume on Religion: A Comparative Analysis* (Stockholm, 1966), including the literature lists, pp. 21-24.

12. Butler, pp. 11-12, 14-16.

13. David Hume, *A Treatise of Human Nature*, edited by L. A. Selby-Bigge (Oxford, 1928), Book I, part iii, section 2: "'Tis only *causation*, which produces such a connexion....'"

work is an inclination of the mind. Hume took the inertia that Butler and others had discovered in the "external" world and transposed
it to the mind.[14] It is only because of a "subjective" inclination, an
"inertia of the mind," that we desire at all to reason from this world
to another. The miracles, for example, which some peoples (i.e.,
primitive ones) take to be signs of supernatural intervention, arise as
stories because of the needs of primitive imagination. Such stories
satisfy curiosity and awaken an agreeable sense of wonder. They are
not a result of reporting events in the outer world.[15]

The effects of Hume's reasoning on a Butler-type apologetics
were grave. It took an argument from experience that was thought to
be neutral and reinterpreted that experience in such a way that the
argument became invalid.

In this situation apologetics was inclined to go in one of two
directions if it was to find an alternative apologetical stance. There
was a tendency, on the one hand, to retreat into a mere confession
of Christian truth, without any attempt to do apologetics. One
could even emerge with the idea that there is an incongruity between Christian confession and its presumed intellectual defense.
In my own circles we call this attitude "fideism."[16] A different line
of action, on the other hand, was to attempt to place apologetics
upon a new foundation, one that would free it from criticisms
like those advanced by David Hume. According to my best
knowledge, it was the Scotsman James Orr (1844-1913) who ini-
tiated this latter trend, at least for the English-speaking world,

---

14. See Herman Dooyeweerd, *A New Critique of Theoretical Thought*, I
(Philadelphia, 1953), 291, 292, 297.

15. See Anders Jeffner, *Butler and Hume on Religion: A Comparative
Analysis* (Stockholm, 1966), pp. 112-25.

16. See Cornelius Van Til, *Christian-Theistic Evidences, In Defense of
Biblical Christianity*, VI (Philadelphia, 1976), p. 34.

drawing upon resources from the idealistic traditions in Germany and Britain.[17]

To illustrate this newer thinking, we must employ a different image. The image we have used before is that of someone who attempts to vault a stream (or perhaps a canal, as it is done in the Netherlands) with the aid of a pole. If his pole is long enough and if he can get a strong enough grip on it, all he must do is to establish sufficient momentum in order to jump safely to the opposite bank. We saw Hume argue against this view along the following lines: "Yes, indeed, sir, that is nice; but I am sorry, sir, you don't have a pole and the other bank is in point of fact a product of your own imagination. We have enough to do simply to keep moving on this side of the stream!" The newer image we may employ, in order to visualize the approach of James Orr, is this: A surveyor comes and observes the near bank of the stream with utmost care. He observes that it is such that he can make sense of it with his surveying instruments. He then asks himself, reflecting upon what he has done, "What is it that makes this rational understanding possible?"

It is, as I have suggested, the latter route that James Orr took. Given our experience, what is it then, he asks, that lies at the very foundation of its possibility?[18] This kind of thinking is what is called "transcendental."[19] Am I incorrect in thinking of James Orr as the first, at least in the English-speaking world, to employ a transcendental method in apologetics?

James Orr argued that to understand the world of our experience it is necessary to postulate certain axioms (presuppositions) drawn

---

17. Van Til, pp. 36 ff.

18. James Orr, *The Christian View of God and the World*, tenth edition (Edinburgh, 1908), pp. 103 ff.; see also pp. 94 ff.

19. Van Til speaks of the "high standard" set by Orr's use of transcendental method in apologetics (Van Til, p. 47).

from the Christian world and life view. The first of those axioms is the God who has revealed himself in Jesus Christ. The second is the Biblical (Christian) doctrine of creation and of man. The third is the Christian view concerning the sin and disorder in the world.[20]

These presuppositions are postulates. As postulates they are not drawn simply from experience, as if we could take off from our experience of sense and rise to a transcendent, divine realm. But Orr does not regard these presuppositions as postulates, on the order of geometrical axioms, from which we might deduce the being of God not only but also that of the world and human existence.

If we simply begin with experience as something neutral, Orr understood, there is no way we can ascend to the absolute being of God. We are always left with something within our experience, with something finite. To this extent Hume was right. If, on the other hand, we seek to deduce the Christian doctrines of God, the world and man, and sin, we must proceed, Orr correctly observed, from a standpoint superior to them. But what is more ultimate than God himself, or more a beginning than his creation of the world and of all things in it?

We must discover a point of departure that does not pretend to be neutral or seek to deduce from ultimate presuppositions, but one that presents us with the key to opening up the meaning of our experience.[21]

---

20. Orr, lectures III, IV, and V.

21. "...a God capable of proof would be no God at all; since this would mean that there is something higher than God from which His existence can be deduced. But this applies only to the ordinary reasoning of the deductive logic. It does not apply to that higher kind of proof which may be said to consist in the mind being guided back to the clear recognition of its own ultimate pre-suppositions. Proof in Theism certainly does not consist in deducing God's existence as a lower from a higher; but rather in showing that God's existence is itself the last postulate of reason—the ultimate basis on which all other knowledge, all other belief rests" (Orr, p. 94; see also Van Til, p. 47).

In my estimation, James Orr did not bring his program to an altogether satisfactory conclusion. I am convinced, nevertheless, that Orr hit upon insights suggestive of methods that are actually being used—or that should be used in apologetics today—if we are to give adequate place to the sovereignty of God and to the authority of his revelation.

Orr gained insight, for example, into what we might call the boundary character of the Christian starting point for thought. He was aware of the anomalies that arise for the human mind if it transgresses the boundary between what is immanent to the world, i.e., what is within the world, and what transcends it as its absolute origin.

In his book *The Christian View of God and the World* (1893), Orr reviews some of the objections a simple-headed rationalism has urged against the idea of a God who transcends the world in infinite majesty. What was God doing before he created the world? Why did he create it just at one moment and not at another? I am certain that you have heard these and other questions like them. Wisely, like Augustine and Calvin, Orr refrained from attempting to answer such questions head on. Even asking them, he said, suggests that one is on the wrong track, that he has an erroneous idea of the relation between time and eternity. One should not seek to answer such questions but should reflect upon why it is that one should not even ask them, and upon the adequacy of his understanding of the boundary between God and man.[22]

Reflecting on the boundary, we can see that there is indeed a boundary idea which is itself not a product of our thinking nor which is even penetrable to our thinking, but which is necessary to that thinking if it is not to proceed in a wrong direction. Thus, any disturbance at the boundary will have repercussions within the limits of the boundary. Thus, too, in order to make it possible to survey the

---

22. Orr, p. 129.

terrain adequately, one will have to obtain a proper idea of the boundary. If he fails in this all-important regard, his survey points will be off, and he will obtain a distorted picture of the terrain he is attempting to map out.

James Orr's position is, in my estimation, not quite so good as the one I have sketched here. His writings employ this transcendental method, however, or are at least so suggestive of it that I can honestly class James Orr as a bona fide forerunner of the kind of apologetics I am describing.

A "bare-bones" description of this method might run as follows: Lose the handle on the true transcendence standpoint and you will no longer be able to obtain a unified view of the created cosmos. Your view of the cosmos will be driven in opposing directions. There will come into being contradictory viewpoints which do not truly belong to the cosmos in its created goodness but which are distortions of it.

This pattern comes to more or less clear expression in James Orr's argument for the Christian faith from history.[23] The Christian, Orr says, finds the central point of reference for his life and thought in the God-man, Jesus Christ, who is the crown of the revelation of God. If one refuses to place Jesus Christ at the center, there comes into play a process within history, unavoidable in its consequences, in which there is a descent from Christian conviction to bare humanism, from humanism to agnosticism, and from agnosticism to despair.[24]

It is characteristic of history, Orr said, to carry things to their extremes.[25] Thus, letting go of the Christ will lead to ever more dire consequences. One will be faced with ever more extreme choices, as

---

23. Orr, lecture II, "The Christian View and its Alternatives."

24. Orr applies the "method of appeal to history" (Orr, p. 43; see also pp. 40 f., 64 f.).

25. Orr, p. 43; see also pp. 45, 47, 48, 51, 53.

the dialectic of history deepens. One will be faced, as we have said, first with the choice between Christ and humanism, then with the choice between Christ and agnosticism, and finally with the extreme choice between Christ and despair.[26] It is at this final point, at the nadir of despair, Orr said, that reason can again assert itself and begin its ascent again to the God-man Christ, in whom alone is the key to reason and meaning.[27]

Kindly note that this argument does not require one to rise above the boundary between God and man. It only requires that one have a proper idea of the boundary.

Kindly note also that this argument does not attempt a direct confirmation of the Christian position, of the centrality of Christ for life and thought. It assumes the Christian position as the proper starting point, as that in which there is the idea of the boundary, the proper expression of the relation between God, man, and the cosmos. Lose hold of this transcendence point and a process will inevitably be set into motion within the world, within history, a process that is dialectical in character, leading to necessary choices between ever more extreme alternatives. That a departure from the Christian starting point leads inevitably to irrationalism and despair is taken as indirect proof of the validity of this starting point. A Christian view of the boundary, involving a view of the relation of immanence and transcendence, becomes the foundation for a presuppositional apologetics that uses an indirect method of proof for the Christian faith.

Orr's indirect method of proof has allowed me to include him among the apologists who do not take a neutral position outside of the citadel of the Christian faith in order to defend it, but who

---

26. "History presents us with a series of alternatives" (Orr, p. 44; see also pp. 44 ff., 47 ff., 51 f.).

27. "...I am at present concerned...not to refute Pessimism, but rather to show how, as a first step in an upward movement back to Christ, by its own immanent dialectic it refutes itself..." (Orr, p. 54; see also p. 64).

mount a defense of Christianity while remaining solidly within its walls.[28] Accordingly, the defense of the Christian faith is not made to depend upon something outside of that faith, as if one required an "objective standard" in the sense of a neutral standard, a yardstick, if you will, that does not itself depend for its validity upon the Christian faith. Instead, the defense of the faith must proceed upon the standpoint of that faith itself. It must present the Christian position as the only one upon the foundation of which our experience is intelligible. Orr argued that it is only by taking Jesus Christ as one's starting point that one can avoid landing up in agnosticism and eventually in despair. For this reason it is possible to number Orr among those whom we today call "presuppositional apologists," even though we must register some disappointment with the way he carried on his argument.

James Orr was capable of mounting an argument from history because of developments that had taken place in current philosophy. He learned, to mention one, from the British philosopher Thomas Hill Green (1836-1882).[29] Green complained that British philosophy had gone to seed in David Hume. He sought to reconstruct it by drawing on the idealistic tradition represented by Immanuel Kant (1724-1804) and Georg W. F. Hegel (1770-1831).[30] Of the two it was Hegel who had carried to their end tendencies within the developing idealistic movement and had intimately connected Reason with the course of history. For Hegel history was the story of Reason (or Absolute Spirit) coming to self-awareness by way of a dialectical

---

28. Robert D. Knudsen, "Progressive and Regressive Tendencies in Christian Apologetics," in *Jerusalem and Athens*, edited by E. R. Geehan (Philadelphia, 1971), pp. 275-98; see also pp. 280-83.

29. See Orr, pp. 59, 104, 125.

30. G. W. Cunningham, *The Idealistic Argument in Recent British and American Philosophy* (New York, 1933), p. 42.

development.[31] That cannot be said of James Orr. There are points at which Hegel influenced Orr, however. The very fact that Orr used an argument from history as he did points to this influence. For it was particularly in Hegel that Reason was no longer identified, as in Descartes, with mathematical thinking, nor identified, as in the thought-sphere represented by Newton, with reasonable assumptions understood along the lines of a mechanical model; in Hegel, Reason became intimately associated with history, and history became the stage upon which Reason came to expression in its dialectical unfolding.

Orr agreed with Hegel that the totality, the point of concentration, of all meaning is rational Reason; furthermore, leads to Jesus Christ. If Christ is not placed at the center, there is an inevitable fall into unreason and despair.[32]

We can learn, however, from respects in which Orr differed from Hegel. For the latter, despair was necessary to Reason. It was only as Reason passed through an entire series of way-stations of despair that it could come to itself, that is, attain complete self-consciousness.[33] Even though there are similarities between him and Hegel, Orr takes a position here that Hegel would have rejected out of hand. According to Orr, Reason can pertain apart from despair. One descends into despair only as he rejects Christ and falls into the grip of a power that leads him from reason to unreason, from meaning to meaninglessness. What serves to trigger this necessary movement need not happen. One need not reject Christ. Furthermore, one may restore Christ to his rightful place and thus overcome the despair. Further

---

31. G. W. F. Hegel, *Phenomenology of Spirit*, translated by A. V. Miller (Oxford, 1977), pp. 488-93; see also p. 591.

32. Orr, pp. 63 f., 215 ff., 39, 40, 43 ff.

33. "The self-knowing Spirit knows not only itself but also the negative of itself...." (Hegel, p. 492, *passim*).

still, at the nadir of despair, Reason can again take over and lead us again to meaningful existence.[34]

James Orr, as I have pointed out, is influenced by Hegel's idea of dialectic in history. Unlike Hegel, however, he uses dialectic only in a negative sense. The dialectic, the necessary development whereby one is gradually forced to decide between ever sharper antithesis, comes into being only when the true concentration point of meaning has been abandoned. It is a sign that the true transcendence point has been lost. Restore this true point of reference, and the dialectic disappears.

Now it is just this negative use of dialectic that I have singled out as a contribution on Orr's part to Christian apologetics.[35] Lose the true concentration point and you will of necessity fall into difficulties, the presence of which is an indirect proof of the validity of the true starting point. The centrality of Christ is testified to by the meaninglessness that issues upon rejecting him. I should certainly not suggest that we follow Hegel, for whom meaning was found only in an encounter with meaninglessness. It is James Orr whom we say is an early advocate of a method employed by presuppositional apologetics.

How James Orr conceives of reason, however, leads to some difficulties. For him the fullness of meaning is rational. Its loss means unreason and despair. The necessary development leading from reason to unreason, however, must itself be an expression of some kind of reason (what one might call an "immanent logos"), a tendency

---

34. Orr indeed speaks of two movements in history, a downward one leading away from and an upward one leading to Christ. The pattern, however, is that of a trough, in which unbelief brings one down, and out of which a straight-line ascent is possible, "retracing the stages of the earlier descent" (Orr, p. 64). A simple descent and/or ascent would be rejected by full-blown Hegelianism as "abstract."

35. Knudsen, "Progressive and Regressive Tendencies," pp. 281, 283, 291.

that gets one in its grip. Finally, reason must be thought of as the force that guides the mind of man, having seen the futility of unreason, to the fullness of meaning in Christ.

That Orr thinks of reason in these ways poses problems. If reason is that which is abandoned in the descent toward unreason, how can it also function as that which provides the framework of this descent itself? If it is the goal to which the process of history leads, how then can it function as the force that drives this process along? Hegel would certainly have objected to allowing these facets of reason to lie next to one another, as Orr left them. If Orr was to retain his purely negative use of dialectic, however, he could not draw these strands together in a universal rational process. The descent from reason to unreason could not be thought of as a constitutive part of the odyssey of reason leading to Christ.[36]

If reason is a universal force guiding the historical process towards Christ, however, would there not be an inclination to view the dialectic, itself part of the historical process, as making a positive contribution, and not only as providing a sign of the abandonment of reason for unreason? Understanding experience in the light of the postulate of sin and disorder would allow one to ascribe an exclusively negative meaning to dialectic, interpreting it as the result of a sinful rejection of the God-man. If one does this, however, can he think of the ascent to Christ as a tendency of universal human reason?

Another related question arises concerning Orr's view of history. Orr must think of history as that in which everything is driven to

---

36. We have already stated that Orr's line of thought would be rejected as "abstract," indeed, as "undialectical," by consistent Hegelians. Had he taken the consistently Hegelian route, the descent to despair would have been far more than a warning signal that the true starting point had been abandoned. He would have had to include, as many contemporary theologians do, the shadow of unbelief together with the sunlight that streams from the God-man, Christ.

extremes—a "reason" in history. It might be argued, on the contrary, that history is a great leveler.[37] The exalted ideals of men and women, their exalted personal ideals, are dissipated by the need to adjust to the historical situation, where compromise appears to be the rule rather than the exception, if one is to be effective and is not to isolate himself, depriving himself of historical power. Observations along this line were important, at least, for Hegel's philosophy of history.[38] In any case, it may be questioned that history, as by an inner law, brings everything to its purest expression.

To retain the force of Orr's apologetical reasoning, however, it is not necessary to make history carry the entire burden, making it display a kind of dialectical structure that is untrue to the actual course of events. We may view history within the broader context of God's creation, where it holds true that if you lose the handle on the true transcendence point, you are unable to see the cosmos in its true origin, its integrality, its coherence. You are bound to set up one aspect of the cosmos against another, making it impossible to establish the proper reference points to carry out your survey operation successfully.[39]

One might argue, in fact, that placing the entire burden on the historical process is itself one-sided. It is a consequence of isolating one aspect of the created order of reality at the expense of others.[40]

We should attempt to place James Orr's apologetical insight, his negative use of dialectic, within a broader context. We observe that it is not only history but all of our experience that is dependent upon the light of God's revelation if we are not to fall into insoluble prob-

37. According to Hegel, anything sticking up out of history had to be mediated and included in the historical process.

38. Hegel's early moves to reconcile ideals and experience are traced by H. S. Harris, *Hegel's Development: Towards the Sunlight* (Oxford, 1972).

39. L. Kalsbeek, *Contours of a Christian Philosophy* (Toronto, 1975), pp. 109 ff.

40. Robert D. Knudsen, *History* (Cherry Hill, N.J., 1976), pp. 38 ff.

lems. We must see all of our experience in God's light if we are to gain a proper boundary idea and are not to fall into meaninglessness. But this observation leads us to take a closer look at Orr's view of the relationship between reason and revelation.

It is certain that James Orr gave an important place to reason. It is reason that we observe at work in the history of mankind, leading it ever higher, to ever higher insights.[41] What, then, of revelation? Orr's view of reason led him to make statements that differed very little from those of his predecessors. The Hebrew-Christian religion, which Orr regarded as the true one, taught for ages that God is one, an ethical and personal being with whom man has personal fellowship. These are insights which reason through the ages had slowly been approaching, moving ahead, often with short and uncertain steps, but always advancing towards the truth.[42] Because of his view of reason, Orr did not always escape, therefore, the deistic notion that revelation presents earlier and to a wider audience that which reason of itself is able to discover.[43]

Important to Orr's position as a whole is his view that reason at its apogee, at its high point, always rises above itself toward the infinite.[44] At the high point of reason there is the union of the finite and the infinite, the human and the divine.[45] This unity is manifested in Jesus Christ.[46] Indeed, for James Orr, Christ becomes the one towards whom reason leads, the one who is the embodiment of reason at its highest point of development. According to Orr, it was the

---

41. Orr, p. 95.

42. Orr, pp. 87 ff.

43. Christianity is "…really the higher truth which is the synthesis and complement of all the others.…" (Orr, p. 11; see also pp. 12 f.).

44. Orr, pp. 113, 156 ff.

45. Orr, pp. 141, 244, 246.

46. Orr, p. 284.

great service of Idealism to point out the affinity between the divine and the human, something that Christianity had already long proclaimed in its message concerning Jesus Christ.[47] Because of his view of reason, Orr comes to think of Christ as the goal of a universal tendency in history towards participation in the divine. This contrasts with his own tendency to interpret all of experience in the light of Christian presuppositions.

His manner of thinking unfortunately allowed Orr to employ that kind of "foot-in-the-door" reasoning that we discover in earlier apologetes. You are familiar with the image of the door-to-door salesman, who first tries to get his foot in the door and then to get completely inside the house. Like many of his predecessors, Orr thought that if he could induce his opponent to go a certain distance with him, that opponent might well find it congenial to proceed yet further. A case in point is his refutation of the thought of a leading agnostic of his day, Herbert Spencer (1820-1903). Spencer, he reports, taught not only that we do not know God (*ignoramus*) but that, because of the intrinsic limitations of the mind, we cannot know him (*ignorabimus*). Inconsistent with his own agnosticism, Orr retorts, Spencer admits that there is an absolute, of which everyone is aware. If Spencer is inclined to proceed this far, what is to prevent him from proceeding further? It is, furthermore, only a step from thinking of the absolute as a being (ontological) to thinking of it as ethical will, and indeed only another step to thinking of it as personal identity.[48] All this parallels the upward course of reason, from being, to the ethical idea, to personality (spirit) as the fusion of the divine and the human.[49]

---

47. Orr, pp. 120 f.

48 Orr, pp. 80 ff., 84, 86, 92.

49. Orr, pp. 64 f., 120 f.

From the perspective we have gained, we may shed some light on Orr's argument from history. If one abandons the Christ, he abandons the One in whom is manifested the openness of the human to the divine, the God-man. If one then replaces that with humanism, namely, with the idea of man on his own, closed off hermetically from the divine, he is bound to go on from there to agnosticism and despair.

What we have pointed out concerning Orr's view of reason must affect our evaluation of his position. In spite of his presuppositional approach, Orr employed neutral ideas of reason which then supposedly became Christian ideas as they were extended to infinity.

In this connection I very often refer to Orr's definition of sin. One of his postulates, you will remember, was that of the sin and disorder in the world. What, then, does he understand by sin? For James Orr, sin is that which absolutely ought not to be.[50] Thus, by reason, we are able to obtain an idea of what is good, just as we can advance to the idea of God as an ethical being. We are able to arrive at the idea of sin when we have extended this ethical idea to infinity, as the expression of what ought to be absolutely or unconditionally.[51] Sin is the transgression of this ultimate norm. It is what absolutely, or unconditionally, ought not to be.

We have commended Orr for having attempted to erect an apologetic upon a Christian foundation. One ought to defend the Christian faith without taking a position outside of that faith. This is, at least, the tendency we observed in Orr's thinking. We also commended him for having developed a method in harmony with this idea, namely, what we have called a "negative use of dialectic."

---

50. Orr, p. 171.
51. Orr, pp. 166, 171.

Because of his acceptance of a philosophy of human reason, however, we discerned a tendency in his thinking to miss opportunities offered by his better insights.

If he was to be true to his radical Christian intentions, Orr should not have thought of God's revelation as a vanguard after which reason marches, slowly perhaps and with stops and starts, but with sure progress toward the truths that revelation has broadcast earlier and to a wider audience. The relation to God and his revelation should not have been viewed as the capstone of a self-transcending reason; instead, every idea should have been examined as to what was already at work in it, as to the fundamental religious antithesis underlying it.

The latter approach requires that one explore in depth, that he penetrate beneath the surface of an idea, even one that might give the impression of being neutral, valid apart from the truth of the Christian faith.

Orr pointed in this direction when he explored the idea of the boundary. What idea of the boundary, of the relation of the Creator to the creature, is at work already in any view that confronts us? In his thinking, has one in reality transgressed this boundary, attempting to set something created in the place of God? As presuppositional apologists have pointed out, this is the pattern of human apostasy described by the apostle Paul in the first chapter of Romans.

Let me conclude by summarizing some of the consequences for apologetics of taking a position such as the one I have associated with James Orr's better insights. I speak negatively and then positively

1. Faced with an apologetical situation, we do not first seek to establish contact with another and then seek to move in our thinking toward the Christian faith. We inquire, on the contrary, as to what is already at work in any

position, including our own. That is to say, we inquire as to the presuppositions that are already at work.

2. Faced with any apologetical situation, we do not look for a common ground with an opponent. We understand that those who object to the Christian faith are themselves impelled by a faith and that this faith is based upon a religious commitment.

3. Faced with any apologetical situation, we do not stop short of pointing out this ultimate commitment. We penetrate, spiraling down to the religious motivation, in order to show that what is at work is a basic antithesis.

4. Faced with any apologetical situation, we do not only point to contradictions in another's thinking. We attempt to show that it is only by proceeding religiously according to the Biblical message that one can lay hold of the true transcendence standpoint and that one can obtain a view of the boundary from which God's creation, including man, can be seen as to its true origin, its true unity, and the true relationships of its aspects.

JOHN H. GERSTNER

Augustine on Irresistible Grace

"...for them that were weak He reserved His own gift whereby they should most irresistibly will what is good, and most
irresistibly refuse to forsake it."

Introduction

THE IRRESISTIBILITY OF GRACE was opposed by the Roman
Catholic Church at the time of the Reformation "with greater vehe-
mence than any other doctrine."[1] In so doing it considered itself
faithful to the official dogma of the Middle Ages, especially defined
at the Second Synod of Orange in 529. It is true that at that Synod
the church had felt herself faithful to Augustine against the encroach-
ments of Semipelagianism, many of its statements being taken directly from Augustine's works. The Synod had indeed achieved a
Semiaugustinianism at least against the Semipelagian pressures that
were ultimately to conquer during the rest of the medieval period.[2]

---

1. L. Berkhof, *The History of Christian Doctrines* (Grand Rapids,
   1953), p. 150.

2. Berkhof, p. 149. See also J. P. Redding, *The Influence of St. Augustine
   on the Doctrine of the II Council of Orange concerning Original Sin*
   (Washington, 1939). An indication of just how far the Middle Ages
   had strayed from Augustine is provided by B. B. Warfield: "Confusion
   became so confounded that the Confession of Faith which Pelagius
   presented to Innocent was inserted quite innocently into the *Libri
   Carolini*, and was even produced by the Sorbonne in 1521 against

But in denying the irresistibility of grace, Orange fell short of the great doctor of grace, Augustine.[3]

Bettenson observes that Orange anathematized "predestination to evil (which A. did not explicitly teach, though it seems implicit in much of his doctrine and was emphasized by many of his followers)."[4] As we shall later show, Augustine did indeed teach predestination to evil. This is one of the reasons for contending that he taught the irresistibility of grace.

There is no doubt that Orange II denied the irresistibility of grace. The question is whether it learned that from Augustine. Loofs does not think so. He finds Catholicism unable to take or leave Augustine so that it took the name and left the saint.[5] Louis Berkhof maintains that Orange II "vindicated a modified Augustinianism,"[6] though noting that "the irresistible grace of predestination was supplanted by that of the sacramental grace of baptism"[7] and that Semipelagianism gradually conquered Semiaugustinianism in the church.

Luther as Augustine's own" (*Hastings Encyclopedia of Religion and Ethics*, New York and Edinburgh, 1910, II, 220).

3. E. Portalié, S. J., *A Guide to the Thought of Saint Augustine*, translated by R. J. Bastian, S. J. (Chicago, 1960), p. 177.

4. *Documents of the Christian Church* (New York and London, 1947), pp. 85, 86.

5. Portalié, p. 178.

6. Berkhof, p. 142.

7. We are afraid that Berkhof makes a rather common mistake here that sacramental grace necessarily supplants decretal grace. This is not only a false antithesis (for God can decree grace through sacraments) but emphatically Augustine taught both predestinating grace and sacramental grace (often predestinating grace through sacramental grace). As Warfield observes: according to Augustine, "those who are of the 'called according to the purpose' are predestinated not only to salvation, but to salvation by baptism" (*A Select Library of Nicene and Post-Nicene Fathers of the Christian Church*, hereafter designated NPNF, New York, 1887, V, lxxv).

We agree with Loofs, but Portalié argues strenuously against him. We feel that Portalié must be answered. But first he must be heard.

Portalié develops three Augustinian principles that bear on our inquiry. First, against Pelagius, Augustine insisted on the "absolute sovereignty of God over the will."[8] But second, the freedom of choice, even under grace, was carefully safeguarded. Third, Augustine reconciled this paradox of sovereignty and freedom.

God's absolute sovereignty in Augustine, Portalié absolutely establishes, but it is his second point, how Augustine safeguards free will, which concerns us. Portalié is impressive because he not only knows Augustine so well but acknowledges the saint's predestinarianism to a great degree. He even admits that Augustine's foreknowledge amounts to predestination, citing *De dono perseverantiae*, "For the disposition of future works in His foreknowledge, which cannot be deceived or changed, is absolute and nothing but predestination."[9] Consequently, it is with force that this conclusion comes: "Now Augustine always proclaims that this preparation[10] leaves the soul master of its destiny, at the same time assuring its consent: 'Not because it is not in the choice of man's free will to believe or not to believe, but because in the elect the will is prepared by God.'" Thus even after this preparation the will *can* refuse ...."[11] Needless to note, it is not Augustine who says that the will "*can* refuse," but Portalié, who is confident that Augustine infers it. Portalié 's reasoning here is that Augustine never retracted the self-determination of the will and none

---

8. Berkhof, p. 192.

9. 17, 41.

10. Portalié had already noted that Augustine referred to Proverbs 7:35 more than thirty times.

11. Pp. 202, 203. *The Predestination of the Saints*, 5, 10. Another statement which impresses Portalié is: "Whoever has received the efficacious grace of faith gives his consent only with complete independent will" (p. 198).

of his later works deny it. Portalié grants that Augustine sees God as having power to direct the choice, however.[12]

It is strange that Portalié does not see that the problem is with *him,* and not with Augustine. Augustine sees no problem between divine sovereignty and responsibility, though the choice is determined. The Jesuit scholar even sees that Augustine sees no problem, for Portalié 's third point is to show how Augustine reconciles grace and free will. First, Portalié observes, Augustine's will never determines itself without a motive; second, God controls the motives which come into the mind; and, third, God knows what the will will choose or reject. So God's determination is by means of the choice of motives. Jonathan Edwards could not have said it better and Aurelius Augustinus did not say it differently, but Portalié does not seem to get the point, though his church surely did. The Roman Catholic Church never accepted this doctrine, Portalié admits, but the doctrine is not fatalistic, he insists.

Our critique of this formidable attack on Augustine's irresistibility doctrine seems quite obvious. What kind of doctrine is a *self*-determination of a will which is determined by motives? And if the soul is determined by the motives, how can it not be determined by them; that is, how can it reject what it chooses? How can it resist what it does not resist? And why does Portalié not notice that it is he—and not Augustine—who denies irresistibility? And how can God control and yet be resisted? All three of Portalié 's points are well taken: for Augustine, God is absolutely sovereign; for Augustine, the will truly wills; and for Augustine, God carries out his sovereignty over the will by control of motives. One fears that some hidden agenda controls Portalié and the Roman Catholic Church here. Only, it is not so hidden. They are concerned that men not be reduced to machines (as they suppose would be the case were irresistibility true). Their last

---

12. *The City of God,* XIV, 43.

bastion of refuge from that danger, with an Augustine on their hands, is to hang in there for resistivity of the human will even though, as Loofs rightly claims, this is tantamount to rejecting St. Augustine.

We will present arguments showing that Augustine did maintain irresistibility. The proofs are ten in number. First, the Bible explicitly teaches the doctrine. Second, the nature of the will requires it. Third, the divine omnipotence, fourth, predestination, and, fifth, foreknowledge unmistakably imply irresistibility. Sixth, operative grace, seventh, baptismal regeneration, and, eighth, conversion itself cannot be understood apart from this doctrine. Ninth, the perseverance of the elect could not certainly occur if there were no such grace. Finally, Augustine declares it blasphemous to deny this doctrine.

1. The Bible Explicitly Teaches the Doctrine

We are usually more interested in the way Augustine interprets the Bible than the mere texts he cites. Nevertheless, for Augustine the Bible was the only ultimate authority, and when he cites proof texts, these texts as cited are assumed to prove. In this manner he appeals to Biblical authority throughout his writings. For the sake of convenience we will present one long, typical statement from his *Against Two Letters of the Pelagians*,[13] which is a veritable anthology of texts on our subject. We will let it suffice as characteristic of other works. In the next chapter he interprets these texts to show that "From such Scriptures grace is proved to be gratuitous and effectual."

> "For that very pride has so stopped the ears of their heart that they do not hear, "For what hast thou that thou hast not received?" They do not hear, "Without me ye can do nothing;" they do not hear; "Love is of God;" they do not hear, "God hath dealt the measure of faith;" they do not hear, "The Spirit breatheth where it will," and, "They who are led by the Spirit of

---

13. NPNF V, 422, 423.

God, they are the sons of God;" they do not hear, "No one can come unto me, unless it were given him of my Father;" they do not hear what Esdras writes, "Blessed is the Lord of our fathers, who hath put into the heart of the king to glorify His house which is in Jerusalem;" they do not hear what the Lord says by Jeremiah. "And I will put my fear into their heart, that they depart not from me; and I will visit them to make them good;" and especially that word by Ezekiel the prophet, where God fully shows that He is induced by no good deservings of men to make them good, that is, obedient to His commands, but rather that He repays to them good for evil, by doing this for His own sake, and not for theirs. For He says, "These things saith the Lord God: I do not this for your sakes, O house of Israel, but for mine own holy name's sake, which has been profaned among the nations, whither ye have gone in there; and I will sanctify my great name, which has been profaned among the nations, and which ye have profaned in the midst of them; and the nations shall know that I am the Lord, saith Adonai the Lord, when I shall be sanctified among you before their eyes. And I will take you from among the nations, and gather you together out of all lands, and will bring you into your own land. And I will sprinkle upon you clean water, and ye shall be cleansed from all your filthiness, and I will cleanse you. And I will give unto you a new heart, and a new spirit I will put within you: and the stony heart shall be taken away out of your flesh, and I will give you a heart of flesh. And I will put my Spirit within you, and will cause you to walk in my righteousness, and to observe my judgments, and do them."

2. The Nature of the Will Requires It

If the will is not a distinct faculty and is literally identified with the affections, then the irresistibility of grace is obvious in Augustine.

This is a highly debatable point—though the irresistibility issue by no means rests on it—but if Augustine is ultimately deterministic, it will follow that he is deterministic here; that is, if the affections determine the will because the affections are the will, then the will is as the affections certainly, determinedly, irresistibly so. If the will is the affections, as the affection so is the will. If the will is not a separate power able to choose other than it is affectionately inclined to do, then it chooses as it is inclined, as it feels. This would be the natural, the inevitable, the irresistible thing to choose, though the very terms *inevitable* and *irresistible* are strange when applied to what is utterly natural.

In his greatest work the will is the affection:[14]

> But the character of the human will is of moment; because, if it is wrong, these motions of the soul will be wrong, but if it is right, they will be not merely blameless, but even praise-worthy. For the will is in them all; yea, none of them is anything else than will. For what are desire and joy but a volition of consent to the things we wish? And what are fear and sadness but a volition of aversion from the things which we do not wish? But when consent takes the form of seeking to possess the things we wish, this is called desire; and when consent takes the form of enjoying the things we wish, this is called joy. In like manner, when we turn with aversion from that which we do not wish to happen, this volition is termed fear; and when we turn away from that which has happened against our will, this act of will is called sorrow. And generally in respect of all that we seek or shun, as a man's will is attracted or repelled, so it is changed and turned into these different affections. Wherefore the man who lives according to God, and not according to man, ought to be a

---

14. *The City of God*, XIV, 6.

lover of good, and therefore a hater of evil. And since no one is evil by nature, but whoever is evil is evil by vice, he who lives according to God ought to cherish towards evil men a perfect hatred, so that he shall neither hate the man because of his vice, nor love the vice because of the man, but hate the vice and love the man. For the vice being cursed, all that ought to be loved, and nothing that ought to be hated, will remain.

In itself the will is a *media vis*, intermediate good, potentially capable of good or evil, depending on the person who uses it. It is an expression of the man, whether before or after the fall, in this world or in the next. The difference is always and only in the person himself. Where his affections are, there he is and his will with him. The will does not denote part of the psuche; "rather it is the human psuche in its role as a moral agent," says Rist, citing Augustine's interpretation of Luke 2:14, "men of good will as meaning goodness of the will."[15]

Nevertheless, Rist tries to hold out against irresistibility. Although he clearly recognizes that the will is nothing but the man, he yet fancies that the man can resist the man. While one wonders what is pulling this thinker out of his own orbit, the answer comes a little later. "How can we be held responsible for our sins," he asks, "if we are slaves of sin and have no freedom whatsoever in the sense of autonomy, no ability to act of our own accord in the direction of escaping from the necessity of being evil?"[16] Augustine's point is precisely that we do have all the freedom we want, all the autonomy we desire. Our choice of sin is free as well as responsible because it is our choice—the choice of our depraved natures, which we love. What Rist wants is precisely what an irresistible grace alone can give, for

---

15. Rist, "Augustine on Free Will and Predestination," in R. A. Markus, editor, *A Collection of Critical Essays* (Garden City, N.Y., 1972), p. 220.

16. Rist, p. 224.

this is a change of the person who loves his sin into one who hates it. His bondage is of his own willing; he must be delivered from himself, as it were. The question is, "How can we be held responsible for our sins if we are slaves of sin and have no freedom whatsoever in the sense of autonomy, no ability to act of our own accord in the direction of escaping from the necessity of being evil?" The answer is: we can be held responsible for our sins if we are slaves of sin *because we choose to be slaves of sin*. We have no violation of our freedom whatsoever in the sense of *autonomy because we do have complete freedom and absolute autonomy in choosing to be slaves of sin*. We have no ability to act of our own account in the direction of escaping from the necessity of being evil because *it is of our own accord that we do not escape from this "necessity" of being evil.*

3. The Divine Omnipotence Implies Irresistible Grace

As Portalié stresses, for Augustine the divine sovereignty was absolute.[17] How, then, could the weak, non-will of fallen man stand against him? Or, if it is said, "It was the renewed will which stood against him," why would a renewed will stand against its Renewer?

See how Augustine handles the *locus classicus* of the sovereignty of the human will, Matthew 23:37 ("How often would I have gathered thy children together, as a hen gathers her young, but thou wouldst not!"). Of course, this did not mean that the wills of the "chicks" were against coming to the call of mother hen—as if "when the weakest stood in the way with their want of will, the will of the strongest could not be carried out."[18] If the will of the chickens cannot resist the call of their mother, how can the will of the weakest sinners resist the call of their God? What, then, was the meaning of Christ's observations? It was not the chickens, says

---

17. See *On the Merits and Remission of Sins, and on the Baptism of Infants*, II, 32, in NPNF V, 12 ff.

18. *Enchiridion*, xcvii.

Augustine, but their owners who were the problem. "*Jerusalem* was not willing that her children should be gathered together, but even though she was unwilling, He gathereth together as many of her children as He wished...." It never crossed the mind of the African that little baby chicks would ever resist the will of the Great Hen of Heaven.

Another classic text often thought to frustrate the divine will is I Timothy 2:4, "who wishes all men to be saved."[19] Augustine shows that it is not those whom God wills to save who are unwilling but interpreters who do not rightly divide the word of truth who err. This text does not teach that God is not willing to permit some to perish—"not that there is no man whose salvation He does not will"[20]—but that there is no one *class* of mankind which is not included in divine electing grace. After surveying the context of this Scripture, which alludes to all classes of people, beginning with kings, Augustine shows that it is that kind of universality to which the text refers. This leads him to point out that this is no uncommon use of "all" in the Bible. The statement of John 1:9 that Christ "lighteth every man" does not mean that every man is enlightened but that every man who is enlightened at all is enlightened by Christ. Likewise, and even more obviously, when Scripture says that the Pharisees tithed "every herb," it does not mean each individual plant but all varieties of herb.[21]

God is able to convert opposing wills. The very titles of chapters 29 and 30 of *On Grace and Free Will* tell the story, "God is able to convert opposing wills, and to take away from the heart its hardness"; "the grace by which the stony heart is removed is not preceded by good deserts but by evil ones."[22] But chapter 31 comes right to

---

19. *Enchiridion*, xcvii.

20. *Enchiridion*, ciii.

21. *Enchiridion*, ciii; Luke 11:42.

22. NPNF V, 455, 456.

our point, "Free will has its function in the heart's conversion; but grace too has its."

Lest, however, it should be thought that men themselves in this matter do nothing by free will, it is said in the Psalm, "Harden not your hearts;" and in Ezekiel himself, "Cast away from you all your transgressions, which ye have impiously committed against me; and make you a new heart and a new spirit; and keep all my command-ments. For why will ye die, O house of Israel, saith the Lord? for I have no pleasure in the death of him that di-eth, saith the Lord God: and turn ye, and live." We should remember that it is He who says, "Turn ye and live," to whom it is said in prayer, "Turn us again, O God." We should remember that He says, "Cast away from you all your transgressions," when it is even He who justifies the ungodly. We should remember that He says, "Make you a new heart and a new spirit," who also promises, "I will give you a new heart, and a new spirit will I put within you." How is it, then, that He who says, "Make you," also says, "I will give you"? Why does He command, if He is to give? Why does He give if man is to make, except it be that He gives what He commands when He helps him to obey whom He commands? There is, however, always within us a free will,—but it is not always good, for it is either free from righteousness when it serves sin,—and then it is evil,—or else it is free from sin when it serves righteousness,—and then it is good. But the grace of God is always good; and by it comes to pass that a man is of a good will, though he was before of an evil one.[23]

---

23. NPNF V, 456, 457.

The chapters that follow later are just as vital to our theme ("God does whatsoever He wills in the hearts of even wicked men"[24] and "God operates on men's hearts to incline their wills whithersoever He pleases").[25] Thus, through Esther God changed the king's hostile will.[26]

How, then, can man oppose God's will anywhere, least of all where his will, being renewed, is to will God's will?[27] It must never be forgotten in this discussion that we are dealing with irresistible grace with reference to the human will. If grace is shown to be irresistible in general, it must apply with special relevance to the human will and most of all in the salvation of the human will.

4. Predestination Implies Irresistible Grace

Augustine did more than affirm divine foreknowledge and infer predestination. He taught predestination as well. Indeed, his very doctrine of foreknowledge amounted to predestination, as he himself says, "for the ordering of His future works in His foreknowledge, which cannot be deceived or changed, is absolute, and is nothing but predestination."[28] His "ordering in His foreknowledge" seems more than mere foreknowledge. When foreknowledge becomes foreordering, it is indeed foreordination or predestination. Apparently, they were essentially the same in Augustine's mind—at least for all practical purposes.

There is no question that Augustine taught predestination; the only question is how soon. *When* this doctrine was does not mean so much as *what* it was; but, even here, the evidence favors the early date, though he stressed predestination more as the years passed (and

---

24. Ch. 42.

25. Ch. 43.

26. *Against Two Letters of the Pelagians*, V, 389.

27. *On Man's Perfection in Righteousness*, Ch. 8.

28. *On the Gift of Perseverance*, Ch. 41.

Pelagianism didn't). Still, that is all that Pelagianism did account for—not the doctrine, but the stress on it. Loofs is right again: it is all in *On Various Questions for Simplicianus*:[29] As Augustine wrote in the *Retractations*, "I have tried hard to maintain the free choice of the human will, but the grace of God prevailed. Not otherwise could I reach the understanding that the apostle speaks with absolute truth when he says, 'Who made thee to differ....'"

In the treatment of Romans 9:10-29, he establishes his doctrine of predestination absolutely. First showing that grace brings works, and not works faith, he then shows (ch. 5) that grace brings faith, not faith grace. If it is asked, "Did God foresee that Jacob (not Esau) would believe?" Augustine answers: "He could equally well have foreseen that he would do good works."[30] No, "if the reason for its not being of works was that they were not yet born, that applies also to faith...."

If there remains any doubt about Augustine's doctrine, *The Predestination of the Saints*[31] puts it to rest forever. It is not inappropriate that this should be virtually Augustine's last major work. It all began there, for Augustine is the first great articulator of this teaching after Paul, and what could be more appropriate than that he should be writing about this eternal foundation of the City of God when the City of Man was almost at the gates of Hippo? This was, however, no oversight or last-minute postscript but, as Harnack, no friend of this doctrine, aptly comments: "It is in the bark formed that faith has grown, just as it is not in the material of the stem, but at its circumference, where stem and bark meet, that the sap of the plant flows. Strip the tree, and it will wither! Therefore it is well-

---

29. Loofs, "Augustinus," in *Realenzyklopädie für protestantische Theologie und Kirche* (Leipzig, 1897), I, 279.

30. John H. S. Burleigh, *Augustine's Earlier Writings*, LCC, VI, 389.

31. NPNF V, 493 ff.

meant, but foolish, to suppose that Augustine would have done better to have given forth his teaching without the doctrine of predestination."[32]

In spite of Augustine's indisputable teaching of predestination, how he conceived of it is crucial to our inquiry. That is, if he did not see it as pertaining to evil deeds, this could constitute a double jeopardy for the irresistibility doctrine. Resistance to grace would be evil, of course, and predestination, therefore, would not pertain to evil choices. If irresistibility is itself evil (supposedly, a reducing of man to machine), then it would not fall within the predestination of God either. In a certain sense, God's predestination would control neither resistance to grace nor non-resistance (irresistibility) because both would be evils—one by man and the other by God Himself, *ex hypothesi*. Predestination would be irrelevant, proving nothing directly about the irresistibility or resistibility of divine grace. Thus at the Council of Valence (855) the fathers decided "that in the wicked He foresaw the wickedness because it comes from them; and does not predestinate it, because it does not come from Him."[33] This was virtually a quotation from Augustine. It is not surprising that these fathers could not get beyond statements like that. Augustine meant that God did not predestinate evil in the sense of producing it; he did not mean that He did not predestinate it in the sense of ordaining it permissively. Augustine, single predestinarian that he was, believed in the double decree. God as deliberately chose to let some perish as He chose not to let others. One decision was no more final or any more a decree than the others. As he says, "it would be done did He not permit it (and

---

32. H. Paolucci, editor, *The Enchiridion of faith, hope and love* (Chicago, 1961), p. 166, n. 1.

33. R. Seeberg, *Text-book of the History of Doctrines*, revised translation by C. E. Hay, 2 vols. (Philadelphia, 1905), II, 33.

of course His permission is not unwilling, but willing); nor would a Good Being permit evil to be done only that in His omnipotence He can turn evil into good."[34] Although the way that God carries out one decree is different from the way in which He carries out the other, there is no difference at all in the fact that He carries out both of them. He has decreed that some perish as truly as He decreed that others be saved.

This is the all-important issue with respect to the matter of the irresistibility of grace. If God has decreed (predestinated) all human actions that come to pass, He has decreed that some infallibly (therefore, irresistibly) be saved by free will and that others infallibly be lost by free will.

5. Foreknowledge Implies Irresistible Grace

Augustine taught divine foreknowledge, and that raised a problem for his friend Evodius in *The Free Choice of the Will*: [35]

> I have a deep desire to know how it can be that God knows all things beforehand and that, nevertheless, we do not sin by necessity…Since God knew that man would sin, that which God foreknew must necessarily come to pass. How then is the will free when there is apparently this unavoidable necessity?[36]

The problem was: How could God foreknow man's sin without making it necessary and therefore not a sin? This is a problem to which Augustine devotes himself here and in many other works. But there is one problem that does not arise. That is, if God's knowledge is

---

34. *Enchiridion*, c.

35. III, ii, 4.

36. Cited by William L. Rowe, "Augustine on Foreknowledge and Free Will," in R. A. Markus, editor, *A Collection of Critical Essays* (Garden City, N.Y., 1972), p. 209.

certain, can man resist what God knows will happen? That question cannot arise. Obviously, if God has certain knowledge, it is certain that man will not resist so as to make that knowledge false. This seems obvious enough, but so many are aroused by Evodius's problem (how can sin be necessary and culpable?) that they do not notice what is taken for granted by Evodius and Augustine, namely, that God's omniscience makes resistance to what he foreknows certainly impossible. Whatever the problems may be with reference to determinism and freedom, there is no problem with reference to certainty and irresistibility. That is to say, foreknowledge proves certainty. Resistance to what is foreknown is a non-entity.

One cannot help thinking of an analogous pattern of thought where a doctrine so absorbs the mind that many do not see an attendant fact which is quite obvious otherwise. We are thinking of the dictation theory of Scriptural inspiration. Most people—even inerrantists —object to that so strenuously that they sometimes do not notice that adherents of that view most certainly espouse inerrancy. Most inerrantists are not dictationists—in fact, they are quite opposed to that theory and insist that it is an aberrant view—but they, of all people, should notice that anyone who is shown to be a dictationist must necessarily believe in inerrancy. One can be an inerrantist without believing in dictation, but he cannot believe in mechanical inspiration without being an inerrantist.

Likewise, one may believe in divine foreknowledge and oppose "determinism," but he cannot believe in divine foreknowledge and oppose irresistibility. Most people who hold to foreknowledge oppose determinism, whether rightly or wrongly, but surely they cannot deny irresistibility. Just as a mechanical inspirationist must believe in inerrancy, so a believer in divine eternal omniscience must believe in irresistibility, though most of them try to oppose determinism.

We have seen that Portalié does precisely this. He asserts absolute sovereignty and even determining of human choices by motives controlled by God, but yet denies irresistibility. This is manifestly inconsistent. If Augustine teaches absolute sovereignty and control by motives, then he teaches irresistibility. If Portalié is going to put into Augustine's mouth what he never himself wrote, then Portalié must have Augustine assert resistibility and deny that God does have perfect future knowledge or perfect control by motives. If Augustine is doing what Portalié says, he is inconsistent here. And if Augustine is inconsistent here, his whole system falls apart, for he is a theologian of sovereign grace from start to finish. God is either sovereign or he is not, and if man has an ultimate veto power over his most important endeavors for the salvation of man himself, then God is not sovereign and man will never know sovereign grace.

For Augustine, God's eternal foreknowledge is of what he has eternally decreed to do. His foreknowledge, therefore, logically rests on his predestination. J. M. Rist has observed that foreknowledge is "prior" to predestination.[37] There is in Augustine what we may call predestination I and predestination II. If Augustine says plainly that God's foreknowledge is of the gifts which he will give, then he has predestinated these gifts prior to foreknowing them (predestination I). Apparently, Augustine also thinks of a formal predestination (II) of what God foreknows. Surely, *On Baptism* (IV, 3, 5) makes it plain enough that foreknowledge is based on predestination, "For, according to His foreknowledge, He knows whom He has foreordained before the foundation of the world to be made like to the image of His Son,

---

37. Rist, p. 219 ff.

many who are even openly outside, and are called heretics, are better than many good Catholics."[38] Here, clearly, God foreknows whom he has foreordained.

God's foreknowing of reprobates would be of the same nature.[39] He foreknew those to whom he would not give gifts (predestination I) and then formally predestinated (II) them to reprobation.[40] As Berkhof says, with reference to the non-elect, Augustine "conceives of the decree of God as one of pre-termission only."[41] This is the famous single predestination of Augustine, to be sure, but here we note only that even single predestination (in a double decree) in Augustine is logically prior to foreknowledge.

Whatever the relation of foreknowledge to predestination may be, it, according to William L. Rowe,[42] does destroy free will as Evodius feared. Although we are not persuaded of Rowe's argument, it would obliterate any possibility of resistibility. If foreknowledge destroys free will altogether, it certainly destroys any form of free will such as resistance.

So, if Rowe is correct, irresistibility is a fact indeed. This would be curing a headache by decapitation. Effective as that would be for the headache, we think that Augustine cures the headache without such drastic surgery. Let us examine the Rowe analysis. Evodius's type of argument he states in six propositions:

---

38. IV, 3, 5.

39. *Enchiridion*, civ.

40. *Enchiridion*, xxvi represents all men as reprobated in Adam to "endless punishment" so that predestination to life is from this state of fallenness. Rist sourly comments: "God, argues Augustine, makes us wish all men to be saved...[making us] more merciful than God Himself" (p. 239).

41. P. 140.

42. "...we have sufficient grounds for rejecting the argument Augustine presents" (p. 214).

1. God has foreknowledge of all future events.
2. Hence, if a man is going to sin, God foreknows that he will sin.
3. Whatever God foreknows must necessarily happen.
4. Hence, if God foreknows that a man will sin, he must necessarily sin.
5. But if such a man must necessarily sin, there is no voluntary choice in his sinning.
6. Therefore, such a man does not have free will.[43]

Rowe sees Augustine as denying premise 5. He can say that again because Augustine writes it hundreds of times. Rowe's refutation is that Augustine says that necessity does not prevent the will from willing what it will (for example, cease sinning). According to Rowe, this seems to have the fault of an obvious criticism. So he introduces an unobvious one, which he cites G. E. Moore (not himself) as thinking of as meaningful. That is, that one may "will to will" to stop sinning and not be able in the same way that Rowe is unable (though willing) to run a four-minute mile. This is supposed to be a refutation of Augustine whereas even Pelagius could see that "willing to will" and willing are the same thing. If a man once wills to will to cease sinning, he has willed to cease sinning. Not only that, but if one wills to cease sinning, he has ceased sinning because sinning is in the will. And if he wills to will to cease sinning, surely he wills to cease sinning.

Rowe, having totally missed Augustine, now returns in imagined triumph to defend Evodius' thought that God's foreknowledge is incompatible with free will.[44] Since in this essay we are only trying to interpret Augustine, not defend him, we will make only the briefest reference to Rowe's critiques and our response. It comes down to this: that what God foreknows will be, but not be necessary, in itself. That is, following Aquinas, Rowe would say that God foreknows

---

43. P. 210.
44. P. 214.

contingent events which are not necessary in themselves. Therefore, he concludes that Augustine is wrong in saying that the foreknown things, the choices, were necessary. As an argument against Augustine this is sophistical. Augustine is only arguing that it is necessarily true that whatever God foreknows will certainly come to pass. It is necessary that these things (even if they be contingent in themselves) will come to pass. So, it is absolutely necessary that the contingent choice will be what it will be. Evodius is not relieved, and Augustine is not embarrassed.

6. Operative Grace Is Irresistible Grace

Augustine speaks of three kinds of grace: "prevenient grace" (which produces a sense of sin as the Holy Spirit uses the law for that purpose); "operative grace" (with which we are especially concerned, producing faith in Christ which brings justification); and "co-operating grace" (which enables the renewed will to work with the Holy Spirit in sanctification).[45]

Operative grace especially concerns us because this is usually what is in mind when the word *irresistible* is used.[46] Nevertheless, it should be noted in passing that for Augustine, no form of grace is really resistible. God is sovereign everywhere and in all forms of grace. Prevenient grace produces its designed effect, which is preparation for the receiving of saving grace. Sometimes Augustine actually uses the term for operative grace, observing that obviously grace must go before faith. This it always does insofar as God gives it. The sinner presumably does not want to be convicted of sin. For Augustine pride went before the fall and keeps man fallen, but nonetheless he is convicted of sin to the degree that prevenient grace comes to him. If he is not convicted to the point of conversion, it is not that he has successfully resisted prevenient grace but that grace has not

---

45. *On Grace and Free Will,* 33.
46. See Berkhof, pp. 139-40.

come in sufficient degree. Likewise, after conversion the saint does not resist "co-operative grace." It is "co-operative grace" which leads him to cooperate to the degree to which it enables him. That far and no further. He is irresistibly drawn toward sanctification as far as the sovereign God of grace chooses. Even before the fall man had sufficient grace, but had he had efficient grace he would have continued upright as the martyrs did [47] and the saints in heaven will. God is never resistible (as Augustine often reminds us) and least of all in what concerns him most—grace. "God is sovereign in grace."

Why, then, is "operative grace" the point of greatest concern? Because at this point only the good will is totally non-functioning. It is dead (free to sin but not freed to do virtuously). In prevenient grace the will is freely, though sinfully, active, and in co-operative grace it is graciously active, but here the will has no relevant role. It does not act but is acted upon. It is totally passive when this grace comes.

And this is what the Pelagians, the Semipelagians, and even the Semiaugustinians cannot admit, or man's last vestige of pride is stripped away. The emperor would have no clothes. The Pelagians—the consistently proud—fought true grace in all its forms and saw the dangers in any concession toward Augustine. The Semipelagians were not that proud, and settled for human freedom within the limits of a non-controlling foreknowledge. The Semiaugustinians followed Augustine to the brink of the abyss, giving up all human ability to the point of mere—but ultimate—veto power. The will could not do it all; the will could not do it even partly; the will could only undo it! Modest enough for human sinners, they thought; but, it was not enough for the Bishop of Hippo.

---

47. "You see, then, that God makes men good, that they may do good" (*Admonition and Grace in Fathers of the Church*: Saint Augustine, IV, 289).

Faith itself is the gift of God. Augustine is constantly maintaining this against the Pelagians, who saw faith as a reward. No, it is the gift which leads to reward. Whence comes the will to believe? Asks Augustine,[48] "If we say that it is not the gift of God, we must then incur the fear of supposing that we have discovered some answer to the apostle's reproachful appeal, 'What hast thou that thou didst not receive? Now, if thou didst receive it, why dost thou glory, as if thou hadst not received it?'" It is an intermediate power itself, and the *good* will must come from God.[49] A freed will is a new creation. Grace does not only enable us to do what we will but to will.[50] God, for example, gave Adam "help without which he could not continue therein if he would; but that he should will, He left in his free will."[51] Adam could have stood by his free will,[52] but he did not, though he would have done so had he been given efficacious grace. "The aid without which a thing does not come to pass and the aid with which a thing comes to pass" (*adjutorium sine qua non* and *adjutorium quo* are differentiated in chapter 34.

Even the desire of the good is itself a gift.[53] God causes the desire. "If without God's grace the desire of good begins with ourselves, merit itself will have begun—to which, as if of debt, comes to assistance of grace; and thus God's grace will not be bestowed freely, but will be given according to our merit. But that He might furnish a reply to the future Pelagius, the Lord does not say, 'Without me it is with difficulty that ye can do anythin'; but he says, 'without me ye

---

48. NPNF V, 108, 109.

49. *On the Spirit and the Letter*, 60; see also *On the Free Choice of the Will*, II, XVIII ff.

50. *Admonition and Grace*, 32.

51. *Admonition and Grace*, 32.

52. *Admonition and Grace*, 28.

53. NPNF V, 399.

can do nothing....' For when the Lord says, 'Without me ye can do nothing,' in this one word He comprehends both the beginning and the ending." Before the chapter is over, Augustine has shown that the saint does not even "think" anything of good of himself.[54] Three chapters later the finishing touch comes, "Man does no good thing which God does not cause him to do."[55]

Yet how does all of this divine activity in operative grace remove a final human veto? Theoretically man can still say no to all that God was doing. But how could God give this gift, create the desire, renew the person, incline the soul, all to produce faith, only to have the end-product an act of anti-faith? To be sure, Augustine did not say expressly that all veto power is removed.[56] Presumably he did not need to say so. After all this divine build-up, what other response was possible? The Mountain labors and brings forth not even a mouse? We cannot help saying at this point that such a notion would indeed seem blasphemous to the Bishop of Hippo, if not absurd.

7. Baptismal Regeneration Spells Irresistible Grace

If baptismal regeneration occurs—as Augustine taught in almost all he wrote concerning salvation[57]—then irresistible grace must follow irresistibly. There are two mysteries: first, that any church could teach one and not the other, and the even greater mystery that anyone could think that Augustine taught one and not the other. Any veto power exercised by a regenerated soul would have to be a veto of

---

54. NPNF V, 400.

55. NPNF V, 400-1.

56. We admit the indisputable fact that Augustine allows a later fall from grace into apostasy. However irresistible grace may be at this point, it is not irresistible forever, we grant. Nevertheless, there can be no doubt that when saving faith is first born of grace in the soul, grace is at that time utterly irresistible.

57. *On Baptism*, I, 12, 20.

what it just voted for. It could not conceivably vote against the grace (the grace having already been introduced into the soul regenerated through baptism), but only against itself. That is, the soul could not veto grace by its own acceptance of grace. It must have voted "yes"—in other words, before it voted, "no." This would not be a veto but a motion to rescind. The grace was resisted, but only after it had been irresistibly accepted.

Augustine teaches the baptismal regeneration of absolutely any who are baptized and the non-regeneration of any who are not baptized. The infants of the baptized who are not themselves baptized must be lost while reprobates, such as Simon Magus, were born again by water. "For the Church had herself given birth to Simon Magus through the sacrament of baptism; and yet it was declared to him that he had no part in the inheritance of Christ. Did he lack anything in respect of baptism, of the gospel, of the sacraments? But in that he wanted charity he was born in vain; and perhaps, it had been well for him that he had never been born at all."[58]

Thus, though some instantly reject what they have an instant before accepted, they were first changed by the laver of regeneration. In the words of Warfield, "…in all its operations alike, just because it is power from on high and the living spring of new and re-created life, it is *irresistible* and *indefectible*."[59]

The uniqueness of Augustine's doctrine may be much of the cause for debate on irresistible grace. Unlike the general Reformed tradition, which teaches that if you have it (irresistible grace) you never lose it and if you lose it you never had it, the reformed Augustine believed only that if you had *election* you would not ultimately

---

58. *On Baptism*, I, 10, 14.

59. "Introductory Essay on Augustine and the Pelagian Controversy," in NPNF V, lxix.

lose grace but ultimately persevere in it. So there are two points at which Augustine teaches the irresistibility of grace: first, when one is regenerated, and, second, when the elect die.

8. Conversion Itself is Irresistible

Our present topic deals not so much with the doctrinal theory as with the way the theory is carried out in actual conversion. This is the laboratory aspect of the principle which will show that in the souls of men no less than in the pages of Holy Writ grace is irresistible.

It is, after all, grace that actually establishes a true freedom of the will or freed will.[60] Free will has no power of itself alone to come to God; for that, grace is necessary. But grace is also adequate to free the will, and when it comes it frees. This good will comes from God,[61] and when it comes, men come running.[62]

In the process of describing this freedom in Christ, Augustine says of the saints that, having been set free, "they have a free power of choice, by which they serve God, and are not prisoners of the devil."[63] His work *On Free Choice of the Will* attributes this to all men. Here "free power of choice" is the possession of saints and refers to their ability to serve God. If there is a verbal confusion here in locating free will in sinners and saints alike in *On Free Choice of the Will* and in saints only in *Admonition and Grace*, the confusion is easily penetrated. Augustine would say that all men have free will, but that only saints have a free will to serve God. Sinners have a free will only to serve Satan. The service of God is liberty and the service of Satan is bondage, but each is freely served or served by a free will.

---

60. *On Grace and Free Will*, 31; see also *On the Spirit and the Letter*, 52.

61. *On the Merits and Remission of Sins*, II, 28.

62. *On the Grace of Christ*, 15.

63. *On the Free Choice of the Will*, p. 288.

9. Perseverance of the Elect Demonstrates Irresistible Grace

If predestination proves the irresistibility of grace, perseverance shows how it is communicated to the elect. If the eternal election of some to everlasting life proves that they will not refuse to live forever, perseverance shows that that irresistible decision will be made in this life. If there is a gift of perseverance, it can only mean that the elect will persevere in grace, and that means equally certainly that they will not resist it. If grace is not irresistible, perseverance is not certain. If perseverance is certain, irresistibility can be no less so.

On the Gift of Perseverance was the very last great work of Augustine, as if his own persevering to the end was an illustration of what he wrote throughout his years. It begins with the interesting, though unconvincing, remark that if perseverance was obtained through prayer, it could not be lost by obstinacy.[64] Of course there are many things which are received by prayer that are lost by obstinacy, including saving grace in many instances (according to Augustine). What he apparently means here is that so long as the saint is praying he is not perishing. If perseverance is by prayer, it will not be lost by obstinacy, indeed, because a praying person is not a resisting person but a believing person. This is a tricky point, but it cannot be denied that it is a genuine application to *perseverance* as to no other aspect of salvation. Persevering prayer precludes perishing.

This also establishes irresistibility, irresistibly; for if a person is persevering in prayer, he is irresistibly drawn thereto. The *Contra Gaudentium*[65] stresses the same aspect. The *Enchiridion* illustration of Jacob and Esau is especially appropriate, "He who says, 'I will have mercy on whom I will have mercy,' loved Jacob of his undeserved grace, and hated Esau of his deserved judgment. And as this judgment was due to both, the former learnt from the case of the latter

---

64. 10-15.
65. 16-18.

that the fact of the same punishment not falling upon himself gave him no room for glory in any merit of his own, but only in riches of the divine grace; because it is not in him that willeth, nor of him that runneth, but of God that showeth mercy. And indeed the whole face, and, if I may use the expression, every lineament of the countenance of Scripture conveys by a very profound analogy this wholesome warning to everyone who looks carefully into it, that he who glories should glory in the Lord."[66]

Suarez attempted to avoid the inevitable argument for irresistible grace found in Augustine's perseverance doctrine, but J. P. Baltzer has shown its futility.[67] More recently, Sister Mary A. Lesousky has attempted the same thing, no more successfully. In fact, she (citing F. Cayré, *La contemplation augustinienne*) has even tried to take the "pessimism" out of Augustine. In another work by this same author who has deep understanding of Augustine, there is an enlightening statement: The insistence with which Augustine has emphasized the weakness of fallen man has been called *pessimism*. It is necessary to realize that many of his expressions, inspired by the love of refuting the proud Pelagian who opposed him, are excessive and even erroneous if taken literally; but we cannot see pessimism (in his teaching, at least in the moral sense).... The doctrine of Augustine has nothing depressing— far from it—if one does not isolate certain particular propositions, important in other respects, from the whole of his teaching, and if one gives, in a particular way to the doctrine of *wisdom* the complete part it held for him in the actual order of humanity, fallen assuredly, but redeemed and redeemed by a God-man.[68] We cannot help won-

---

66. xcviii.

67. J. P. Baltzer, *Das heil: Augustinus Lehre über Prädestination und Reprobation* (no place, no date; located in Speer Library, Princeton Theological Seminary).

68. *De dono perseverantiae*, translated and introduced by Mary A. Lesousky (Washington, 1956), pp. 268, 269.

dering, knowing what Augustine said to the Pelagians who opposed him, what he would say to these modern Pelagians who "agree" with him!

Augustine himself raises a more difficult problem in a strange statement in *The City of God*: "Take two men who are equally disposed in body and soul…If both are tried by the same temptation and one yields to it …while the other perseveres…what is the cause of this if not their own free wills, since both had the same disposition of body and soul?" But what was the ultimate explanation? Why did one succumb? "Was it because his will was a nature, or because it was made of nothing? We shall find that the latter is the case. For if a nature is the cause of evil will, what else can we say than that evil arises from good or that good is the cause of evil? And how can it come to pass that a nature, good though mutable, should produce any evil—that is to say, should make the will itself wicked? [69]

This is quite cryptic apropos perseverance, yet the meaning seems clear. Man's soul is nothing and could fall away at any moment, according to Augustine. Only God preserves it. What makes one man persevere and another not is that one is preserved and the other is not. Man, left to himself, would surely resist grace as he resists all good. Only an irresistible grace can account for perseverance.

10. Denial of Irresistibility is Blasphemy

…who will be so foolish and blasphemous as to say that God cannot change the evil wills of men, whichever, whenever, and wheresoever He chooses, and direct them to what is good? But when He does this, He does it of mercy; when He does it not, it is of justice that He does it not….[70]

Augustine wants to know "who will be so foolish and blasphemous as to say that God cannot change the evil wills of men, which-

---

69. *The City of God*, XII, 6.

70. *Enchiridion*, xcvii.

ever, whenever, and wheresoever He chooses." Pelagius was that foolish and blasphemous; the Semipelagians were that foolish and blasphemous; and the Semiaugustinians at Second Orange and Mayence were that foolish and blasphemous. Trent was that foolish and blasphemous when it said that "while God touches the heart of man through the illumination of the Holy Ghost, man himself neither does absolutely nothing while receiving that inspiration, *since he can also reject it*, nor yet is he able by his own free will and without the grace of God to move himself to justice in His sight." [71] And contemporary Roman Catholic doctrine can be so foolish and blasphemous as to write, "Everyone, however, may be sure of receiving sufficient grace to obtain his own salvation…." [72] This is a rejection of irresistible grace with a vengeance. It rejects even the necessity of it. Men have sufficient grace without it, thank you.

And Second Vatican is most foolish and blasphemous of all. For this Council, "God is the Father of all men," there being a "universal design of God for the salvation of the human race."[73] There are no references to damnation—the closest approach is the statement that those who "knowing the Catholic Church was made necessary by God through Jesus Christ would refuse to enter her or to remain in her could not be saved." This is almost certainly a benign form of Catch 22. That is, if anyone refuses to be baptized, can he really "know" that "the Catholic Church was made necessary"? The Eastern Orthodox, Protestants, Jews, Hindus, Buddhists, Moslems,[74] and, indeed, all men of good will are beneficiaries of the work of Christ,

---

71. H. J. Schroeder, O.P., *Canons and Decrees of the Council of Trent* (St. Louis and London, 1941), p. 32.

72. Wm. Abbot and J. Gallagher, *The Documents of Vatican II* (London and Dublin, 1966), pp. 567, 586.

73. Abbot and Gallagher, pp. 32, 33.

74. [Editor's Note] The term "Moslems" was commonly used to refer to Muslims in English texts from the sixteenth to mid-twentieth centuries. We have retained the original term as it appeared in the title's first publication.

who gave "His life as a ransom for the many—that is, for all."[75] "This all holds true not only for Christians but for men of good will in whose hearts grace works in an unseen way. For, since Christ died for all men and since the ultimate vocation of man is in fact one, and divine, we ought to believe that the Holy Spirit in a manner known only to God offers to every man the possibility of being associated with this paschal mystery."[76] As usual, Second Vatican tries to appear not to have abandoned Christianity altogether, by inserting a "*possibility* of being associated with this paschal mystery" (italics mine). But where is the mere possibility if the work of Christ (who died for all) is beneficial to all and when the grace of God is at work in all? The Council is talking, though not frankly, about universal grace, far removed from the doctrine of St. Augustine.

Conclusion

Our conclusion is that Orange II was only Semiaugustinian when it held out for the resistibility of grace, where it held out. It had departed from Augustine at a point so crucial that it could not be called Augustinian. It is no surprise that the Middle Ages gradually moved toward Semipelagianism and that Roman Catholicism at Trent fell back into Semipelagianism and at Second Vatican fell back into what amounts to Pelagianism.

As for Augustine, we will say that he is Calvinistic or Augustinian at the point of regeneration, Roman Catholic on the possibility of a fall from it, and Calvinistic or Augustinian again on perseverance as it pertains to the predestinated. In the main, Augustine was an Augustinian on the irresistibility of grace.

---

75. Abbot and Gallagher, p. 587.
76. Abbot and Gallagher, pp. 221, 222.

CORNELIS VEENHOF

Church and Church Unity

It is a fundamental Scriptural idea with regard to "the church of God in Christ" (I Thess. 2:14) that it is the *body of all believers*.[1] Through faith believers are incorporated into the body of Christ. The body of Christ is his church or congregation (Col. 1:18, 24) as, conversely, the church of Christ is also his body (Eph. 1:22, 23). Church and *body of Christ* are thus indicative of the same reality.

All Reformed churches have reiterated and emphasized this Scriptural view in contrast to the Roman Catholic idea. According to the Catholic idea, the church is a hierarchically ordered institution concentrated in the Pope. The Reformed churches have confessed without exception that the one holy catholic apostolic church is formed by the communion of *all* believers as they are spread out and dispersed over the face of the earth.[2]

---

1. The description of the church as "church of God in Christ" is the most inclusive and most adequate. Usually the church in the New Testament is called the "church of God." The addition "in Christ" explains *why* and *how* the church can be the church of God, namely, through its being "in Christ."

2. I give evidence for these assertions in Appendix III of my book *Volk van God, Enkele Aspecten van Bavinck's Kerkbeschouwing* (Amsterdam, 1969). Bavinck summarized this Reformed outlook with the words: "the universal catholic church is the meeting of all believers of *all* times among *all* nations from *every* country, in *all* churches" (pp. 21-29).

In the Belgic Confession this truth is formulated thus: "We believe and confess one catholic church which is a holy communion of
all true Christian believers." In the Latin translation of this confession produced at the Synod of Dort, the word *all*, although quite
unnecessary, was specifically added.

In Holy Scripture the word *church*, or, as one reads it in most
Dutch translations, *gemeente*,[3] first of all means *catholic* or *universal*
church, which includes all believers. This is especially so in Ephesians
and Colossians. But just as frequently the word means the "*local*" or
"particular" congregation.

The relationship between the universal church and the local congregation is unique. According to Scripture the universal church does
not subdivide into a great number of local churches. But neither is the
former the sum total of all local churches which are spread out over
the world. The uniqueness of this relationship consists in the fact that
every local church also possesses everything that makes a church
church.

Through the Holy Spirit and the inspired Word of God, every
congregation, no less than the universal church, has direct communion with its Lord, the crucified and risen Christ. The congregation,
no less than the universal church, partakes of the salvation which
Christ obtained for his own. To it are also given the full gospel, the
two sacraments, and the office bearers whom Christ will use as office
bearers of the local congregation.

Probably the best way to describe the relationship of the universal church to the particular church is that a congregation is an *expression* of the universal church not in the *quantitative* sense but in the
qualitative one. Paul addresses his second epistle to the Corinthians

---

3.   The Dutch—non-Roman Catholic—Bible translations have
      congregation for the Greek word *ekklesia*, probably because the word
      church might be confused with the Roman Catholic view of church.

to *the* church "as it is in Corinth" (II Cor. 1:1). If there were only local congregations, then that would not diminish their being fully church.[4]

It is also true that the church reaches its highest and richest expression in the local congregation. According to Scripture, the proclamation of the gospel is the focus of church life. The church is born and nourished through the preaching, which is its principal task in the world. This preaching is done first of all in and by the local congregation to its members. But it is also proclaimed to those who do not know Jesus as well as to those who have estranged themselves from him. The same goes for the administration of the sacraments, which is entrusted to the congregation and is performed exclusively in its midst. Moreover, the prayers and singing of the congregation are elements of the worship service of the local church as it gathers in one location. In view of the above, it can be said that the church is best exemplified as church when believers gather as a local congregation before the pulpit and around the table of the Lord.

That the local church reaches the fullness of its "being church" comes to expression most clearly when one focuses on the "calling" of the church. This calling can best be described with the word *service*. In the first place *service* means "to serve God in Christ Jesus." Moreover, intimately connected with that, it means to serve the brethren and all those God places as neighbors on the path of the members of his church. Service is the continuous service of all with everything that church is and has through God's grace. Such service only happens, and can only happen, to people with whom one has come into personal contact. This means that it can only happen in and through the local church. All service of the distant neighbor,

---

4. See *Volk van God*, chapter 8, *particuliere* and *universele Kerk*, and Appendix V about the concept *ekklesia* in the New Testament.

which can be realized indirectly by means of missionaries and workers in development programs, is hypocritical if the service of the local church of which one is a member is not a concrete reality.

It ought to be unmistakably clear to anyone who has even an elementary knowledge of Scripture that it is God's will that believers show forth in deed the unity in Christ which exists among them. Believers are one "in Christ," but they also have to be one "in fact" in the practice of life. In addition, the unity of the church means that the indicative "you *are* 'in Christ' the one and indivisible church" is undeniably connected with the imperative "you *must* now also become in the concrete reality of life the one and indivisible church."[5]

Paul declares with regard to the church, "You are one body, you receive one Spirit, you are called to one hope, you have one Lord, one baptism, and one faith, and your God and Father above is with you and in you all." But especially with regard to this matter, he exhorts believers of all times patiently to bear with one another in all humility and gentleness and to strive to maintain the unity of the spirit through the bond of peace, until all come to oneness of faith and the knowledge of the Son of God (Eph. 4:1 ff.).

The great seriousness of this apostolic exhortation imposes itself upon us when we realize that Jesus Christ stakes the matter of his Kingdom on the one crucial issue of its unity. Just before his crucifixion, did Christ not pray that the Father would give him as a "reward" for his suffering and death the *visible* unity of his church?

---

5.   The indissoluble connection between indicative and imperative plays a dominant role in the Biblical message and must also play a part in our faith life. Particularly illustrative is what Paul writes in I Corinthians 5:7, "So get rid of the old yeast, and make yourselves into a completely new batch of bread" (NIV). Such a saying cannot be explained logically.

My prayer is not for them alone. I pray also for those who will believe in me through their message, that all of them may be one, Father, as you are in me and I am in you. May they also be in us so that the world may believe that you have sent me. I have given them the glory that you gave me, that they may be one as we are one: I in them and you in me. May they be brought to complete unity to let the world know that you sent me and have loved them even as you have loved me (John 17:20-23 NIV).

For those who understand how Scripture views the relationship between the universal church and the local church, it ought to be clear that the call to believers to implement their unity as given in Christ has first of all to do with the local church. This, of course, is self-evident, for believers meet each other personally and constantly in the same place. There they are placed by God next to one another, united with each other, and responsible for each other—*everyone* without exception. If Christ were to write a letter to the congregation of a city or to the congregation of part of a city or village or region, then this letter would be directed and sent to the community of all believers who live there. Therefore, as children of one Father and thus as brothers and sisters of Jesus Christ, they must first and foremost show themselves as one congregation and one church in word and deed.

The unity of the local church is thus primary, and unity among different local churches secondary. This unity can be realized regionally, in the country, or worldwide. It can be concretized in ecclesiastical meetings such as classes and synods. But can there be true unity among local churches if believers in one locality refuse to unite? Has then the idea of unity among local churches not become hypocritical?

Thus, all efforts to unite believers must first and foremost be directed to ecclesiastical unity, the unity of the local church, and secondly to the unity of the national and universal church. Basically it is hypocritical for Christians to cooperate in every manner, such as in media, in politics, and in other organizations and even denominations, if they refuse to bring about that one unity which is basic to any further cooperation. We must begin to realize that it is a sin in God's eyes for churches which confess the same confession of faith in the Word of God to continue to exist alongside of—or worse, in enmity with—each other. At the same time, it is offensive to "those who are outside." Can we seriously expect the blessing of the Lord if we persist in this sin?[6]

All efforts to establish the Kingdom which the congregation receives as a task from its Lord, Jesus Christ, must especially be directed to the unity of his church, for which he prayed. As I have already said, this concerns in the first place the establishment of the local church as a community of all believers. But this also concerns "interchurch" relationships.[7]

There is something demonic in the fact that particular, historically developed, and therefore historically relative denominations with their own major assemblies, committees, and other agencies obstruct this unity or even make it impossible, instead of promoting

---

6. In no way do I mean to condemn the cooperation of believers in many fields. I mean here the cooperation which is a substitute, a pseudo-legal consolidation or camouflage of ecclesiastical disharmony. I do not mean to condemn the cooperation which is practiced with sorrow and with the realization of the sin of church disunity.

7. I use the word *interchurch* here in its original and true meaning, thus as analogous to the terms *international, intercontinental interdepartmental,* etc. Here a relationship among "equals" is indicated. In its original and true meaning, the word *interchurch* indicates a relationship among "churches." To describe a group or a society or an organization as "interchurch" because members of different churches participate in it is, strictly speaking, incorrect.

in every possible way the unity of the local churches as ordered by God. As concerns the promotion of this unity, hierarchicalism in whatever form has been detrimental. Whether this hierarchy is represented by the Pope or by a major assembly actually makes no difference. By its very nature, every hierarchy is a human effort to make the national or global church a powerful organizational unity. But as with every trespass of God's commandments, hierarchy brings about the opposite of what is intended. Herman Bavinck once wrote a devastating but thoroughly justified criticism of this destructive evil that recurs again and again in the church. "The idea of a church hierarchy," he said, "that wants primarily to unite Christianity has actually throughout the centuries created division and caused splits." The history of the Roman Catholic Church, the founding of the Dutch Reformed Church in 1816, and the formation of the *Gereformeerde Kerk* are ample proof of the truth of what Bavinck said. All Reformed Christians should furthermore seriously take to heart what Bavinck goes on to say, namely, that Protestantism denies its own confession "if it seeks to maintain the unity of Christianity by means of hierarchical pressure."[8]

Another fatal barrier to the true unity of the church is found in the ever-recurring evil of absolutizing one's own denomination. This evil usually shows itself in camouflaged fashion, but as a result is that much more dangerous. It reveals itself in the proud pretense that one's own church is the one and only true church. Sometimes this pretense goes so far that those who are not members of this only true church are disqualified as "outsiders." In addition it is even asserted that there is no community of faith between members of this true church and Christians outside and that therefore no communion of the saints can be exercised.

---

8.   H. Bavinck, *Gereformeerde Dogmatiek*, IV, third edition (Kampen, 1918), 345.

The error of such absolutizing also reveals itself in the hidden effort to expand, consolidate, and obtain influence for one's own denomination or group. According to this frame of mind, church unity can only be pursued rightly if we see to it that every believer is active only in his "own church."

An objectionable side-effect of the absolutizing of one's own denomination is often an unusually sharp and constant criticism of other denominations. It is a criticism that obviously is motivated to justify the separate continued existence of one's own denomination and to consolidate its position internally and externally.

Those who are caught in the grip of this absolutizing have little understanding of the catholicity of the church and are fundamentally sectarians and separatists. They do not realize that there is no "church of our own" that is true church and that a "church of our own" can easily become "a chapel of Satan's." Such persons do not realize that in this world a "church" does not, may not, and can not exist other than the one and only church of our Lord, Jesus Christ. For a Christian there should be no other desire and prayer than to be and remain forever a living member of this church.

If we wish to follow Scriptural direction in our effort at church unity, we must always keep in mind a few matters of decisive significance. First, the existing institutional church may never be regarded as *normative*. Historically formed and developed denominations that are therefore also relative are indeed the *starting point* of all ecclesiastical dealings. Of course, one can never begin to undertake anything except out of the ecclesiastical situation in which one finds oneself at the outset of this activity. But a starting point differs fundamentally from a norm. Therefore, a starting point may never become a norm. The norm which constitutes the basis of the quest for church unity is exclusively that challenge which Christ gave, namely, that all who are by true faith incorporated in his body should also and especially be *one* in the church.

The implication here is that as long as the unity of his body, coveted by Christ, has not been reached, every believer must regard his congregation with all its committees and decisions as temporary.[9] When somebody wants to perpetuate his church and remain a member of it no matter what, he makes "his church" an idol. Should ever a Biblically valid church union occur, then something new emerges, just as, when two rivers come together and continue to flow between the same two banks, a new river is formed in which the two rivers merge. In such a case, ecclesiastical names are of secondary importance.

Furthermore, it is necessary that in the attempt to reach church unity we neither go back confessionally behind the dogmatic decisions reached prior to the great Reformation of the sixteenth-century nor regard these as antiquated. In this Reformation the Spirit of God has lit again the spark of the gospel as it occurred in the beginning of the Christian church. According to Bavinck, in no confession has "Christianity in its religious, ethical and theological character come into its own; nowhere is it so deep, so wide, so spacious, so free, and so truly catholic as in the Reformed churches."[10] Continuing, Bavinck asserts in the same vein:

> In this confession more than in any other...grace is completely sovereign, more overwhelming than all sin, indepen-

9. The general synods of the *dolerende Gereformeerde Kerken* in Holland were always called "temporary." Regretfully, after 1892, with the uniting of the *dolerende* and *afgeschieden* churches, the *Gereformeerde Kerken* have not maintained this usage.

10. H. Bavinck, *Gereformeerde Dogmatiek*, I, first edition (Kampen, 1895-1901). The second edition (Kampen, 1906-11) was very much revised and expanded, though the successive editions from that point on are the same as the second.

dent of sex, age, race, nation, and even the will of man. No other boundary has been put to the love of the Father, to the grace of the Son, and to the communion of the Holy Spirit than that which has been established in the consistently wise and holy counsel of God. No part of life is excluded from recreation, and no human being need despair for the gospel is given for all creatures.[11]

The Reformed confessions have always emphasized especially the wonder of the justification of the sinner by grace alone, on the basis of the sacrifice of Jesus Christ, as well as the implications of this confession. This justification by grace through faith was always for Luther the *articulus stantis vel cadentis ecclesiae*, a truth on which the church stands or falls. Luther claimed that one could neither add anything to or subtract anything from this truth even if heaven and earth should fall, "On this truth everything rests that we teach and show in our life to pope, devil, and world. Therefore, we have to be absolutely certain with regard to it and not doubt, lest everything be lost and pope, devil, and everything that is against us achieve the victory and the right."[12] Calvin completely agreed with Luther in this respect. According to Calvin, the justification of the sinner is the heart of the gospel. If knowledge of it disappears, then according to Calvin the glory of Christ will become dim, the gospel nullified, the church destroyed, and the hope of eternal life wiped out.[13]

---

11. H. Bavinck and P. Biesterveld, *Bede on Rede* (Kampen, 1895), p. 40.

12. *Articuli Smalcaldici, Das Ander Teil* 5; see J. C. Müller, *Die Symbolischen Bücher* (Gütersloh), p. 300: *"Und auf diesem Artikel stehet alles, was wir den Pabst, Teufel and Welt lehren und leben. Darum müssen wir der gar gewis sein und nicht zweifelen, sonst ist alles verloren und behält Pabst und Teufel und alles wider uns den Sieg und Recht."*

13. See *"Responsio ad Sadoleti epistulam," Opera Calvini*, V (Brunsvig, 1863-1900), 396-97, where Calvin writes about justification by faith

In their confessions the Reformed churches returned to the "origin," namely, to the gospel as it was preached by Jesus Christ and the apostles. They wanted to restore the "old image" of the church, *vetusa ecclesia facies*,[14] which meant, above all, believing, confession, and preaching justification by grace through faith alone: *sola gratia, sola fide.*

The great historian, lawyer, statesman, and confessor of the gospel, Groen van Prinsterer, played a dominant role in the struggle that occurred during the previous century in the Dutch Reformed Church, to return it to its true confession and thus to bring to the fore the true unity of the church. Because the work of this great man in the Kingdom of God has become better known and more appreciated in the United States, but above all because his work is very relevant, I would like to relate something of what he had to say about this subject.

In his continuous labor for the restoration and development of the Dutch Reformed Church, Groen van Prinsterer had ideas basically similar to the reformers. He, too, sought this restoration in believing and confessing the truth of the gospel of Jesus Christ. And, therefore, he sought to recover the confession of the old "martyr church," which up until that time had professed the gospel. Just as for the reformers, justification by faith was for Groen van Prinsterer the dominant element of the Christian religion. Says Groen, "Without the doctrine of freely given grace, which confesses Jesus Christ as true God and accepts his death as the true redemption for sin, there cannot be a Reformed or even a Christian church."[15]

"*sublata eius cognitio, et Christi gloria exstincta est, et abolita religio, et ecclesia destructa et spes saluta penitus eversa.*"

14. Groen, *De Antirevolutionaire en Confessionele Partij in de Nederlandse Hervormde Kerk*, translated by A. J. Dam (Goes, no date), p. 16. The words, cited from Adolphe Monod, were wholeheartedly taken over by Groen.

15. Groen, *Het Regt der Hervormde Gezindheid* (Amsterdam, 1848), p. 20.

Moreover, Groen told his fellow believers and opponents, the church has determined what it believes and confesses as divine truth not *because of* its creeds, but *according to* its creeds. The confessions are never *norms* for the church, for only the Word of God can be a norm; but they can be "prescriptions," "rules," "guidelines" for preaching and teaching.[16] The confessions are the symbolic writings offering the congregation a guarantee that the faith of the church is presented—not an arbitrary belief of a preaching or movement—and that preaching and teaching will be not only *from* and *about* but also *according to* Scripture. The creeds are guidelines "as application of the Protestant rule 'the Bible, the whole Bible and nothing but the Bible' to the being and need of every group which bases itself upon the unity of faith and commitment."[17]

Along with Groen van Prinsterer, believers will in their efforts for church unity desire "*the broad*" but also the "*clear*," the *Scriptural* and the *confessional* use of the creeds of the Reformed churches.[18] This is indeed the "God-glorifying confession" that comes from the heart of those churches that have reformed themselves again (*de ge-reformeerde Kerken*). Therefore, this is its "trademark," its "banner," and its point of unity.[19]

16. As can be seen here, Noordman's well-known characterization of the confession as the "rule of speech" in the church was already introduced by Groen van Prinsterer.

17. Groen, *Adres aan de Algemeene Synode der Nederlandse Hervormde Kerk* (Leiden, 1842), pp. 5-6.

18. Groen, *Adres*, p. 19. Groen van Prinsterer describes the meaning of these words at the end of the address when he says: "Maintaining of the main truth of the Gospel and, as a means thereof, maintaining of the Forms of Unity, with regard to the being and the principles of the Reformed doctrine, in the spirit of the authors and of the Dutch Reformed church:" (p. 51). In his fine work *De Verbindende Kracht van de Belijdenisschriften* (Kampen, 1969), Dr. Nauta gives a detailed description of Groen's idea with regard to the character and authority of the confessions.

19. Groen, *Adres*, p. 2.

In the attempt to realize the unity of the church, we have to be deeply convinced that, according to Scripture, it is important to be ruled by the "mind of Christ." Thus, all involved will become like-minded, having unity of will and effort and conquering selfish ambition and vain conceit (Phil. 2:4). In other words, the concern is primarily with the crucifying of the flesh with its evil works, such as feuds, quarrels, jealousy, partiality, dissensions, and the like. And, conversely, the concern is positively to reveal the fruits of the Spirit, which consist of love, joy, peace, patience, kindness, goodness, faithfulness, gentleness, and self-control (Gal. 5:19-23).

In *Gereformeerd* circles, when dealing with church unity, we have often put the emphasis upon agreement of doctrine to the neglect of the above-mentioned apostolic admonition. Furthermore, with doctrine under discussion, the argument was mainly about dogmatic questions. And in this regard there was often intellectual manipulation.

It cannot be stressed enough that the absolutely primary rule for realizing church unity is conquering selfishness with all its side-effects: self-will, ambition, self-concern, hunger for power, pride, and so forth. Conversely, this means putting into practice selflessness with all its implications and ramifications.

I have commented upon the church and the problem of church unity in the Reformed community. I want to conclude here with a reference to Groen van Prinsterer, a man who loved the Dutch Reformed Church deeply, who sketched its position and calling clearly and incisively, and who worked during his entire life for growth and unity with all his knowledge and strength.

In his beautiful *Het Regt der Hervormde Gezindheid*, Groen speaks about the two alternatives which confronted the Dutch Reformed Church in his time: "Either a true reformation in the denomination will be the call to those who have left to rejoin; or we will be forced to split due to total injustice, in which the necessity of a choice between confessing or denying the Christian faith will be made clear for all who love and acknowledge the truth, as it is taught in the doctrine of our church." [20]

What Groen van Prinsterer really wanted, what he hoped and prayed for, was that the Reformed Church would regain the place which it once occupied "in the development of God's Kingdom on earth." But the retaking of that place, he proclaimed to his fellow believers, will only be possible "when the renewed church gives testimony to the living and eternal Word of God; when it shows its agreement with the confession which is expressed in its midst by word and deed; when it again shows fidelity to the good confession (I Tim. 6:12, 19) which is sealed on the hearts of believers by the Holy Spirit; already sealed by the blood of many martyrs before it was written in the symbolic writings of the church as an expression of communal faith, as guide for communal labor, and as the unchangeable life force of the congregation with the clarity and warmth of those who know in whom they have believed."[21]

---

20. Groen, *Het Regt*, pp. 137-38.

21. Groen, *Het Regt*, p. 196. Groen van Prinsterer has written much about the church and its struggles in his time. His most important works are *Adres aan de Algemeene Synode der Nederlandsche Hervormde Kerk* (1842), *Aan de Hervormde Gemeente in Nederland* (1843), and *Het Regt der Hervormde Kerk* (1848). The latter can be regarded as the ecclesiastical equivalent of Groen van Prinsterer's *Ongeloof en Revolutie*. I have described Groen's church struggle in my *Kracht en Doel der Politiek* (Goes, 1948), pp. 39-68.

GORDON J. SPYKMAN

A New Look at Election and Reprobation

Introduction

SOONER OR LATER, IT seems, every course in Reformed theology reaches that critical "moment of truth" when the doctrine of predestination comes up as the topic of the day. One of those sessions stands out in my memory. It happened several years ago as I was teaching a class of graduate students. That interchange was a real eye-opener, touching off within me a chain reaction of reflections on the doctrine of election/reprobation. As a teacher who tries to learn from his students, I decided to devote this chapter to explicating some of the seminal ideas born out of that moving experience.

Thinking back to that day in class, the very mention of reprobation evoked intuitively a strongly negative response. Antipathy toward the question of predestination as expressed by those students was deep-seated and adamant. With near unanimity they stated their position: there is no way of dealing with this issue, especially its shadow side called reprobation, in a healthy Biblical way. This reaction, as I sat back to assess it, was part and parcel of a total attitude toward decretal theology. It took about a week of class time to clear the air.

That lively theological interchange did not take place in a vacuum. The students had done their homework, which included a reading of the following passage:

The doctrine of reprobation follows naturally from the logic of the situation. The decree of election inevitably implies the decree of reprobation. If the all-wise God, possessed of infinite knowledge, has eternally purposed to save some, then He *ipso facto* also purposed not to save others. If He has chosen or elected some, then He has by that very fact also rejected others.[1]

Such theologizing, the seasoned end-product of a long tradition of scholastic thought, lay at the bottom of the problem which was plaguing the class. If predestination in history is understood as the re-run of a pre-written script that can be traced back to a set of decrees in the eternal mind of God, with election as a picking-and-choosing process superimposed upon us from above and reprobation a rational negative inference drawn from this its positive counterpart, then, as these students sensed it, there is no way to extricate ourselves from the agonizing dilemma of the supra- and infra-lapsarian problem. Theology then drifts easily into abstract speculation. Dark and ominous shadows fall over the Biblical teaching on election/reprobation. The whole issue of predestination gets reduced to an overwhelming guessing game. Then, too, the sovereign grace of God engenders a gnawing sense of anxiety instead of hope and comfort and security.

That classroom episode was not an isolated case. It is fairly typical of the restless mood which often surrounds what Calvin called the *decretum horribile* (the awesome decree).[2] Accordingly, many find this article of faith almost unthinkable, let alone preachable, teachable, and livable. Were those students right,

---

1.   L. Berkhof, *Systematic Theology* (Grand Rapids, 1946), pp. 117-18.

2.   J. Calvin, *The Institutes of the Christian Religion*, Battles-McNeill edition (Philadelphia, 1960), III, xxiii, 7.

after all? Has the Calvinist tradition, for all these many centuries, been overburdened with the unbearable weight of a troublesome caricature? Is the doctrine of predestination merely the monstrous brainchild of decretal theologians? Are we victims of a colossal misconception? Or is there a way of reconciling more happily the teachings of the Reformed confessions on predestination with the truth of Scripture? Is there just possibly a better way of "handling aright the Word of truth" concerning the realities of election/reprobation?

My purpose in taking yet another look at this controversial topic is to suggest a reformulation of the structural contours of this enduring theological issue. It would be sheer pretense, of course, to think that we can reduce this question to rationally manageable form, or to imagine that by rigorous analysis we can intellectually resolve the mystery of the mighty acts of God. For in its depth dimension, God's "ways are past finding out." I submit, however, that it is possible to re-contextualize this question, to re-articulate our Biblical-confessional framework-of-reference for dealing with it, and thus to restate this doctrine in such a way that, relieved of some of the dubious scholastic constructs which until now have often encumbered it, we can learn to theologize on it with renewed openness and joy as the very *cor ecclesiae*, the very heartbeat of the church.[3]

The question we face then is this: Have we perhaps painted the Biblical idea of election/reprobation into a faulty picture of reality? For predestination is not an isolated doctrine, standing alone, unrelated to a full-orbed life-philosophy. Therefore, it cannot be dealt with independently as a self-contained issue. It is connected integrally and coherently with some overall world view. For viewpoints on theological matters, while rooted in basic religious principles and directed by Biblical teachings, take on their definitive structure and

---

3.   G. C. Berkouwer, *De Verkiezing Gods* (Kampen, 1955), p. 13.

coloration from the larger confessional perspectives within which they function.[4]

Too often Reformed thinkers have overlooked this fundamental, all-embracing idea. They tended to assume rather uncritically that it is possible to engage in theology without being self-consciously aware of the philosophical assumptions which always shape the direction of our thinking. Theology, however, cannot stand alone. And it is too important to be left to theologians who are unclear about their philosophical assumptions. For theology always rests upon a philosophical base. Overlooking this, too frequently Reformed thinkers tended to bypass a serious consideration of the prolegomena commitments which informed the patterns of their theologizing. They failed to make explicit the comprehensive world views which are real and present in their work, and which serve inescapably as theoretical models for dealing internally with the more specifically theological issues, such as election/reprobation. As Troost puts it, clear distinctions in theology "can be worked out with a certain assurance of justification only in the context of a theology that proceeds from a biblical life-view and is philosophically reformed," to which he adds: "To date, there is no such theology, as far as I know."[5]

---

4. See F. Klooster, "Predestination—A Calvinistic Note," *The Banner*, November 23, 1979, where, in his concluding remarks, he points to "the larger questions concerning the nature of God and his relation to history," adding that "one's entire view of God and his relation to history will call for deeper reflection." Also J. Daane, *The Freedom of God* (Grand Rapids, 1979), p. 479: Election "...is as comprehensive as salvation itself because it characterizes the totality of God's dealings with his people, his church, his world."

5. A. Troost, "The Relation between Word-revelation and Creational Revelation," *Circular of the International Conference of Institutions for Christian Higher Education*, No. 18 (April 1980), p. 32.

This shortcoming, I submit, helps to account for the fact that we have inherited truncated doctrines which suffer from theological tunnel-vision. Undergirding such theologies are dubious methodologies which generally resort to rationalistic belief-structures to control the valid drawing of conclusions or rely upon positivistic approaches to Scripture which employ fragmentary exegetical data as a set of self-evident truths from which certain logical deductions can be drawn.

A hasty perusal of the voluminous body of predestination literature will quickly impress even the casual reader of the bewildering array of theological insights amassed by the fathers. Their work leaves no stone unturned in the search to uncover right doctrines. One can hardly avoid the conclusion that certainly by now all the countless pieces of this giant theological puzzle are on the table. But what we still lack is a theoretical paradigm to which we can appeal in putting all these pieces together into a well-knit, meaningful totality. The urgent challenge for constructive theology today is therefore to settle upon a unifying Reformed world-and-life view which can serve as a catalytic agent for rethinking the Biblical doctrine of election/reprobation.

I propose that we make this challenge a matter of high priority, if we are really serious about gaining greater clarity on the issue at hand. In this decade of our Lord, the 1980s, the time appears to be ripe. Drawing upon the varied insights of Augustine, Thomas, Calvin, Bavinck, Kuyper, Van Til, Dooyeweerd, Barth, Brunner, Berkhof, Berkouwer, and others, I believe we have reached a point in Western Christian thought which calls for a new initiative. After all that has been said in the past, advancing the discussion now requires a more holistic approach to the doctrine of predestination, one which can help to account for our life experience in God's world in the light of his Word, seeking thus to do justice to the norms of Biblical revelation and to honor the claims of the Reformed creeds. Failing in this, it should not surprise us if students in theology, surveying the field, continue to despair of ever unraveling all the tangled threads and then conclude that the reality of election/reprobation finally "dies of a thousand qualifications."

A Look at Calvin

In setting out to update and reframe this dogma of the church, I propose that, as a point of departure, we turn first to Calvin. Note the following three motifs in his theology which, as background ideas, can serve as helpful pointers in reformulating the question at hand.[6]

First, we find Calvin repeatedly stating and demonstrating what he takes to be a basic principle of Biblical hermeneutics. On the one hand, he holds, we must seek to say no more than the Bible says, lest we fall into speculation. Here he warns against "human curiosity" which "will leave no secret to God that it will not search out and unravel...No restraints can hold it back from wandering into forbidden bypaths and thrusting upward to the heights."[7] On the other hand, says Calvin, we must try to say no less than Scripture says, lest we impoverish its message. Here Calvin has in mind those who "require that every mention of predestination be buried; indeed, they teach us to avoid any mention of it, as we would a reef."[8] It is noteworthy that Calvin underscores this fundamental rule of interpretation precisely within the context of his discussion of election/reprobation.

Directed therefore by the light of Scripture, as we seek to understand the unfolding drama of election/reprobation within our various life situations, our theologizing must take as its criterion "the full

---

6. See W. Niesel, *The Theology of Calvin* (Philadelphia, 1956), pp. 159-81.

7. Calvin, III, xxi, 1.

8. Calvin, III, xxi, 3.

counsel of God," no more, no less. For the Scriptures serve as indispensable "spectacles"[9] for bleary-eyed, sinful men so that they may begin to see clearly not only God's handiwork in creation, but also his electing/reprobating will at work in history. God's Word alone sets the parameters, fixes the bounds, and establishes the limits within which we are to "work out our salvation with fear and trembling"—which includes working out our theology of predestination. Quoting Calvin: "I desire only to have (all men) generally admit that we should not investigate what the Lord has left hidden in secret, that we should not neglect what he has brought into the open, so that we may not be convicted of excessive curiosity on the one hand, or of excessive ingratitude on the other."[10]

Second, not only *what* one says on the doctrine of predestination is important, but also *where* one says it. Its Placement within the total structure of one's theology often speaks volumes. On this point it is therefore significant that Calvin introduced a striking shift of location in his elaboration of this doctrine as he moved along from the earlier versions of the *Institutes* to its final definitive edition. This change involved transferring his discussion of predestination out of Book I on "the Knowledge of God as Creator" to Book III on "the Christian Life." Accordingly, he chose finally to deal with election/reprobation after his treatment of justification, sanctification, faith, and Christian freedom. Handling predestination in its original place suggests a rather abstract, arbitrary, non-historical view of this decree. Coming up, as it now does, near the close of Calvin's theology of redemption, it bears a much more concrete, experiential, confirmational character. It is designed to reassure believers that their salvation is not an accidental circumstance or a capricious turn of

---

9.   Calvin, I, vi, 1.

10.   Calvin, III, xxi, 4.

events. Rather, from beginning to end it was and is and ever will be in "good hands."

This insight gained by Calvin during the course of his theological pilgrimage was soon lost, however, on his followers. From Theodore Beza, Calvin's successor at the Geneva Academy, onward, most orthodox theologians belonging to the tradition of Reformed scholastic theology reverted to the position Calvin had abandoned.[11] Predestination emerged as the regnant structuring principle of their theologies. This development affected not only the spirit and style of their doctrines of election/reprobation, but also dictated a decretalist transformation of theology as a whole. Entire theologies were constructed around the pivotal idea of double predestination and the equal ultimacy of election and reprobation, with every other point of doctrine logically derived by rational argumentation, deduction, and inference from these primary starting points. This radical departure from Calvin's freshly evangelical approach has permeated the thinking of large segments of the Reformed community down to the present time.

A third point in Calvin's theology worthy of special attention in elucidating the theme of this chapter is his emphasis on relational theology. Calvin opens the *Institutes* with these lines: "Nearly all the wisdom we possess...consists of two parts: the knowledge of God and of ourselves."[12] If this were Calvin's last word instead of his first or if this were his only word, then he could justifiably be read as compounding our problems rather than alleviating them. For then these "two parts" could be construed as two parties, God, and man, without a normatively structured relationship between them. Then we would be doomed either to speculation, which intrudes upon the maj-

---

11. See B. G. Armstrong, *Calvinism and the Amyraut Heresy: Protestant Scholasticism and Humanism in Seventeenth-Century France* (Madison, 1969), esp. pp. 37-41.

12. Calvin, I, i, 1.

esty of God, or to agnosticism, which repudiates God's coming out to us in his revelation, or to historicism, which seeks the answer within the world of our experience. If Calvin had left us with a "missing link" between God and ourselves, we would then have to struggle with the yawning chasm between an unrelated two-part view of reality. In fact, however, Calvin rejects all pretended ignorance of God, since "the universe is for us a sort of mirror in which we can contemplate God, who is otherwise invisible."[13] He also rejects historicistic speculation, saying that "we ought not to rack our brains about God; but, rather, we should contemplate him in his works."[14] We therefore know God not *ad intra*, as he is in himself, but *ad extra*, as he manifests himself in his outgoing words and works. The question, therefore, is not "Who is God in his essence?" but "Who is God in his relationship to us?" The best understanding of Calvin is that which sees God's revelation as the abiding covenantal boundary and bridge between man and his Maker. His view of the Christian religion therefore demands the recognition of a three-part world view: God, his Word, and the world. God's Word, revealed in creation, in Scripture, and in Christ is the dynamic bond uniting the creator with all his creatures, just as the Holy Spirit is the living bond uniting us to the incarnate and glorified Word made flesh. Calvin's thinking is pervasively relational. Accordingly, every theological truth has an anthropological correlate, and every anthropological truth has a theological correlate. The boundary which assures a proper distance between these two covenant partners and the bridge which at the same time establishes communion between them is the abiding Word of God.

A Mixed Tradition

The choice we face between a two-factor (God and cosmos) and a three-factor (God, Word, and cosmos) world view carries with it

13. Calvin, I, v, 1.
14. Calvin, I, v, 9.

far-reaching consequences. The former opens wide the door to meta-physical, decretal speculation. The latter offers greater promise for a relational, covenantal theology. Scholastic theology tends to follow a two-factor line of thought. It deals extensively with the two *relata*, God and man, with an exhaustive inquiry into the ontology of these two essences. In reaction, much of contemporary existential theology locates its center of gravity in some almost indefinable *relatio*. It concentrates on relationships ("I-Thou"), often reducing issues to situational relativity. In the process the distinctive reality of the *relata*, of creator and creation as they stand over against each other, fades into a blurred irrelevancy.

Traditional Reformed theology tends to err in the direction of a two-factor perspective. It upholds the unique reality of the two *relata*—the creator/creature distinction. Its thinking does not reflect great consistency, however, in defining in a normatively structured way the covenant relationship which stands at the center of its theology. Either the norm tends to get pushed up transcendentally into God himself, making it inaccessible; or it slips down into man and his world, accompanied by subtle hints of historicism; or the specter of voluntarism emerges, conceiving of God's acts as direct interventions by his absolute power and arbitrary will, bound to nothing, so that he can do capriciously whatever he pleases; or we end up constructing our own theoretical bridges between the God-side and the man-side, resulting in a perpetual balancing act between divine sovereignty and human responsibility. Predestination literature is replete with evidence of such dialectical tensions.[15]

---

15. Concerning Reformed theologians in the tradition of scholastic orthodoxy, forced to choose between God and man as subject in salvation, H. Berkhof says "that they lacked the theological categories with which to grasp the uniqueness of the biblical-covenantal (inter-subjective) mode of speaking." (H. Berkhof, *Christian Faith*, Grand Rapids, 1979, p. 482.)

On a two-factor world view, the election/reprobation issue gets suspended in a bi-polar tension between time and eternity, with nothing in between. Then the central Biblical emphasis on the concrete terms of covenant fellowship gets shortchanged. The result is often a tug-of-war situation between man and his Maker. We either eclipse divine sovereignty, Arminian style, or we eclipse human responsibility, labeling it hyper-Calvinism. To avoid these extremes, we try to maintain an uneasy, strained, and often unstable balance between them. With only two factors almost anything can happen. We can drift in the direction of a deist-like determinism or in the direction of a refined humanism. Without that third intermediate factor God and man easily become either competitors or cooperators. The revelation/response model then loses its sharp focus. As a consequence, we either overload the divine circuit or overload the human circuit. Either way we then find ourselves blowing out Biblical, confessional, and theological fuses. A consistent two-factor view cannot avoid either eternalizing the issue at hand or historicizing it. For it must locate decisive moment of salvation history either in eternity, beyond time and therefore also beyond our reach, thus committing us to an impossible speculative excursion; or it must locate this norm within the historical process with its flux and flow.

Only on a three-factor world view, centered on God's inter-relational Word for covenant-keeping and covenant-breaking, can theology enrich our understanding of the urgency, responsibility, profundity, and surety of our faith responses. The genius of Reformed theology, therefore, comes through at its best in its conscious efforts to do justice to the *relata in relatio*. It speaks not only of covenant *partners*, but also of the covenantal *partnership* which binds the parties together. This mediational emphasis in theology is therefore not a novel idea, foreign to the Reformed tradition. On the contrary, the basic ingredients for such theological renewal are ready at hand.

What I am proposing is simply that we make explicit what is already implicitly there; that we take this assumed, yet often "missing," link and capitalize upon it more fully in working out the doctrine of election/reprobation. Such a perspective, focusing on the crucial religious importance of God's Word as the covenantal bond between God and his world, offers very promising methodological possibilities for restructuring our predestination theology. It recognizes that God holds himself to his Word and that he also holds us to that Word. We can then speak more meaningfully of covenantal faithfulness on the part of God, including both his electing and reprobating Word, and covenantal faithfulness/election or unfaithfulness/reprobation on the part of man.[16] Election/reprobation then comes to play a more integral and stable role within the total context of God's dealings with mankind.

This pivotal position which Scripture ascribes to the Word of God has not been absent from the Calvinist tradition of the past century. In fact, it finds substantial, though largely latent, support there. Kuyper, however, makes the point clearly in these words: "All revelation assumes (1) one who reveals Himself; (2) one to whom he reveals Himself; and (3) the possibility of the required relation between these two."[17] Note also what the seasoned Reformed theologian Bavinck says:

> The Christian world view holds that man is always and everywhere bound by laws set forth by God as the rule for life. Everywhere there are norms which stand above man. They find a unity among themselves and find their origin

---

16. See N. Shepherd, "The Biblical Doctrine of Predestination," *The Banner,* March 21, 1980, pp. 15-16 and March 28, 1980, pp. 18-19 for suggestions along these lines.

17. A. Kuyper, *Principles of Sacred Theology* (Grand Rapids, 1965), p. 257.

and continuation in the Creator and Lawgiver of the universe. These norms are the most precious treasures entrusted to mankind. It is God's decree that these divine ideas and laws be foundations and norms, the interconnections and patterns for all creatures. To live in conformity to those norms in mind and heart, in thought and action, this is what it means most basically to become conformed to the image of God's Son. And this is the ideal and goal of man.[18]

This relational idea has been underscored emphatically by Gerrit Berkouwer since the middle of this century in his monumental *Dogmatic Studies*. Woven tightly into the very fabric of his theology is the *correlative* motif—the intricate correlation between God's work and man's in the way of salvation. This connecting-link concept is so crucial to Berkouwer's thinking, points in the right direction. Yet it never gets firmly structured. It tends to waffle, oscillating back and forth, as though still caught in the bi-polar tension of a two-factor world view which vacillates between divine initiative and human response. Therefore the center of gravity in his theology is subject to gradual shifts from a kind of objectivism (revelation from God transcendent) in the early Berkouwer, through a stress on correlation (God and man in interaction) during his middle years, to a kind of existentialist emphasis (revelation filtered through human experience) during his later career.[19] Thus the structured centrality of God's Word as the pivotal functioning reality within a Bib-

---

18. H. Bavinck, *Christelijke Wereldbeschouwing* (Kampen, 1904), pp. 90-91 (adapted translation—G.J.S.).

19. See H. Berkhof, "De methode van Berkouwers theologie," in *Ex Auditu Verbi* (Kampen, 1965), pp. 40-53.

lical world view fails to exercise a consistently stabilizing effect on Berkouwer's theology.

Still, epistemologically, Berkouwer issues some important reminders on the question at hand in his discussion of the *grensprobleem*. In seeking to respect the boundary-line for theological reflections on predestination, "precisely then the hermeneutic question arises in connection with the very structure of the Biblical witness." Our limiting concepts in theologizing on election may not be borrowed from logic, reason, tradition, or experience. Instead, "the boundary-line lies undoubtedly in God's revelation," which is discoverable through concrete exegesis of the gospel. But is there no Word of God prior to this Word?" Berkouwer suggests an affirmative answer (when pointing to Jesus Christ, whom he calls *de grens* en *de weg* (the "boundary" and the "way"). Only, he warns against making this part of "a metaphysical system for explaining the world"—perhaps betraying his aversion to philosophical considerations. It would have been helpful if a Biblical world view had been allowed to play a more formative role in Berkouwer's theology.[20]

We find a more consistent development of these foundational ideas in the famous Dutch Neo-Calvinist philosopher Herman Dooyeweerd. He holds that "in Christ the heart bows under the *lex* (in its central religious unity and in its temporal diversity, which originates in the creator's holy will), as the universal boundary (which cannot be transgressed) between the Being of God and the meaning of His creation. The transcendent totality of meaning of our cosmos exists only in the religious relation of dependence upon the absolute Being of

---

20. Berkouwer, pp. 15-27.

God."[21] Moreover, of Dooyeweerd's close associate and colleague Vollenhoven, it has been said that his "life-long concern can be summarized, as he himself once did, with these words: God, law, cosmos."[22] This *relatio*, rooted analogically in the covenantal Word of God, should not be construed as a third ontic reality, having an independent existence alongside God and the creation. It is rather the dynamic historical/trans-historical religious point-of-contact and interaction between the revealing God and responding mankind. As Vander Velde puts it, "The creaturely life-line to the Creator is of a religious nature which runs via Golgotha and the empty tomb."[23] Viewing this *relatio* as religious in nature, rather than ontic, should not be construed, however, as rendering it less real than the metaphysical constructs developed by scholastic systems of thought.

To restate the main thesis: our theology of predestination would profit greatly from granting the covenantal Word of God, as a functioning reality and as the religious *relatio* between God and man, a more normative and decisive place as the central operative principle in it.[24]

Since a picture is sometimes worth a thousand words, perhaps keeping the following simple three-factor paradigm in mind will prove to be helpful:

---

21. H. Dooyeweerd, *A New Critique of Theoretical Thought* (Philadelphia, 1969), I, 99.

22. A. Tol, "Vollenhoven as Christian Philosopher," unpublished paper, Calvin College, Grand Rapids, Michigan, 1980, p. 6.

23. G. Vander Velde, "Definitive Theses on the Analogy of Being," unpublished notes, Institute for Christian Studies, Toronto, 1978.

24. See H. E. Runner, who speaks of "the scriptural idea that God puts the Law to, faithfully maintains it" (*The Relation of the Bible to Learning*, Toronto, 1970, p. 27).

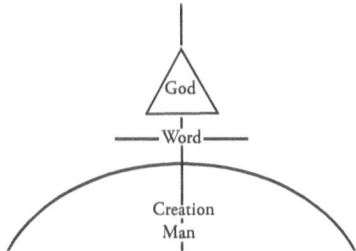

The Biblical Witness

A more significant breakthrough toward such theological renewal could be achieved by taking seriously the analogy used by Augustine, Calvin, and others, which depicts Jesus Christ, God's Word incarnate, as "the mirror of our election." *He* is God's ultimate Word on election/reprobation. We have no Word beyond this Word. He fully reflects the Father's heart and will. In facing up to the Father's electing love in him, we must also, by deflection, account for the question of reprobation. He is the only bridge between God and man. And he is also the boundary—thus far and no farther. "For . . . there is one mediator between God and men, the man Christ Jesus." "No man comes to the Father"—also in settling the question of election/reprobation— "but by Me," says Christ himself. He who has seen Christ has seen the Father. We need look no farther. He is God's first and last Word for the world. All God's dealings with the world—creation, preservation, judgment, redemption, consummation—are through Christ. "All authority"—also in matters of predestination— "is mine," says Jesus. There is "no other name under heaven given among men" to which we can turn for answers. He is the key to election/reprobation. Only a Christocentric theology of predestination will do. "What think ye of the Christ?" is the final and decisive issue on the response side. This is the testimony of Scripture.[25]

---

25. B. Zylstra, "Thy Word Our Life," in *Will All the King's Men* (Toronto, 1972), pp. 154-64.

Election/reprobation is therefore not an "eighth question" to be settled after the "first seven" are settled. It is not as though, having faced up to the questions of believing in Christ, loving him, seeking to serve him, and all the rest, there is still that final, haunting, nagging "eighth" question hanging over one's head: "But am I elect?" Election/reprobation is not an extra, separate issue over and above the others. Rather, the fundamental issue of our relation to God is settled in the process of answering the question, "What then will you do about Jesus?" For we are "elect in Christ." And no one can snatch the elect out of his hand. We need not, nor can we, reach behind the will of God in Jesus Christ in an effort to discover a higher or deeper will of God embedded in his eternal decree. Either he is our "rock and our redeemer," or he is our "stone of stumbling." It is impossible to go over Christ's head directly to the Father, as though there were some way of "going to the top" by making "an end run around the Mediator. What more could God say or do than he has said and done in him? Christ is God's only interface with the world. Hence any theology of election/reprobation apart from this abiding Word of God breaks with the Christocentric world view of Scripture, thereby severing the Biblical connecting link, robbing itself of Biblical concreteness, and finally thrusting itself into the arena of shaky speculation.

Struggling with the Issue

These Christocentric affirmations have not escaped the attention of Reformed theologians. But they have not been fully exploited either. Often the mediating function of the covenantal Word has been suppressed by the powerful influences of scholastic thinking with its two-factor world views. Still, the witness of Scripture to the Word as *relatio* could not be denied. Three-factor mediational motifs therefore continually found their way into Reformed thinking. Often this generated internal struggles. Turretin, for example, concedes, on the one hand, that no decree which "proceeds from (God's) free will can be (called) God absolutely and in himself," although it can be called God relatively according to "the mode of relationship." On the other hand, he holds that the decrees "must be in God essentially," since "they do not differ in reality from the very essence of God" and "are rightly said to be identical with his own essence." Thus, "the decree is nothing other than God himself decreeing."[26] Clearly, Turretin is struggling with the very question at hand, whether God's decree (Word) is to be understood as intrinsic or extrinsic to God himself. The former position goes hand in hand with a two-factor, the latter with a three-factor world view.

A similar ambivalence is evident in Heppe as he intuitively posits a certain distance between God and his decrees, which he calls "acts of (God's) will with a tendency toward externalization." He allows for a difference between "the *decretum* and the *essentia* of God," and speaks of "the *res decreta* which is distinguished from God *realiter*." At the same time Heppe identifies the decreeing Word with "God's very nature."[27]

In Hoeksema, too, we find a theological force at work which tends to burst the bounds of the old two-factor scholastic patterns of thought. As he puts it, God is "absolute, sovereignly above all laws and relationships; and we must forever deal with the relative, because we are under law." Accordingly, "there can never be any knowledge of Him if we must establish the condition necessary for such knowledge." But "the Infinite did reach out into the finite. In this revelation we have an adequate *medium* through which...we derive a real knowledge of God."[28] One could only

---

26. F. Turretin, "*Instituito Theological Elencticae*," in J. W. Beardslee III, *Reformed Dogmatics* (Grand Rapids, 1977), pp. 338-41.

27. H. Heppe, *Reformed Dogmatics* (Grand Rapids, 1978), pp. 136-39, 147, 192.

28. H. Hoeksema, *Reformed Dogmatics* (Grand Rapids, 1966), p. 6.

wish that in Hoeksema, as in other Reformed scholars, this mediational locus given to God's Word-revelation had functioned in a more consistently normative way.

Daane addresses this same issue. He recognizes that scholastic, decretal theology, working within a two-factor world view, renders a meaningful relationship between the decreeing God and a decreed world impossible. He therefore posits "a gap between the reality of God as he necessarily is and the reality of the decree," which "gap is traversed by God's freedom...Thus understood," Daane continues, "the free decision of God's decree bridges Lessing's gap between the eternal and the historical."[29]

Though not broached directly, this same question is implicit in Boer's gravamen concerning reprobation. In his call for a revision of the Canons of Dort, "little or no attention is given to the doctrine of election," and "this was done of set purpose," says Boer. For he holds that the doctrine of reprobation requires "a biblical and theological underpinning" distinctively different from that of election. There are no substantial parallels between them. There is indeed an eternal background to election, for "the salvation of God's people lies anchored in their election from eternity." There is no such background, however, to reprobation, which would compel us to look to "any other area than that of human responsibility within the dimension of history."[30] In Boer's theology, only eternity (election) and history (reprobation) come into play, without reference to God's mediating Word of election/reprobation. Accordingly, his writings are not so much concerned with challenging decretal theology itself as with seeking an adjustment within it. This leads Boer then finally to advocate a decretal understanding of election over against a historical understanding of reprobation.

---

29. J. Daane, *The Freedom of God* (Grand Rapids, 1979), p. 77.

30. H. Boer, in *Agenda of Synod: Christian Reformed Church* (Grand Rapids, 1980), pp. 335-39.

The committee report which was drafted in response to Boer's challenge seeks to hold together in tenuous balance a complex cluster of very intriguing historical, exegetical, and doctrinal ideas. While God's eternal decree is the "efficient cause" of election, it is only the "deficient cause" of reprobation. Reprobation, understood as "preterition" (passing by some), is rooted in an eternal decree; but, understood as "condemnation," it takes place "only on the basis of what men actually do in history," and is "not the result of a decree of God." So, it may be said concerning reprobation that "God rejects those who reject him," although—and this is the mystery of election—"God does not reject *all* who reject him." Thus, reprobation is basically a form of "limited election." It is "a single (complex) decision" in which reprobation is not "a separate decree," but "an action of God which is involved in, and therefore a facet of, the one decree of election." According to Dort, the question "When did (does) all this happen?" is inappropriate. For "the decree in question is an eternal decree of God," which "does not stand in some before-and-after relation to what takes place in history."

It is not easy to bring the varied aspects of this report together into a unified perspective. Many of its insights seem to assume a two-factor, scholastic outlook upon reality. But the report also creates openings for a more promising three-factor view on election/reprobation. It sometimes suggests symmetry, a kind of soft equal ultimacy, between election and reprobation. At other times it stresses a certain disjunction between them. Repeatedly it sets this issue within the Biblical framework of the history of redemption: "…The Canons begin with history—not with the eternal decrees of God, not with the decisions of God from before the foundation of the world, but with our actual, historical, human condition." And "the first thing said about our human condition is that it is the condition of fallenness…All of us, says Dort, are deserving of condemnation…" Yet, also repeatedly, "another level" is introduced, that of eternal decrees. Once again, we are struck by the problem of "the missing link."

I submit that the committee report could have delivered more fully on its promising insights if it had recognized consistently the structured normativity of God's covenantal Word at the very crossroads of the divine-human encounter. Then, in addressing the question "Why does God deal with his creatures the way he does?" instead of answering, "We simply have no answer," confessing only "that there is some good reason, but we do not know the reason" and that "we stand here before mystery," an appeal could be made to God's faithfulness to his abiding Word. The report holds that "God's election includes the means as well as the end," the means being "the preaching and teaching of the Word. But does not that very Word also hold as the means unto judgment? God's Word is "a two-edged sword." Reprobation is the other side of God's decreeing Word of election. Thus understood, the statement in the report that reprobation is "an inescapable aspect or facet of the biblical doctrine of election," could come to its own more clearly. Moreover, the view that "there is an eternal decree on God's part to the effect that he who sins shall perish, unless in some way the sentence of condemnation shall be lifted...," and that "the decree of reprobation (include) God's eternal decision that he who sins shall perish unless his sins are atoned for and forgiven..."—this view would stand firmer if it were anchored in God's mediating Word.[31]

Drawing upon this report, our starting point must be the Biblical witness to the actual, historical, human condition of universal reprobation resulting from mankind's fall into sin. Thus, reprobation is not a second consideration which follows sequentially upon a primary consideration of election. Methodologically, we are to begin not with "limited election," but with the human predicament of un-

---

31. Boer, pp. 359-401.

limited reprobation into which the mass of mankind was corporately plunged as a result of our original sin.[32] Reprobation is therefore not so much a mystery as the awful enigma of covenantal unfaithfulness, from which believers are delivered by God's electing grace. The "greater mystery"[33] is election.[34] Therefore, rather than moving from election to reprobation, we would do better to follow the pattern of the central historical motifs in Biblical revelation, namely, creation/fall/redemption. This means listening, *first*, to God's two-sided Word of election/reprobation as given with creation (his "Yes" with a threatening "No" side to it); *second*, his reprobating Word of judgment in the aftermath of man's fall; and *then* God's redeeming counteraction in the reiteration of his "Yes" Word unto the election of a renewed humanity in Christ Jesus.

New Directions

With the preceding discussion as background, what remains for this concluding section is to sketch briefly the structured contours of this unfolding doctrine of election/reprobation. I offer it within the context of a three-factor world view as an alternative to traditional two-factor views of reality. It was this position which helped set the minds of my troubled students at rest. Let me now outline its main lines of thought in a series of sequenced steps.

(1) The decree of election/reprobation is to be viewed not as intrinsic, but extrinsic to God. Its locus is not God's inner Being, but

---

32. Klooster, p. 8: "The fall and sin are the perspective from which God views the race in his eternal predestination." See also H. Kuiper, *Calvin's Doctrine of Predestination* (Grand Rapids, 1977), pp. 83-86.

33. Boer, pp. 396-97, footnote 23.

34. For a contrasting position, see N. Punt, *Unconditional Good News: Toward an Understanding of Biblical Universalism* (Grand Rapids, 1980), where the author develops the thesis that "the elect are all persons except...."

his outgoing works. It belongs to his revelation, by which he comes out to us as his creatures. We are not to seek to enter into the eternal mind of God, but to listen to his Word. If we view God's predestinating Word as embedded in eternity, it remains forever hidden and inaccessible, for God "dwells in light unapproachable." It is unthinkable apart from his relation to the cosmos. We can reflect theologically on its reality concretely only in a creational way. We must therefore recognize a certain distance between God and his decreeing Word. Otherwise, we slip into Gnostic speculation, get enmeshed in enervating (*supra-* and *infra-lapsarian*) problematics, and turn history into a charade. Our noetic order must comport with the ontic order: God, his Word, the cosmos.

(2) The decree of election/reprobation is anchored in God's covenantal Word. For us there is no other Will behind this Word. God accomplishes all things by this Word of his power. This Word—first spoken in the act of creation, then republished in Scripture, and ultimately personified in Christ—is the mediational bond, link, and religious lifeline between God and the world. It holds a position-in-between: under God, above the cosmos, to which we in our lives must answer. As such it must be given a normatively structured central place in our theology, functioning there as a bridging and limiting concept. It has a concealed depth to it on its God-side (the "secret will" of God). On our side is its revealed dimension (the "revealed will" of God). Of God's Word we must therefore say that on its concealed side there is more than is revealed to us; but it is more of the same. For God's Word is "as good as gold"—as good as God himself. There is continuity between the revealed dimension and the concealed depth of God's Word. Thus the "secret will" and "revealed will" do not cover two different categories of things. Such a part/part approach gets us nowhere, as though some things are "secret" and others "revealed." Rather, there is a "secret" depth and a "revealed" dimension to all God makes known to us. And in his Word God has

opened his whole heart to us— "he who has seen (Christ) has seen the Father," for "in him was revealed the fullness of the Godhead bodily." Whatever lies outside of this is contraband. But most importantly, this decreeing Word, this *relatio* which holds the *relata* (God and the world) together, is a completely sufficient revelation. Seeking a detour around this Word ends either in eternalism or historicism. Apart from this *analogia* between Creator and creature, theology becomes either anthropocentric or theocentric without a Christocentric focus.

(3) For the doctrine of predestination this means that the bridging Word of God stands from the beginning as the electing/reprobating Will of God. And it will so stand to the end. It has both a "sunny side" and a "shadowy side" to it. From the dawn of history, it embraced both God's "Yes" and his "No." It is both a forthright affirmation and a warning negation. Reprobation was not a Word added later as an afterthought. It, too, is original. "Obey me," God said—his Word of election. "Or else," said God in the same breath—his Word of reprobation. Reprobation is the "or else" side of God's love command. Recall Genesis, "God saw everything that he had made, and behold, it was very good"; so "eat freely of every tree"—God's Word of election. But we must not overlook the other side of the same story, "But of the tree of the knowledge of good and evil you shall die"—God's Word of reprobation. See Deuteronomy 30:15-20 for a further unfolding of this same revelation. From the start, therefore, God's two-sided Word of election/reprobation was real and vocal and active. All the elements of that covenantal Word were in place from creation onward: the promise, the condition, the reward, and the penalty. It was a matter of life (election) and/or death (reprobation).

(4) By our corporate fall into sin, with all mankind, brought down upon us God's "or else" Word. As a result, in Adam, our rep-

resentative head, we all became reprobate. That required no added decree on God's part; it is a consequence given with, and built into God's original and abiding Word. God was simply executing faithfully his part in the everlasting covenant. His Word, "sharper than any two-edged sword," descended in judgment. Condemnation came to rest upon all men (hence the great relief of Romans 8:1— "no condemnation"). God does justice to human responsibility. His Word, which "does not return empty," placed the whole human race under the universal sentence of reprobation. Therefore, we may not underestimate the radical effects of the fall. It is the "sufficient cause" of reprobation. It brings on the effectuation of the "No" side of God's Word. True to that Word, God rejects all who (continue to) reject him.

(5) Election, however, is just as great a reality as reprobation. By his electing grace God reaffirms the original intent of his Word. He does not (continue to) reject all who reject him. He reiterates the "Yes" side of his decreeing Word. Through the enabling power of the Spirit, who "blows where he wills," the affirmative side of God's Word overcomes the reprobating effect of the negative side of his Word. God's good Word is bound to have its way with the world. For God wills a renewed humanity within a renewed creation. Both are now "groaning in travail—together, awaiting their redemption." A fallen creation restored—that is the front side of God's Word triumphing in sovereign grace over the universal judgment leveled by the backside of God's Word. The same well-meant Word of reconciliation comes to all men. Why do some continue to reject it? That is the enigma of reprobation. Why do others come to accept it? That is the real mystery, the mystery of election. The ultimate reference point for both is the ever-faithful Word of God. There is mystery enough on our side of God's Word without seeking it in eternal decrees within the mind of God himself beyond the Word which he has given.

(6) This view of election/reprobation honors the basic thrust of trinitarian teaching in the Scriptures—the God who is "above all" (Father), and "through all" (Son), and "in all" (Holy Spirit). Though every work of God is pervasively the work of all three persons, various works are ascribed prevailingly to one or another person in the triune God. Accordingly, Scripture relates the principle of initiation to the Father, the principle of mediation to the Son (the mediating Word in both creation and redemption), and the principle of implementation to the Holy Spirit.

(7) In sketching this alternative view, we must take into account certain classic passages in Scripture on the doctrine of predestination. As samples, think of the Biblical references to "being elect in Christ from before the foundation of the world" (Eph. 1:4), to the crucifixion of Jesus being "according to the definite plan and foreknowledge of God" (Acts 3:23), to inheriting "the kingdom prepared for you from the foundations of the world" (Matt. 25:34), and to the "good works, which God prepared beforehand, that we should walk in them" (Eph. 2:10). What are we to make of such texts? Do they not, as often assumed, point unmistakably to eternal decrees in the mind of God? They certainly do confirm Christian conviction that there is a deeper background to history. Things don't just happen. But is a decretalist interpretation our only choice? The question of the meaning of such passages cannot be settled simply by a positivistic method which limits itself to an empirical study of the exegetical data provided in Scripture. Larger issues come into play. The way we read such lines in Scripture depends largely on the hermeneutic glasses we wear in approaching Scripture, on the pre-understanding we bring to it, on the world view into which we integrate our interpretation of such Biblical givens. My present contention is that the demands of such Biblical teaching can be more properly, adequately, and meaningfully satisfied within the framework of a three-factor than a two-factor world view. Such references to pre-temporal,

trans-historical reality do not compel us to reach all the way back into God's eternity. (Obviously, we are stumbling here over our own language, being limited in every way by the horizon of our creaturely experience.) Taking the covenantal Word as our ultimate confessional reference point discloses adequately the meaning of such Biblical passages. God's Word is his decree. We need not reach back any further than that.

(8) The thesis here being developed helps put the question of "double predestination," as advocated by Augustine and many theologians after him, in a better Biblical light. It seeks to honor as a right insight the idea that God maintains his sovereignty in reprobation as well as in election. A three-factor world view offers potential for handling this question of "double predestination" in a way which overcomes many of the disturbing problems inherent in a two-factor world view. It does so by anchoring both sides of the issue in God's sovereign mediating Word of election/reprobation rather than by driving them back into a set of eternal decrees. Thus, it allows us to honor both the structural commonality (the same Word is "a savor of life unto life" and "a savor of death unto death") and the directional antithesis ("I will put enmity") involved in God's one decreeing Word of election/reprobation.

(9) Similarly, this three-factor view opens up the possibility of taking a fresh look at the question of "equal ultimacy." This idea doubtless also carries with it a certain right insight. It is intended to resist theological reflection which, on the one hand, eternalizes election, while, on the other hand, historicizing reprobation. In the measure that the traditional idea of "equal ultimacy" arises out of the context of a two-factor world view, however, its choices are severely limited. The decisive touchstone must then be either in God or in man. Its intent is clearly to honor God's sovereignty over all, reprobation as well as election. God has a hand in both, an equal hand. Such thinkers sense intuitively, and rightly, that God's involvement

in the lives of men cannot be simply reduced to or absorbed into the historical drama. The norm cannot be pulled down into creation. The only option left then is to locate the norm eternally in the inner Being of God. Thus, election and reprobation get incorporated in the rigorous symmetry of a decretal theology.

The three-factor framework of reference for dealing with our theology of predestination offers relief in the midst of such troublesome problems. Locating the revealed norm not in eternity, not in history, but in God's mediating Word recognizes a certain kind of equal ultimacy in the question at hand. God's Word is the one Word of election/reprobation, his love command: "obey me" (election) and its other side, "or else" (reprobation). The two sides of this one Word are equally ultimate in the sense that they were given simultaneously as integrally constitutive aspects of the single, abiding Word of God. Yet, there is also a certain non-parallel, non-equal, non-symmetrical connection between them. For the "Yes" side of God's Word reveals his original intent for the world ("I will be your God, you be my people"), the ceaselessly ringing affirmation of the gospel ("God was in Christ reconciling the world unto himself"), and the final destiny of creation ("all in all"). Election echoes the overtone of God's Word ("not wishing that any should perish") and reprobation the undertone ("depart from me"). As the two sides of God's single Word of love, reprobation is a revelation of his justice and election a revelation of his mercy.

PART THREE

Politics

"*The living and powerful Word of God sets us in the light of the Truth: it discloses to us that our life in its integral wholeness is religion. Christian political life is therefore an aspect of our single-hearted life-walk before God.*

But the Word of God does not merely reveal to us what our life is; by the grace of God it also begets us to new life. That is, it makes life-service of God again a reality (in principle).... Our political life is properly seen only when it is viewed as one aspect of our whole-hearted God-testedness, which God Himself has given back to us in his Son."

— H. Evan Runner, *Scriptural Religion and Political Task*, pp. 162-3.

James W. Skillen

Politics, Pluralism,
and the Ordinances of God

Dr. H. Evan Runner's book *Scriptural Religion and Political Task* was one of the first that helped me to begin thinking normatively (out of principle) about a Biblical view of political and social life. "The Christian," he said, "may not accept as norm anything other than what God has ordained for the peculiar 'life' of the State. Accordingly, the Christian political task is to come to a recognition of that specific aspect of authority which God in His creation-ordinance delegated to the State."[1] But, as Runner pointed out later in the book, "Everywhere we look we neither hear nor see anything of a people of God, an Order of Creation, the Office of man restored in Christ, but only find our Christian people scattered in all camps making use of the usual tools of the [political] trade.... What, indeed, is the meaning of all this?"[2]

The key to a revival of Christian social and political life today must be a revived understanding of God's ordinances—God's normative will for all of life, including politics. We are grateful that H. Evan Runner helped to introduce many of us to a tradition of Christian thought and life which has led to a revival of concern for God's ordinances for all of life.

---

1. *Scriptural Religion and Political Task* (Toronto, 1974), p. 36.
2. Runner, p. 109.

The centuries between the Protestant Reformation and the French Revolution were marked by both religious vitality and a decline in Christian influence in many areas of social and cultural life. That might sound paradoxical, but the seeming paradox can be understood if we take note of what Christians were doing and how they were doing it during that time. At the risk of overgeneralization, I want to offer the following brief account or characterization.

Until the time of the French Revolution, both Protestant and Roman Catholic Christians possessed an outlook on life that was rooted in centuries of medieval tradition. Christians saw themselves as *riding through history* on their way toward a supernatural destiny. The various social structures and patterns that defined their lives were accepted, for the most part, as the natural and God-given "furniture" of *this* world. The institutional church was the primary vehicle which carried them toward their ultimate destiny in the Kingdom of God. As Christopher Dawson put it,

> ...it hardly entered into men's minds that the existing order could be radically transformed. The European social order was an organic development—the result of centuries upon centuries of unconscious growth. The family and the state, kingship and authority, the different orders and classes with their functions and privileges, were not artificial creations. They had always been there and had gradually changed their form under the influence of new circumstances and different environments. And thus they were regarded as part of the natural order, ordained by God, and were accepted as men accepted the changes of the seasons and the other laws of nature.[3]

---

3. Christopher Dawson, *The Gods of Revolution: An Analysis of the French Revolution* (New York, 1972), pp. 10-11.

When the conviction began to grow toward the end of the Middle Ages that the church was corrupt and heading in the wrong direction, it brought forth tremendous internal reform efforts. The most visible of those efforts occurred in the sixteenth-century, and we now refer to them as the Reformation and the Counter-Reformation. The church had to be reformed, Protestants believed, so that it could continue to serve as the proper vehicle of orthodox Christian faith. Political, economic, and other social consequences flowed from the reform efforts, but those consequences were not the primary preoccupation of most Protestants. The major focus of attention in Protestant circles for the next several centuries was on the character of the church and its confession, and even that concern suffered frequent derailments into dead orthodoxy and hypocrisy.[4]

With what now appears to have been an almost sudden shock, the French Revolution burst upon the European scene at the end of the eighteenth-century. One of the most striking revelations brought forth by the Revolution was that human beings do not simply ride through history, but actually *make history*. The revolutionaries, in fact, believed so strongly in their own autonomous power and freedom to make history that they thought they could start almost from scratch in doing so.

It is to Groen van Prinsterer's credit, early in the nineteenth-century, that he was one of the first modern Protestants to begin to reflect with deep seriousness on the meaning of human history-shaping power in this world. He saw that Christians were mistaken in thinking of themselves primarily as members of a church that rides through history. That was part of the problem with Christianity as it had existed for so many centuries. The revival of faith during the

---

4.   This is the charge of Groen van Prinsterer and other revived Calvinists in nineteenth-century Holland about whom we will see more below.

Reformation, said Groen, "eventually expired in dead orthodoxy and hypocrisy and moral decline, and...room was thus made for unbelief to spread in, especially among the classes whose mental habits predominantly influence the progress of ideas. It is this unbelief which brought about the Revolution."[5] "What had become of the warmth and fervour of the evangelical persuasion, which earlier had borne so much fruit in deeds of faith? In its stead we find the spectacle of narrow superstition, or intolerant hypocrisy or fondness from mere tradition for forms of doctrine."[6]

Christians ought to see themselves as people called by God to *make* history according to his will, Groen believed.[7] Only with such an attitude would Christianity truly live. As Groen gained insight into this simple truth, he began to recognize that different, competing spirits were at work in the shaping of history. And the spirit of the French Revolution was at odds with the Spirit of Christ in all areas of life.[8] The Christian battle could not be carried on simply by preserving an orthodox church in the world, but would have to be carried on in politics and education, in journalism and science.

Recognizing that God by his Spirit was calling Christians out of their somewhat passive journey *through* "secular" history, Groen urged his fellow Christians to reread the Scriptures in order to understand the responsibility that the people of God have to shape the

---

5. From the translation of part of Groen's *Ongeloof en Revolutie* prepared by Harry Van Dyke and Donald Morton: *Lectures VII and IX from Unbelief and Revolution* (Amsterdam, 1975), p. 39. The edition of the complete Dutch volume to which I will be referring is *Ongeloof en Revolutie*, edited by H. Smitskamp (Franeker, no date).

6. Groen, *Lectures VIII and IX from Unbelief and Revolution*, pp. 7-8.

7. See especially the closing pages of *Ongeloof en Revolutie*, pp. 322-27.

8. Groen, *Lectures VIII and IX from Unbelief and Revolution*, pp. 17-18.

history of this world to the glory of God.[9] Just as a declining and corrupt church in the Middle Ages occasioned the Reformation, so the shock of the Revolution was one ingredient in the revival of Calvinism in northern Europe in the nineteenth-century.

With this issue of human responsibility for shaping history, we confront one of the most important challenges of modernity. It is one thing for people to try to adjust themselves to a seemingly unchanging order of nature; it is something else for them to contribute to the continuing creative changes in human life. To see themselves as the makers and shapers of history carries with it important assumptions. The revolutionaries held one set of assumptions: human beings are endowed with certain inalienable rights, including the freedom to govern themselves as they see fit. Social and political life should consist of whatever free individuals make of those areas of life. The guiding principle is the promotion of each person's freedom and autonomy.

That set of assumptions, as we know, has become the basic framework for thought and action in the modern world. Even Christians tend to accept that view of social and political life. After all, it seems pious enough to believe that God endowed human beings with sacred worth as individuals and that each should be as free as possible to live his or her life. The problem, however, is that this view of history and human responsibility acknowledges no principles or rules for life that do not flow out of the autonomous personality.

---

9. Groen did not entirely free himself from the older attitude which accepted past historical patterns and institutions as a revelation of the will of God. For a criticism of the "historicism" and "organicism" in Groen, see the excellent article by Herman Dooyeweerd, "Het Historisch Element in Groen's Staatsleer," in H. Smitskamp et al., *Groen's "Ongeloof en Revolutie": Een Bundel Studiën* (Wageningen, 1949), pp. 118-37.

Autonomy means that the "self" claims to be the only rightful "law-maker" for its own life. Autonomy means being a law unto oneself.

The revival of Calvinism, expressed in the life work of Groen van Prinsterer and then of Abraham Kuyper, was a fundamental challenge to that basic liberal and revolutionary outlook of modernity.[10] True human freedom and responsibility in history, they asserted, is possible only through submission to *God's ordinances*.[11] Human beings cannot escape the "heteronomous" character of creaturely life. The true law of life comes from outside the human will; it comes from another—from the will of God. That is what "heteronomy" means. The heteronomous character of God's will stands in direct opposition to all claims of human autonomy.

The key to human responsibility in history, then, as Kuyper saw it, is not for human creatures to try to hold on forever to seemingly unchanging patterns of social life; nor should they launch out into the future with the conviction that they are free to create social and political life in any autonomous ways they choose. Rather, human beings must give shape to an ever unfolding creation by seeking to respond obediently to God's ordinances for different areas of life. Moreover, this kind of responsibility is not simply an option that Christians may choose to pursue if they want to do so while they ride through history on their way to another world. God, through his common grace that extends to the whole world, is calling all creatures, his people above all, to fulfill their creaturely callings. The

---

10. Regularly Kuyper criticized the spirit and consequences of liberalism and the Revolution. See Dirk Jellema, "Abraham Kuyper's Attack on Liberalism," *Review of Politics*, 19 (1957), 472-85.

11. This language is everywhere in Kuyper's writings, but see especially the section, "Ordinantiën Gods," in his *Ons Program* (Amsterdam, 1879), pp. 116-29. Also see Kuyper's *Lectures on Calvinism* (Grand Rapids, 1961), pp. 70-71.

Christian life consists of *obedience* to God's ordinances, and not merely of an orthodox confession *about* God's ordinances.[12]

Abraham Kuyper believed with Groen that Biblical Calvinism could make a major, systematic contribution to life in the modern world.[13] But Calvinism itself would have to be continually reforming. Reformed Christianity was not a pure and clean package that could simply be protected and handed down through an otherwise corrupt and changing history. Calvinism had to be liberated from various unbiblical chains that still held it in check. Not the least of the bondages in which Calvinism found itself in Kuyper's day was the old Roman and medieval view of politics which did not allow for the legitimate unfolding of political life in accord with God's ordinance of public justice. The unhealthy alliance of church and state which, back in Calvin's day, had led to such things as the burning of Servetus at the hands of the Genevan government because of his heretical convictions was something from which Calvinism had to be set free. As Kuyper put it:

The duty of the government to extirpate every form of false religion and idolatry was not a find of Calvinism, but dates from Constantine the Great, and was the reaction against the horrible persecutions which his pagan predecessors on the imperial throne had inflicted upon the sect of the Nazarene. Since that day this system had been defended by all

---

12. Kuyper's most systematic treatment of common grace is in his three-volume work *Gemeene Gratie* (Amsterdam, 1902-04). The best article on this subject is S. U. Zuidema's "Common Grace and Christian Action in Abraham Kuyper," in Zuidema's *Communication and Confrontation: A Philosophical Appraisal and Critique of Modern Society and Contemporary Thought* (Toronto, 1972), pp. 52-105. See also Henry R. Van Til, *The Calvinistic Concept of Culture* (Grand Rapids, 1964).

13. See especially Kuyper's *Lectures on Calvinism*, pp. 9-40.

Romish theologians and applied by all Christian princes. In the time of Luther and Calvin, it was a universal conviction that that system was the true one....

Notwithstanding all this, I not only deplore that one stake, but I unconditionally disapprove of it, yet more so if it were the expression of a special characteristic of Calvinism, but on the contrary as the fatal after-effect of a system, grey with age, which Calvinism found in existence, under which it had grown up, and from which it had not yet been able entirely to liberate itself.[14]

Out of this nineteenth-century revival of Calvinism in the Netherlands, we get one of the most helpful interpretations of the modern secularization process. On the one hand, Kuyper, along with many Catholics and other Protestants, was a vigorous opponent of secularization, if by "secularization" we understand the outworking of the spirit of liberalism which claims that human beings have no master in history, no ordinances from God to bind them, and that they are autonomous in their freedom to shape politics, art, science, education, and all of culture. But unlike most Catholics and many Protestants of his day, Kuyper was a strong promoter of the secularization process if by "secularization" we mean the freeing of different life spheres from ecclesiastical control.[15] Kuyper believed that politics, art, science, education, and other areas of life should be free to unfold in obedience to God's ordinances. Each sphere of life had to be free of direct control by any other so that each could learn obedience to God's special ordinances for each area of life. Artists must be free to obey God's norms for art; they must not be locked up into obedience to what ecclesiastical officials believe to be good art. Teachers

---

14. Kuyper, p. 100.
15. Kuyper, pp. 46-54, 59-66.

and scholars must be free to respond obediently to God's ordinances of truth for the entire creation; they must not be under orders to teach and publish only what ecclesiastical office bearers approve as scientific truth.[16]

Clearly this whole framework of thought presupposes that the open field of human action is not a field without boundaries or an arbitrary openness without limits. On the contrary, the dynamic, creative, supple character of human action is always either obedient or disobedient to divine ordinances. The norms are not created by autonomous individuals. Nor can those norms be fulfilled by some central, controlling authority on earth, be it a church, a state, or a multinational corporation. The development of diverse human talents reveals the true character of creatures who are called to action, called to respond, by a multiplicity of creational ordinances or norms.[17] God is the author of human creatures who cannot escape family life, who cannot avoid speaking and singing in complex languages, who would not know themselves apart from intricate economic exchanges, who are driven to build amazingly sophisticated political systems, and who do a host of other things both individually and in communities. Blindness to the full, norm-laden reality of

---

16. Kuyper, *Souvereiniteit in Eigen Kring* (Amsterdam, 1880). On this subject of "sphere sovereignty" and also on some other important themes, see the two articles on Herman Dooyeweerd's philosophy by Jacob Klapwijk in *The Reformed Journal* (February, 1980, pp. 12-15, and March, 1980, pp. 20-24).

17. On the meaning of historical, cultural responsiveness to divine norms or ordinances in the sense in which I am discussing it here, see Herman Dooyeweerd, *Roots of Western Culture: Pagan, Secular, and Christian Options*, translated and edited by Mark Vander Vennen and Bernard Zylstra (Toronto, 1979), pp. 66-72. See also Bob Goudzwaard, *Capitalism and Progress: A Diagnosis of Western Society*, translated and edited by Josina Van Nuis Zylstra (Toronto and Grand Rapids, 1979), pp. 204-14.

social institutions and organizations is due to an individualistic (nominalistic) predisposition that does not allow one to *see* reality. From the other side, every attempt to collectivize that social diversity for the purpose of economic efficiency, or for national solidarity, or for some imagined aesthetic or social harmony, reveals blindness to the same reality. Singing cannot be economically collectivized. Thinking cannot be politically confined. Family love cannot be submerged in ecstatic worship or in cultic discipline.

It all sounds so simple; it seems so obvious; but this view of life, which we might call "principled pluralism," has captured very little attention in the West, and it has nowhere been more systematically articulated than in the Kuyper tradition, especially by those associated with Herman Dooyeweerd and D. H. T. Vollenhoven.[18] The acknowledgement of divine ordinances as norms for a diversity of social spheres is only slightly and occasionally reflected in our North American civil, criminal, and constitutional laws. Teaching of the social sciences in most Christian as well as non-Christian colleges and universities does *not* begin and end with inquiry about the character and demands of God's ordinances.[19]

But, you see, the powerful import of acknowledging God's ordinances is precisely that we must work at *obeying* them; in other

18. An excellent introduction to Dooyeweerd's Kuyperian Calvinism is his *Roots of Western Culture*, noted above. See also L. Kalsbeek, *Contours of a Christian Philosophy: An Introduction to Herman Dooyeweerd's Thought*, edited by Bernard Zylstra and Josina Zylstra (Toronto, 1975).

19. Especially valuable on modern social thought is Chapter 8 of Dooyeweerd's *Roots of Western Culture*, "The Rise of Social Thought," pp. 189-218, and the first five chapters of Goudzwaard's *Capitalism and Progress*, pp. 1-54, where he discusses the emergence of secularized rationalism in the West between the Renaissance and the French Revolution.

words, we must shape history according to those ordinances and not merely ride through history proclaiming that they exist. The only option besides obedience is disobedience. Justice must be *done* by us, not merely spoken as a word from our lips. Stewardship is God's demand upon our farms and shops and corporations, not simply a word to be used for rhyming our Sunday hymns. Nurturing love calls our homes and schools to account; it is not just a term to help us organize our thoughts at prayer time.

The power behind the idea of "sphere sovereignty" is not Abraham Kuyper's genius or some Dutch philosophical peculiarity. It is rather the simple but overwhelming power of God's voice speaking forth through his Son in all his sovereignty. Sphere sovereignty means nothing more sophisticated yet nothing less important than the fact that God is the only sovereign of this world and that all his ordinances must be obeyed.[20] Individuals are not sovereign; the state is not sovereign; the church is not sovereign. God alone is sovereign. And that God—Father, Son, and Holy Spirit—calls his creatures to a host of different tasks, most of which can be fulfilled only in communities, through institutions, by means of organized societies, each having its own proper offices of authority and accountability.[21] Thus, each task, each special human community, each peculiar and precious association, is never simply at our disposal. It is guarded by the Sovereign and granted its own subordinate sovereignty in the same way that

---

20. On the different meanings of sphere sovereignty, see Dooyeweerd, *Roots of Western Culture*, pp. 40-60.

21. Dooyeweerd's detailed, philosophical exposition of this Kuyperian social philosophy is in Vol. 3 of his *A New Critique of Theoretical Thought*, translated by David H. Freeman and H. De Jongste (Philadelphia, 1957). For a brief introduction, see my "Herman Dooyeweerd's Contribution to the Philosophy of the Social Sciences," *Journal of the American Scientific Affiliation*, 31 (March 1979), 20-24.

every sparrow of the air and every lily of the field is called into existence and guarded by the heavenly Father.

The individualistic and collectivist humanists blaspheme God by shouting autonomy and turning their backs on the reality of God's creation. Christians violate God's commandments when they confess with pious voice that God is sovereign, but then cast their votes, buy their homes, sell their stocks, or run their schools and colleges by considering only the demands of the American way of life, or asking only about the requirements of a healthy profit margin, or looking only to the habits and expectations of tradition.

Dooyeweerd speaks of the power of the Word of God as the radical challenge of the basic motive or ground motive of the Christian religion. That Word "lays full claim on one's attitude to life and thought." It "moulds our view of history." It "unmasks today's dangerous community ideology and its totalitarian tendencies." The Christian ground motive of God's Word "posits the unshakable firmness of God's creation order in opposition to the so-called dynamic spirit of our times which refuses to recognize firm foundations of life and thus sees everything 'in change.'"[22]

Consider the cost of taking this radically scriptural Christianity seriously. Ask yourself which side you must join in the tense spiritual battle of our times. Compromise is not an option. A middle-of-the-road stance is not possible. Either the ground motive of the Christian religion works radically in our lives or we serve other gods. If the antithesis is too radical for you, ask yourself whether a less radical Christianity is not like salt that has lost its savour. I state the antithesis as radically as I do so that we may again experience the full double-edged sharpness and power of God's Word. You must experience the anti-thesis as a spiritual storm that

---

22.   Dooyeweerd, *Roots of Western Culture*, pp. 108-109.

strikes lightning into your life and that clears the sultry air. If you do not experience it as a spiritual power requiring the surrender of your whole heart, then it will bear no fruit in your life. Then you will stand apart from the great battle the antithesis always instigates. You yourself cannot wage this battle. Rather, the spiritual dynamic of the Word of God wages the struggle *in* us and pulls us along despite our "flesh and blood."

My effort to impress upon us the scope of the antithesis is also directed at committed Christians. I believe that if Christianity had held fast to the ground motive of God's Word, and to it *alone*, we never would have witnessed the divisions and schisms that plagued the source of all fundamental schisms and dissensions is the sinful inclination of the human heart to weaken the integral and radical meaning of the divine Word.[23]

The basic thrust of Dooyeweerd's comment is that Christians can overcome their accommodation to medieval traditionalism and to liberal/conservative or socialist radicalisms only by taking God's Word seriously. And that Word illuminates and spotlights the creation ordinances for social life which we must then heed. His point, put very simply, is that there is no way to develop or preserve principled, structural pluralism in social and political life without practicing creative, communal, self-critical responsiveness to God's ordinances. Protection of private property and a free press is not sufficient for public justice. Advocating the rule of law, or seeking human rights for individuals, or pressing for educational freedom is not enough. There is no common secular tradition to which we can pledge our troth as Christians and still hope to have truly principled pluralism. It is not enough for us as a Christian community to work

---

23. Dooyeweerd, p. 109.

at developing our homes, churches, and Christian schools in response to God's Word while merely learning to adjust to the major political, economic, and media decisions being made in our society according to other principles.

The liberal/conservative tradition seeks to build society and politics in obedience to a norm of freedom and sovereignty for individuals. It ends up with unresolved tensions between its sovereign individuals and its powerful governments.[24] It ends up, for example, with both state and family claiming prior rights to educate children.[25] It opens the way for the moneyed classes to control most of the public law-making powers. It can find no way to give significant public room to small groups such as American Indians. It finds itself unable to clarify in public law the substantive identity and tasks of such basic institutions as family, school, church, business enterprise, and the state itself.

Just as pragmatically, the socialist and statist traditions attempt to build the social order in obedience to norms of communal solidarity, economic equality, or national security. Contradictions in these systems also abound. National unity is bought at the expense of individual lives and social diversity. The diversity that does exist exists by the grace of the central government or ruling party. National progress as defined by the central authorities becomes the standard that qualifies and directs every occupation. The self-established norms of both traditions are blatantly substituted for the ordinances of the Creator.

The people of God cannot simply ride through a history that is being shaped by these spirits and traditions. And they certainly must

---

24. See the especially helpful discussion of this tension between freedom and self-imposed bondage in the liberal/conservative tradition in Goudzwaard, *Capitalism and Progress*, pp. 142-61.

25. See the position paper "Justice for Education," published by the Association for Public Justice, Box 5769, Washington, D.C., 20014.

not continue to accommodate themselves to these tension-filled systems and expect that God's ordinances will still shine through in their deeds to brighten a dark world. Christians have only one healthy option, and that is to take God's Word so seriously that they refuse to live by any other ordinances or by any other hope than the ordinances of creation and the hope of the Gospel.

Such a response will mean facing up to the shocking fact that the liberal/conservative and socialist traditions are facing a crisis of immense proportions today. The faith of French revolutionaries in their own autonomous power to shape history by starting from scratch is a faith that is now turning sour for many. The humanistic confidence that progress can forever be made on earth without obedience to God's ordinances is a confidence that is turning into despair. Bob Goudzwaard explains that:

> The theme of progress has penetrated western society so profoundly because it was able to present itself as a *faith* in progress, as a religion of progress. That is also why the present-day crisis of the idea of progress has the depth of a crisis of *faith*. There is more at stake than a somewhat reduced confidence in "progress" on the part of western man. His whole life perspective has undergone a shock. The unfulfilled promises of progress have brought about an emptiness, a vacuum, with respect to the *meaning* of life and society. Many among us even experience the demise of the idea of progress as a kind of divine betrayal. The very thing in which we had placed all our trust is turning against us to devour us. And what does one have left when one's gods betray him?

If this observation is correct, then we find ourselves at a very critical juncture in the development of western civilization. No society or civilization can continue to exist without having found an answer to the question of meaning. The emptiness created by the death of the god of progress must be filled with something else. But what will that be? It seems that we have two choices: either the vacuum will be filled by a new, awe-inspiring myth, possibly built around the leaders of a central and large-scale world authority, who are authorized by their populations to direct all available technical, economic, and scientific means to new objectives with which to assault both heaven and earth; or else there will take place a turnaround to Christians and non-christians together, a turnaround which directs us to the Torah or normativity which the Creator of heaven and earth has given to this world as its meaning from the beginning, and which points forward to a new earth, coming with the return of the crucified One. Without such a turnaround I can hardly imagine a real and permanent disclosure of our western civilization.

Therefore our deepest choice appears to lie between an enslaving autonomy and a liberating heteronomy, or, to put it another way, between restricting utopias and the inspiring openness of the biblical *eschaton*.[26]

The work of Groen van Prinsterer, Abraham Kuyper, Herman Dooyeweerd, Bob Goudzwaard, and many others in that line is no more finished and complete, no more sufficient and normative for us today than was the work of Calvin for Kuyper, or of Augustine for Calvin. Groen was too much caught by historicistic traditionalism. Kuyper never resolved problems in his understanding of the relation between an organic nature and God's ordinances, between common grace and special grace. Dooyeweerd left unresolved problems with his interpretations of the historical unfolding process and the relationship of time to eternity. Goudzwaard admits

---

26. Goudzwaard, *Capitalism and Progress*, pp. 248-49.

the tentative and uncertain character of his proposals about the responsibility of modern economic enterprises and the relationship of government to the economy.

But the question is not whether we must become disciples of Kuyper and his followers. The question is: Will we take up the historical struggle of our day in the spirit of Biblical revival? Will we become self-critical about our illegitimate accommodations to the spirits and traditions of our time? Will we quit trying to *ride through* history and begin trying to *shape* history in obedience to divine ordinances? This is our only calling—to serve God and neighbors according to the Creator's ordinances fulfilled in Christ. This is also the only way that we can contribute to a healthy unfolding of a just society—one that will be respectful of the true plurality of God-given associations, institutions, and social relationships.

I am indebted to Dr. Runner, who helped to open the "Kuyper tradition" to me in North America. A thankful response to him requires that we get to work in politics and political science (as well as in other areas of life and other disciplines) in order to understand and obey God's ordinances. That work is an exciting and inspiring service to the Lord.

RICHARD J. MOUW

Providence and Politics

IN HIS STUDY OF the Christian belief in "divine providence," G. C. Berkouwer asks, "On what grounds is it considered possible to perceive God's finger in special events in his story?"[1] This is an important question for all of us who believe that God rules providentially over the historical process, and who believe further that this confession ought not to foster attitudes of quietism, historical resignation, or fatalism.

Everything that happens in history happens within the scope of God's sovereign rule. This has been the universal confession of the historic Christian churches. It is a confession which has been given special emphasis in the Reformed tradition. But this confession has seldom been put forth as a reason for concluding that all events in history should elicit our unqualified approval or acquiescence. God also calls his people to obedience, an obedience which requires them to say, on occasion, "This should not be" or "We should not have permitted that to happen." On what grounds ought we to make assessments of that sort? How do we discern the patterns of God's rule and leading in history?

These concerns have special significance for those of us who study and assess political events and movements. How do we perceive the finger of God in political history? What are our criteria or

---

1.   G. C. Berkouwer, *The Providence of God* (Grand Rapids, 1952), p. 169.

norms for political approbation and disapprobation? These are important questions for the Christian community, and they will be explored in this present discussion.

The Christian belief in divine providence, then, has important applications to political thought. But there is another link between providence and politics which ought to be noted at the outset. Christian confessional statements concerning divine providence are themselves heavily laced with political language. Typically, discussions of God's providential activity have been divided under two sub-headings: God's "sustaining" activity and his "governing" activity.[2] Thus the two dominant images in discussions of divine providence have been those of nurturing and ruling: God is pictured as a life-giver and a political administrator. These images are rooted in some common Biblical pictures of God as parent and shepherd, Lord and King. Variations on these themes are also dominant in New Testament Christological imagery: Jesus is the good shepherd, the life-giving Lamb, the one who would gather Jerusalem as a mother hen gathers her chicks; and he is the prince of peace, the ruler of the kings of the earth, the Lion of the Tribe of Judah.

At least half of the traditional language of providence, then, has been political language—a pattern which in turn reflects some important Biblical emphases. And we would do well to guard against viewing such Biblical language as "mere metaphor." We must of course appreciate and absorb the sensitivities of a book which is, among other things, a poetic book—picturing the deity as riding upon the winds, ruling the waves, and issuing authoritative commands to the fountains of the deep. But the language of governance and rule in the Bible is not exhausted by its poetic contexts. When the Biblical writers portray God as a king, they very often mean to

---

2.   Berkouwer devotes a chapter to each of these two dimensions of providence; see ibid., Chapters 3 and 4.

emphasize a teaching which has much to do with our attitudes toward flesh-and-blood kings and tangible thrones.

The doctrine of providence, then, is in part a political doctrine. Much the same can be said for the closely related theme—also a favorite of Calvinists—of the *sovereignty* of God. To say that God is "sovereign" is to say that he is a ruler, a mighty potentate. In both cases—i.e., the references to divine sovereignty and to divine providence—the area being referred to includes a set of political concerns, in a fairly straightforward sense of the term *political.*

Reformed Christians have not been unaware of the fact that their commitment to a strong emphasis on God's governing activity, his sovereign Lordship over "all things," has practical political implications. They have not been reluctant to confess that God is presently exercising control over political structures and processes. Indeed, in the Reformed churches a common liturgical salutation is that of the opening verses of the book of Revelation, in which the church is greeted in the name of the One who is "the ruler of kings on earth" (Rev. 1:5). There can be no doubt, furthermore, that many Calvinists have explicitly acknowledged that the "profit" gained by a belief in God's providence, as described in Question and Answer 28 of the Heidelberg Catechism, is among other things a matter of *political* comfort—thus, there is no reason why we cannot paraphrase the Catechism in such a way that it assures us that "we may be patient in political adversity, thankful in political prosperity, and with a view to the political future may have good confidence in our faithful God and Father that no politician shall separate us from his love, since all politicians are so in his hand that without his will they cannot so much as move." Reformed Christians are committed to the confession that God is presently active politically, that he is working out his political purposes in the world.

But while many of us would be quick to acknowledge *that* God is presently working in and through the political processes of his creation, we would be less clear on just *how* he is doing so. Furthermore, this is not merely a problem for Reformed Christians; virtually every confessional tradition affirms a belief in divine providence. Thus, the problem of the "how" of God's present political rule is an ecumenical problem.

How is God acting politically today? Is it possible to discern clear traces of his rule over all things in the present political situation? What is the relationship, properly understood, between providence and politics? These are questions I will reflect upon in what follows.

Most Christians would agree that the patterns of God's sovereign rule are explicit and obvious at several stages in the Biblical record. They are obvious, for example, in God's relationship with the unfallen creation as pictured in the first few chapters of Genesis; God reveals his purposes for human beings through his commandments and in his offer of fellowship, his covenant-partnership, with them. And even the fall of the human race into sin does not obliterate the obvious patterns of divine rule as they bear on mundane political happenings. For in response to human rebellion God surprisingly and graciously renews his pledge of benevolence toward his creation, a pledge that takes a specific political shape when God promises Abraham that from his seed will spring forth nations and kings (Gen. 17:6). Thereafter the Lord God gathers unto himself a special people, the nation of Israel, and he makes his political will and purposes known to his people through a series of theocratic arrangements. In its political life Israel clearly discerns the workings of the divine liberator and judge; sometimes these workings are matters of reward and blessing, and on other occasions they are expressions of divine judgment and wrath. But in all of these matters there are discernible patterns which can be properly described as "the politics of God."

Most Christians would also agree that the patterns become less clear in the New Testament. Here it is not as easy to identify in an unequivocal manner the workings of God among the nations. Because the nation of Israel rejected the Messiah, God forsook it— or at least he ceased to work explicitly and openly through that national vehicle. And so, we, as New Testament Christians, lack a national reference point for discerning the political purposes of God in world events.

This does not mean, however, that God is not working in and through the contemporary political scene. On the contrary, most Christians openly confess that God presently governs all things through the kingship of his Son. The problem is not in believing *that* he rules politically; it is in discerning *how* he rules politically.

Some Christians attempt to resolve the difficulties here by seeming to take a certain delight in *not* knowing how to discern the political movements of God among and within the nations. This retreat into willful ignorance might be taken to be suggested by the Belgic Confession's commentary on the doctrine of divine providence:

> [God's] power and goodness are so great and incomprehensible that He orders and executes His work in the most excellent and just manner, even then when devils and wicked men act unjustly. And as to what He does surpassing human understanding, we will not curiously inquire into farther than our capacity will admit of; but with the greatest humility and reverence adore the righteous judgments of God, which are hid from us, contenting ourselves that we are pupils of Christ, to learn only those things which He has revealed to us in His Word, without transgressing these limits (Article 13).

Here we have an excellent statement of those sentiments which have led many Christians to distinguish between God's "revealed will" and his "secret will." There is much to be said in favor of making such a distinction, and it is difficult to fault the Confession for introducing an acknowledgment of human limitations into its discussion of divine providence. Of course, there are matters that God has chosen to hide from us. And when we come up against such matters, it would be foolish and pretentious, if not also sinful, to attempt to "curiously inquire into" such things, attempting to probe "farther than our capacity will admit of."

The rub comes, of course, when Christians attempt to place the *whole* question of God's workings in politics beyond the boundaries of human comprehension. This is a way of viewing things which I have elsewhere labeled "pious agnosticism."[3] It is not difficult to find Christians actually suggesting that this sort of pious political agnosticism is desirable, even a sign of Christian piety. For example, Gordon Clark tells us that in Romans 13,

> when Paul insists that every soul should be subject to the powers that be, he is evidently removing from individual judgment any question as to a *de jure* as opposed to a *de facto* government. Julius Caesar instituted the Roman imperial system by a criminal *coup d'état*; Augustus also had little claim to a throne other than armed force; and Christians, especially the Jewish Christians of the first century, could easily produce arguments against obeying Rome. It will not be forgotten that one of the catch questions put to Christ was, "Is it lawful to pay tribute to Caesar?" Probably most of the Jews secretly believed that it was unlawful. Christ's answer and Paul's statement are justifications of *de facto* government. The powers that be, i.e., the actually existing powers, are ordained of God.[4]

---

3. See my *Called to Holy Worldliness* (Philadelphia, 1980), Chapter 5. In that chapter I treat similar issues to those in this essay, but in less detail.

4. Gordon Clark, *A Christian View of Men and Things* (Grand Rapids, 1952), p. 140.

Clark provides us here with an excellent statement of pious political agnosticism. He does not mean to suggest that *God* makes no distinctions between *de facto* and *de jure* governments—that is, between governments which *happen* to rule and governments which *rightly* rule. Clark undoubtedly believes that there have been, and are, governments which God simply does not approve of. What Clark is warning against is a pattern of thinking whereby *we* get into the business of distinguishing between *de facto* and *de jure* governments. Such a distinction is for God to make; it is not our business. If God does not like the governments of the Soviet Union and South Africa, he will bring them to ruin in his own mysterious way and in his own good time. But in the meantime, it is proper for Christian citizens of those nations to respect their governments as being ordained of God. To repeat Clark's point: "The powers that be, i.e., the actually existing powers, are ordained of God."

There are, of course, problems with this perspective which come immediately to mind. Are there no conditions under which a Christian may justifiably disobey a government? Clark allows that there are such conditions, in the light of the fact that "the Bible several times makes explicit statements and gives several concrete examples" of civil disobedience—e.g. Peter's refusal to obey the injunction that he desist from preaching the Gospel, as well as the examples of Moses' mother, Daniel, and the three young men who were thrown into the fiery furnace. What these examples have in common is that they have to do with political decrees which "conflict with God's laws."[5]

Clark is correct in pointing to Biblical instances of this sort as relevant for contemporary Christian political discernment. The only problem is that, by raising them, he seems to undercut his own insistence that we cannot make a distinction between *de facto* and *de jure* governments. On his account, we can be sure at least that any gov-

---

5. Clark, p. 143.

ernment which forbids the preaching of the Gospel, or places a ban on Christian worship, ought not to be viewed as having the legitimate authority to set such policies. But then it would seem that we cannot simply leave the business of distinguishing between *de facto* and *de jure* governments up to God after all. For we are required to obey the will of God; and sometimes we are faced with situations, as the apostles were, in which it is impossible to obey both God and human government at the same time.

It is important that we try to get clear about the limits which pious political agnosticism would try to place on Christian attempts to discern the present political activity of Jesus Christ. For example, many of us are convinced that it is wrong for Christians to live in silent approval of governmental policies and social practices which promote racism, nationalism, sexism, consumerism, and militarism. We are convinced that a promotion of such patterns is incompatible with a yearning for the Kingdom of Jesus Christ—and so we believe that it is legitimate, even mandatory, for Christians to speak out against such policies and practices. On the other hand, many proponents of the perspective we are discussing do not agree. Why not? Why do they not believe that these are matters which must be submitted to an aggressive Christian critique?

Their answer, it should now be clear, is not that we cannot make *any* distinctions between governments and policies which God approves of and ones of which he disapproves. For they are prepared to make such distinctions themselves at important points. The important disagreement, then, is over *when* we can make such a distinction. Thus, while it is proper to view a political agnosticism at work in this perspective, it is a *limited* political agnosticism. It is not the case, on this view, that *all* of God's political workings are shrouded in mystery. There are at least some policies in the political arena about which we can say with certainty: "This is something which Christ is working to abolish."

Another way of viewing the political workings of God in history is evident in the thinking of those Christians who operate with a rather clearly defined "church/world dualism." Here a very positive assessment is made of "the politics" of the Christian community, while a very negative assessment is given to political developments within "the kingdoms of this world."

Proponents of such a view place a strong emphasis—and rightly so—on the Christian community as an arena within which persons are called to live in radical obedience to the lordship and kingship of Jesus Christ. The Christian community is viewed as a manifestation of "the new order" of things, an order which will someday hold full sway over the creation, but which presently stands in sharp opposition to the reign of sin.

The political order represented by the national governments of this present world is in the grip of demonic "principalities and powers." These forces are doomed. The cross of Christ sealed their fate, and their rule is one that will end in ruin. The present structures of political authority—and all those forces and movements which oppose those structures by means of violence and coercion—are headed for destruction.

On this view, then, two political processes are unfolding in this present age, under the sovereign will of God. The church, the Christian community, as the manifestation of a people-hood which is being realized under the direct rule of Christ, is a sign of the new order; it is a key element in God's preparation for the new age, the perfected Kingdom of Jesus. This "holy nation" is the only political entity which has legitimate status and which is of lasting significance. This is where God is working out his positive political purposes for the world.

In the kingdoms of this world, on the other hand, we have evidence of God's continuing patience with the fallen structures of his creation. The present-day nations are all in the grip of demonic powers.

They are a part of the order that will soon pass away. If they seem to be alive and strong, it is only because God has chosen, for his own good reasons, to be patient with them—much as the executioner patiently awaits the day on which the sentence of death will be carried out.

There are some contemporary Christians who seem to accept this viewpoint without qualification. Others seem to lean in the direction of this viewpoint, without necessarily being willing to carry out its implications to an extreme. For example, Jim Wallis sometimes suggests what appears to be an unqualified version of this viewpoint, as in this passage:

> In a world that does not know God, the church lives in radical antagonism to the existing order of things. The Bible sees the powers of the world in rebellion against God and in domination over human life. The Bible names the prince of the world as the Devil. The church of Jesus Christ is at war with the systems of the world, not detente, ceasefire, or peaceful coexistence, but at war. The church exists to continually confront the world with a new reality—the kingdom of God—that has invaded the world and taken root in the life of the church as God's new community.[6]

Here there is very little room to work with Clark's distinction between *de jure* and *de facto* government. There is only one *de jure* government—and that consists of those patterns of authority which characterize the new community in which Jesus Christ is consciously affirmed as Lord and King. All other *de facto* governments are just that—*de facto* governments. They have no legitimate authority; they are not positive instruments of God's purposes. They exist only by virtue of God's patience; and they will be destroyed when the new order is ushered in with fullness and power.

---

6.   Jim Wallis, *Agenda for Biblical People* (New York, 1976), p. 132.

On this view, then, God's present government over all things has two basic features. First, God is actively ruling the church through his Son, the Lord and King of the church, Second, for reasons known only to himself, he is exercising patience with the political powers whom he has already defeated. Christian political activity, if it is consistent with this viewpoint, follows this same twofold pattern. We are to submit to the political patterns of the new community of the called-out people of God—actively seeking to bring our lives into conformity to his will for his people. And we are also to imitate God's patience with the political powers of the world. We must live in "subordination" to them—not out of respect for a legitimate authority that they might exercise over our lives, but rather out of a spirit of rebellion against them, a rebellion which manifests itself in a conviction that they do not, after all, "matter," since their doom is sealed.

This perspective fails to account for the fact that the Biblical witness does not *simply* contrast the incoming Kingdom with either "this world" or the "principalities and powers" which dominate the world. The divine rule confronts the world in its fallenness and the powers in their rebelliousness; but the ultimate purpose of this confrontation is not the destruction either of the world or of those powers which exercise authority in the world. Rather, the present confrontation is directed toward the *restoration* of the world in its createdness.

This dualistic perspective seems to present us with a scenario wherein "the world" is headed for destruction while the church awaits the victory. The apostle Paul, however, gives us a very different scenario in Romans 8:19-23: For the creation waits with eager longing for the revealing of the sons of God; for the creation was subjected to futility, not of its own will but by the will of him who subjected it in hope; because the creation itself will be set free from its bondage to decay and obtain the glorious liberty of the children of God. We know that the whole creation has been groaning in travail together until now; and not only the creation, but we ourselves, who have the first fruits of the Spirit, groan inwardly as we wait for adoption."

According to this Pauline picture, the distinction between church and world is not to be understood as consisting of the church's anticipating redemption while the world is moving toward its doom. Rather, the whole creation, including the political network of God's world, is groaning for release from bondage—"and not only the creation, but we ourselves, who have the first fruits of the Spirit." The church and the world groan together in anticipation of release from bondage. The crucial difference between them is that the church groans knowledgeably while the world groans in ignorance. This is the source and nature of the church's "confrontation" with the world.

In an important sense, we must view God's present relationship to "the world" not under the rubric of "patience" but of "preparation." Creation, even political creation, is being prepared for the coming of the Kingdom. Of course, it is not always easy to discern just *how* political life is being prepared for the new order. In what ways, for example, was Watergate an occasion of God's preparatory activity in the political world? How are the angry cries of dispossessed Third World peoples to be rightly viewed as the economic groans of God's creation? In what sense is the struggle for equality of both women and men before the law an anticipation of the new order? These are difficult questions—but they are not all equally difficult. It is possible to discern, or at least to suspect that one is discerning, the preparatory activity of Christ in some of these things.

The two viewpoints which we have discussed thus far share some fundamental assumptions. Not the least of their agreements is on this point: that it is extremely difficult to view the current political scene with the ability to discern clear signs of God's redemptive political activity in that sphere. Proponents of pious agnosticism allow that God may indeed be working in that milieu, rewarding some

kinds of governmental decisions and standing in judgment on others—but they are convinced that it is very difficult for us to be certain about where and how God is pursuing these matters. The dualistic perspective views God's activities among the nations under a
single and comprehensive category: God is exercising *patience* with a
state of affairs that will soon pass away. From both of these perspectives, if there are criteria we can employ which allow us to say, "God
approves of this policy," or "God disapproves of that one," these criteria are intimately related to the way in which governmental policies
affect the life of the church. Both the politically-agnostic variety of
Calvinism and radical dualistic thought would agree, for example,
that Christians must specifically resist political policies that restrict
the preaching of the Gospel.

There are other Christians, however, who insist that we can
clearly discern the positive workings of God in the political realm,
even where those dealings have little or nothing to do with the life of
the institutional church. On the contemporary scene this way of
viewing things is especially obvious in those Christians who are associated with "liberation theology," a movement whose adherents are
not reluctant to identify specific forces for social change in the broad
social arena as ones which bear clear marks of divine sponsorship.

Indeed, some contemporary Christians seem to posit a very positive relationship between the workings of God in history and "social
change" as such. In some circles the reaction against Hellenistic versions of "divine immutability" has been so extreme that the impression is given that the positive work of God in history is to be discerned wherever social change is taking place. Some (but not all)
liberation theologians, "process" theologians, and proponents of the
"theology of hope" have adopted a view of divine process which ex-
hibits the strong influence of Hegelianism. Thus we are told that the
Biblical God is "in the open future," that he is at work in all that
"negates the present." Ernst Bloch, whose work has been an import-

ant influence on the "theology of hope," is reported to have once re-marked that "Heraclitus is the real origin of the theology of hope!"[7]

Mary Daly, in developing a perspective that is meant to free religious belief from all that she judges to be "patriarchal," goes so far as to suggest that we no longer think of the term *God* as a noun. Rather, we must direct our allegiance to "the God the Verb," who is "form-de-stroying, form-creating, transforming power that makes all things new."[8] If we take some of her suggestions at face value, it would seem that God is at work wherever old "forms" are being destroyed and new ones created.

The drafters of the "Boston Affirmations," a public statement issued by a group of liberation theologians in 1976, strike a more moderate tone. They do not insist that God is positively at work wherever social change is occurring. God, they tell us, is "active in current struggles to bring a Reign of Justice, Righteousness, Love and Peace"; God's action in history "shatters the barriers of ethnic, class, familial, national and caste restrictions." [9]

On this view, then, it would not be necessary to view a resurgence of Nazism or the rapid growth of a significant Dolly Parton cult as instances of the kind of change in which God is doing a liberating work. There are patterns whereby we can discern the liberating activity of God. God's liberation is occurring where Justice, Righteousness, Love, and Peace are being realized in history. The God of the Scriptures is one who "shatters barriers"—and only certain kinds of barriers at that.

Nonetheless, some critics of the Boston document have not been satisfied with these qualifications. They fear that this document,

---

7. Quoted by M. Douglas Meeks, *Origins of the Theology of Hope* (Philadelphia, 1974), p. 15.

8. Mary Daly, *Beyond God the Father* (Boston, 1973), p. 43.

9. "The Boston Affirmations," *Worldview* (March 1976), pp. 45-47.

along with other expressions of the perspective of liberation theology, manifests a tendency toward an uncritical endorsement of movements in the "secular" arena.

There is something to be said for this line of criticism. Like the pious agnostics, we must acknowledge some element of "hiddenness" in God's workings amidst processes of social change. God is presently bringing about his redemptive will throughout society; he is at work fashioning his complex purposes in the cultural arena, even in processes which promote conflict and radical change. But we must exercise caution in our attempts to discern his movements.

The dualist perspective rightly stresses that God's ultimate redemptive purposes are presently revealed, openly and publicly, in the context of the called-out people of God. In the midst of the life of this people, as Paul put it, "the mystery hidden for ages and generations" is "now made manifest to his saints"—and the mystery is this: "Christ in you, the hope of glory" (Col. 1:26-27). In the Christian community we realize (or ought to realize) the first fruits of what God will bring about for his whole creation, including created culture.

There is an important sense, then, in which we can only know God's cultural purposes—what he is up to in the midst of social change—by "withdrawing" from the world. A proper understanding of God's providential workings cannot be fully gained by a detached "empirical" study of the social process. It can only be attained by experiencing the redemption that is to be found by identifying with the new community of God's people. But this involvement is just the beginning of cultural discernment; for, having turned away from the world to taste the first fruits of the Kingdom, we must return to it to discern the larger work which God is doing there. "Retreat" from the world is not the end-goal of the Christian life; it is a tactic whereby we become properly sensitized for sanctified, discerning involvement in the broad reaches of God's creation. We must be released from the grip of the principalities and powers so that we may better serve the one whose recreating purposes encompass even those powers, "For God sent the Son into the cosmos, not to condemn the cosmos, but that the cosmos might be saved through him" (John 3:17).

This is where the liberation perspective, for all of its dangers, points us in the proper direction: we must attempt to discern the workings of God in the processes of social change. The Belgic Confession rightly warns us against curious inquiries into areas which are hidden from us. But neither may we draw the blinds where God has shed light.

The thoughts that we have just been expressing are crucial for an understanding of a Reformed perspective on providence and politics. There can be no doubt that the element of political agnosticism that we have noticed in some strands of Calvinist views of providence has been closely related to an attitude of political "fatalism." These patterns of political agnosticism and fatalism can be understood and assessed by noting that there are two different streams in the Calvinist tradition, each finding its source in the central Reformed emphasis on the sovereignty of God.

One stream stresses God's sovereign activity in the area of soteriology—i.e., in matters having to do with personal regeneration and sanctification. We might call this stream of thought "Tulip Calvinism." Here the expansive, unrestricted adjectives which are typical of Reformed thought—*total, unconditional, irresistible,* and the like—are limited in their application to the electing and preserving of individuals.

The other stream, which need not stand in opposition to the first, promotes what we might call a "cultural Calvinism." Whereas the former emphasis focuses on the sovereign activity of God in bringing individual persons into his Kingdom, the latter stresses the sovereign lordship of Jesus Christ over all spheres of human activity. When Calvinism is restricted to the soteriological emphasis, Reformed Christians can be content to acknowledge God's sovereign workings in their own personal lives; and they need only add, as a virtual afterthought, that God is exercising his sovereign lordship over the broad movements of history as well—although the manner of doing so is a dark mystery into which we must not inquire.

But where the genius of the second stream of Calvinist thought is recognized and loved, as it has been in the career of H. Evan Runner, we will be reluctant to relegate too much to the realm of mystery; in tones of pious agnosticism. The cultural Calvinist affirms that Christ's sovereignty is revealed not only in his function as the Shepherd of souls, but also in his claims upon our lives as he reveals himself to us as the Lord of history and the King of the nations. On this understanding of divine sovereignty, it is a matter of *obligation* to probe into the secret places, in anticipation of the day when the glory of God will be revealed to the ends of the earth.

Cultural Calvinists, then, seek to avoid fatalism—choosing rather to pursue the way of obedience as persons who are called to labor in, and even to contribute to, the establishment of, the Kingdom of Christ on earth. In this context, a concern with the workings of divine providence is, in effect, a concern over how we are to receive our political marching orders.

In the final analysis, then, we cannot ask about the relationship between providence and politics without asking very practical questions about what it means for us to be responsible for the political dimensions of God's creation. The Reformed confessions do not always make this clear. As we have seen, they often adopt the tone of warning us against making inquiries into that which we cannot comprehend. Indeed, the call to responsible involvement in the political world over which God presently rules is found, not in those sections of the Belgic Confession and Heidelberg Catechism which explicitly refer to the doctrine of providence, but in the discussion, in the final article of the Belgic Confession (Article 37), of "The Last Judgment." There we are told that when the day of accounting comes:

> the faithful and elect shall be crowned with glory and honor; and the Son of God will confess their names before God His Father and His elect angels; all tears shall be wiped from their eyes; and their cause which is now condemned by many judges and magistrates as heretical and impious will then be known to be the cause of the Son of God.

This, ultimately, is the proper context for framing our questions concerning the relationship between providence and politics. This is why we must ask what God is doing right now by way of political activity. This is why we must enter into that glorious experiment in risk-taking—even if that experiment should lead us to suffer at the hands of contemporary "judges and magistrates." It is not because we are curious about that which is hidden from us. Rather it is because we must desperately desire to know the mystery that *has* been revealed to us—so that Jesus will someday confess our names before his Father, and so that it may then be revealed that our present struggle to do his political will is in reality the very "cause of the Son of God."

ALAN STORKEY

Dominant Concepts of Power in Recent British Politics

IT IS A MEASURE of the stature of Dr. Runner's thought that it can be held up as a standard by which the political developments of a nation can be judged. The Biblically anchored insights of his book *Scriptural Religion and Political Task*,[1] which I encountered in the 1960s, were significant not only in my understanding North America but also in my assessing the political situation in Britain. In acknowledgment of a long-term debt, I would therefore like to apply this met-wand to some aspects of the recent development of British political life.

The specific theme is the contemporary meanings of *power* in politics. A concept that was the object of faith in a wide variety of ways during the 1960s has become a source of puzzlement during the 1970s. This change, however, inadequately documented in Britain in the following pages, bears witness to the covenantal strength of Dr. Runner's definition of power and its promise for modern politics.

> POWER is the Word of God as Principle of our integral life … The whole revelation of God in His Word is full of illustrations that man must be weak in order for God to reveal His strength. The power to renew the life of mankind is in the Word of the Living God.[2]

---

1.   H. Evan Runner, *Scriptural Religion and Political Task* (Toronto, 1974).
2.   Runner, pp. 122-23.

The ultimate truth of this view is antithetically shown by the bitterness and destructive nature of much of contemporary politics. The hope is that it can also eventually be shown more fully through assent and submission.

Political Science

Our initial concern is not with the academic study of politics in Britain *per se* but with its influence on political practice. During the last two decades the influence of the academic study of politics upon practical politics has been unprecedented, not primarily because of textbooks, periodicals, and school political education, but because of "experts" in television and the press who have been required to explain and interpret political activity in a supposedly authoritative but neutral way. Thus, some political scientists have moved into the key role of framing the public's perception of politics.

During this period a major trend, evident earlier, was to see politics basically in terms of power, rather than as an explication of the structure of the state.[3] The reasons for this transition were interesting. One reason was that examination of the structure of the state was likely to appear biased along a socialist-conservative divide, removing the possibility of the neutral political science which the status of the discipline demanded. A second was that the growth of political sociology, with its emphasis on *unmasking* the difference between formal structure and "real" relationships, had hyperbolized the distinction between authority and power.[4] Further, the emphasis on empirical studies meant that, provided the concept of power was homogenized, it could be handled as the unidimensional, universal "fact" of

---

3.   The key volume was probably Robert McKenzie's *British Political Parties: The Distribution of Power Within the Conservative and Labour Parties* (London, 1955). McKenzie is one of the key media men in this development.

4.   See, for example, J. Urry and J. Wakeford, editors, *Power in Britain* (London, 1973).

politics which both allowed the illusion of coherence in the discipline and opened up the possibility of quantification. Finally, a Marxist critique emphasized the difference between the economic and class roots of power and the political superstructure created by the threatened bourgeois ruling class.[5] For these reasons, at least, power had become possibly *the* key concept in modern British political sciences, and certainly it has become the normal frame of reference for political commentary.

The public has therefore been assiduously taught that politics is about power, by which is chiefly meant control of the government, and that it is achieved by a quantifiable, atomistic, vote-based calculus at elections. Implicitly it is also conveyed that the overriding concern of politicians is to get in power and stay in power. The tireless psephological machine centering on David Butler, has, in election after election, looked at the forces shaping electoral choice,[6] and this emphasis has been reinforced by the dramatic opinion poll commentary on people's attitudes. Nevertheless, the awareness has also grown that elections change relatively little; a search has started, therefore, for the roots of power in the Civil Service, various elites, the establishment, the major pressure groups, the cabinet, the parties, the financial and business worlds, and multinational companies. What emerges is that powers are pluriform, that they are viewed very differently by various groups, and that they are shaped by the institutions where they are exercised; as a result, the hope of a unifying concept in one discipline has been destroyed.[7]

---

5.   See R. Miliband, *Parliamentary Socialism* (London, 1961) for a presentation of the ineffectual nature of socialism in Parliament and J. Westergaard and H. Resler, *Class in a Capitalist Society* (London, 1976) for a Marxist view of the *real* power relationships.

6.   See D. Butler and D. Stokes, *Political Change in Britain* (London, 1969).

7.   See, for example, J. Bruce-Gardyne and N. Lawson, *The Power Game* (London, 1976).

But something else has also been destroyed. The trust in and emphasis on electioneering, on getting into power (not office), and on using political pressure have led to a degeneration in political norms and principles in the public consciousness and have created a different tone in the national debate. The cynicism evident in British politics today is partly the result of the view of power adopted by academic political scientists.

Normal British Attitudes Toward Power

There are some assumptions about power which are fairly universally held in Britain and rarely reflected on. One is that the government should exercise authority over the nation rather than merely over the polity. Both major parties believe that the government is responsible, in some senses at least, for providing a religious direction for the nation. Reactions to this approach have tended merely to be laissez-faire, that is, to assert that the government should not interfere, rather than to recognize in principle that the sphere of competence of the state and political leadership is limited. Consequently, there has been a tendency throughout this period towards encroachment, the politicization of issues, and the massification of the electorate, as their other institutional roles are subsumed under their role as individual voting citizens. Moreover, political leaders have regarded it as their duty on many occasions to assume national spiritual leadership and formulate its direction.

A second element has been the majoritarian emphasis. The single-member constituency system of voting gives the larger parties, those able to muster over about 23% of the votes, a likely monopoly of parliamentary seats. They therefore claim, from their support in the House of Commons, to speak for the majority of the people, although actually it is possible—and has occurred—for a party to have a majority of seats with the support of less than 30% of the electorate. The response in this situation is to try to manufacture majoritarian party support by deliberately obscuring differences of political faith and coalescing values to the lowest common denominators. This process is regarded as necessary for majoritarian status and is therefore normal. Unfortunately, it leads to the suppression of many kinds of opinions, especially during the election process, and to a deliberate lack of clarity in political debate.

A third factor, which we shall examine later, is the recognition that British elected representatives, in contrast with their U.S. counterparts, have little power independent of their party and government. Attention therefore focuses on the fight for control of Downing Street, which has assumed an intensity and sophistication that dominates most other concerns in Britain.

Power as National Economic Direction

One ethos of power which has had a great impact is that of *government planning as the key to the regeneration of the British economy*. By 1964 the Labour Party's emphasis had switched from nationalization to centrally directed economic planning. A new Department of Economic Affairs, a National Plan, a network of consultative bodies, and a government strategy would, it was hoped, set the economy on a higher growth path. The rapid failure of this initial plan by 1966 was followed by other attempts at government engineering. In December of 1966 the Industrial Reorganization Corporation was created, largely with the idea of making, through mergers, new giant companies like British Leyland able to meet future world competition. [8] The details and results of this approach do not concern us here, although they are rarely judged successful; our concern is with the view of power implied in it.

---

8. See A. Budd, *The Politics of Economic Planning* (London, 1978) for a brief survey and S. Young with A. V. Lowe, *Intervention in the Mixed Economy* (London, 1974) on the IRC.

First, there was a false assumption of the government's competence in economic affairs; it was not possible for the government to control the development of private enterprises; that much was quickly revealed. Second, the predictive powers of D.E.A. economists were swayed by the particular kind of national economic leadership that was deemed necessary at this period, namely, a certain pattern of growth. The control conceptions of power, however, were to be formed in the *ratio* of the age. All men of good sense, it was argued, must come to the conclusion that a National Plan was needed, that industrial bigger was better, and that progress was by planned adjustment. The economic orthodoxy of the time, already in part a response to Russia's seeming success, became that in which the government vested its leadership and its hope. That specific policies rapidly became dated did not shake the underlying faith in a *ratio*, a national economic policy, on which all educated people could agree, through which the government could lead the people into economic success. This planning ideal was rooted in rational efficiency and did not even draw any water from the old Socialist concern for economic justice.

The Conservative Leadership Theme

Conservatism since Disraeli has expressed the ideal that *the political leader should unite the nation under himself.* This theme draws from the Tory monarchist background and is also a response to the Socialist class-divisive challenge. It was, of course, strong in the 1939-45 War, although Churchill's demise in 1945 suggests it was not quite as universally shared as is usually assumed. To some extent both Eden and Macmillan continued the ethos, when it was taken up, after the leadership crisis of Home, by Edward Heath.

This view of leadership is elitist and charismatic; a leader must generate a following. The inspiration comes from the top and is then shared among the population at large. It is personally generated and is more than the authority that derives from a careful definition of political office. In 1970 the pressure for leadership was great both from the media and also from within Heath's own party. His particular response to this theme was twofold. First, he led a crusade of "going into Europe," by which was meant joining the European Economic Community. This fundamental constitutional change was carried out in 1971 on the basis of a simple majority in the Commons with probably two-thirds of the electorate at the time opposed to it. That this decision should be a leadership crusade made without electoral assent to this basic change in the structure of national government led to a period of hostility to the EEC which may not yet be over. The other area was economic; together with his Chancellor of the Exchequer, Anthony Barber, Heath decided that a "dash for growth" and prosperity would unite the nation and give it the necessary dynamic of spirit. This economic indulgence in fact created serious weaknesses in the economy, and after losing the election in February of 1974, Heath was relieved of the leadership in favor of a potentially more charismatic leader, Margaret Thatcher. Her rhetoric does not yet reveal a change in this Conservative ethos of power generated from the top.

The New Barons

During the same period, another conception of power in politics arose which cut across the two we have already examined. Through recruitment and organization, the two great industrial armies of labor and capital were able to enhance their direct political power. The history of the unions' exercise of it was more obvious. In June of 1969, Barbara Castle's white paper *In Place of Strife* was abandoned by the Labour Government under pressure from the union leaders and the union-sponsored MPs. The white paper aimed to establish a recognized legal procedure of industrial bargaining to prevent anarchic industrial relations. From that time onward the unions became more adamant in opposing any legal constraints on their spheres of activity, and the passing of the Industrial Relations Act in August 1971 began a period of extended resistance by the unions to the law and the government. Led by the Transport and General Workers Union, they refused to register under the Act, were taken to court, and fined. The Labour Party meanwhile offered to repeal the Act on return to power, and this was done. Certainly, in practice and usually in principle, the regulation of union activity by law was completely ruled out from that time onward.[9]

The Labour Party, whose National Executive Committee could be, and usually was, dominated by union-appointed nominees, came to identify itself fully with the union position that there were to be no legal controls and that unions had an effect autonomous power which they could use as they and their members saw fit. The immediate result of this was that wage-induced inflation rose to a rate of 25% during late 1974 and early 1975 and that the issue of price control became a central one in 1975. The response of the Labour Government was a unique one. It *negotiated* a Social Contract with the trade unions as equal partners; the terms of the agreement were that the Trades Union Congress agreed to limit annual wage increases (although it had no formal method of exercising control over its member unions) in return for government-imposed constraints on prices and dividends and some welfare and subsidy payments. This bilateral agreement was the kingpin of government policy throughout the late 1970s, and it was argued that only this unique relationship could establish a sound anti-inflationary agreement and industrial peace.

The partisanship of this compact with the union barons and its denial of authoritatively-based office were scarcely seen as an issue at

9. See Robert Taylor, "Scapegoats for National Decline: The Trade Unions since 1945," in C. Cook and J. Ramsden, *Trends in British Politics Since 1945* (London, 1978, pp. 88-108) for one description of this development.

the time. The immediate, appropriate response was cobbled into history with little regard for its partiality and without any contact with a principal base. Necessarily, it produced its inevitable reaction. The forces of capital and management began to organize themselves to redress the balance—or more.

The best way to change the parameters of power is by a lower level of activity in the economy, leaving less pressure on output and a pool of unemployed labor to provide some competition in the labor market. This was tried initially by Heath on the basis of the inverse relationship between unemployment and inflation revealed by the Phillips curve in 1970-71 and was reflected in a recession in the early 1980s with two million unemployed, mainly in the north of England. The effect was to transfer power to the employers, whose position had also been partially strengthened by the abolition of secondary picketing and withdrawal of unemployment pay for strikers. At the same time the tax system had been changed to encourage those with responsible positions and with "successful" salaries. Thus, the emphasis is now on bigger differentials and weaker collective bargaining. There has been no modification of the process of free collective power bargaining, but only of the balance on the political seesaw.

The problem that exists is that the autonomous empires of power have been built up and defended a-normatively and that there have been a-principled political responses to them. It is now normal for interest groups to respond contingently to threats to the status quo which they seek to defend without any principal direction governing their response.

The Hailsham-Jenkins Theme

In recent years a theme has been developed, most notably by Lord Hailsham,[10] about the direction of the Constitution. The argument is that whereas in earlier periods there had been a diffusion

---

10. Lord Hailsham, *The Dilemma of Democracy: Diagnosis and Prescription* (London, 1978).

of power among British political institutions—Lords, Commons, Judges, Local Authorities, Monarch, and Parties—in the postwar era a number of factors have led to a heavy concentration of power in the hands of the party in government. These include the Prime Minister's choice of an election time, the eclipse of common law by statute law, the expertise of the Civil Service available to government, the development of national media politics, the Whips' control of the backbenchers, the fiscal power of the government, and the doctrine of mandate, whereby an election victory, albeit with the support of only 30% of the electorate, is taken as full justification for the adoption of the manifesto program. The centralization of power, argued Hailsham, has effectively destroyed the delicate balance of constitutional power which earlier existed.

In 1979 Roy Jenkins took the argument further.[11] He argued that the "elective dictatorship" that Hailsham had outlined was the result of and was perpetuated by a rigid, and partisan two-party system, which vetoed further constitutional development, like the adoption of proportional representation, not in its interest. He suggested that the way out of this dilemma is a new control party which would break up this ossified pattern and allow relevant constitutional change.

However, specific changes or the formation of a center party does not get to the root of the problem. British constitutional practice and theory have deteriorated because of the approach that has been adopted. Three main strands are detectable. One is an adulation of British historicism. The Conservatives argue that the Constitution has been developed through a long historical process and reflects the unique character of the British—their fairness, maturity, and even bloody-mindedness; it is therefore a system which is balanced, tried

---

11. Dimbleby Lecture, *The Listener*, November 29, 1979, pp. 733-38.

and tested, and worthy of emulation, provided that people adopt good Anglo-Saxon patterns of behavior. This tradition, as Dr. Runner points out, is doomed.

> Having once taken his position within historical development, the conservative is lost...The conservative... could either fall back into a reactionary defense of the ways of *already* vested interests, and thus lose all genuine relevancy, have no significant view about the dynamic, the novel, in history; or he could find himself in the most unhappy position of following along after the more progressive accomplishments of the liberals (or more radical spirits), serving chiefly as a brake upon the dynamic movement of innovation.[12]

The complacency and lack of principal basis of much of this tradition has contributed to the gradual erosion of much constitutional practice. Unless the principle is developed, the practice will merely be bypassed.

The second approach is pragmatic. The virtue of the "unwritten," "flexible" British Constitution is its ability to adapt to circumstances. It can change by practice, by statute, by convention, through case law, or through European law; it is not held in one formal straight jacket, but can pragmatically respond to what is the case by a process which Harold Wilson described as "steering by the seat of your pants."

The outcome of this approach is obvious; it involves the decay of guiding principles for political life. New conventions have suddenly appeared, including that the government should be able to threaten (economically) firms which do not follow advised policy, that resignation should not follow from defeat on a major issue or cabinet splits, and that government can strike a bargain with one interest

---

12. Runner, pp. 92-93.

group over legislation. There is a gradual degradation of constitutional thinking and practice which follows from this pragmatic approach, and already the results are being harvested.

The third and, in the end, determinate approach is that adopted by the two major parties. The Constitution, and especially the single-member constituency method of election (which, incidentally, was discredited and under very strong attack at the beginning of the century), favors and can be made to favor the major parties. As long as they hold power and control most of the rules of the game, they will normally subject the constitutional rules to their party aims. Political power takes precedence over constitutional principle.

The outcome of these approaches is at least as serious as Hailsham and Jenkins suggest. For a generation or more the expedients of power have dominated the consciences of politicians and the consciences of the electorate. Moreover, the centralization of power has led to its more arbitrary use, although the new Commons Select Committees and Lord Denning are at least trying to reverse this trend. In the long term, unresolved constitutional problems and decadent practice are sapping the principal structure of political life.

Power Within the Parties

The views of power within the two major parties differ considerably. Conservative commitment among the electorate tends to be materialist; people hope that "progressive moderation" will keep things as they were without any crises, so that they can go on accumulating wealth.[13] The politicians are entrusted with this process of management, which therefore assumes a normal professional career pattern of promotion by good performances. This process tends to be deferential, and hence the party is able to diminish conflicts of power,

---

13. Runner, p. 53.

which, if they occur, tend to be among charismatic leaders rather than among competing power groups.

The Labour Party is more complex. The same kind of pattern of promotion has existed within the party, especially when it has been in power, but the route to promotion has always involved ideological orthodoxy more than managerial performance. Indeed, there has been a fear that "progressive moderation" is the aim of the leaders of the Labour Party as much as of the Conservatives. The result has been a growing distrust of those in governmental authority when the Labour Party is in power, and consequently attempts to disturb the existing pattern.

The most serious of these, although there have also been attempts by Neo-marxists to infiltrate the party at the constituency level, center on the attempt by Tony Benn to democratize the party structure.[14] His critique is that the leadership is detached from the party and has created its own complacent power base. The remedies are that the leader should be elected by the whole party (not just Labour MPs), that the MPs should regularly present themselves for reelection, and that the manifesto should be written from a wider party base. This view of democracy within the party is, however, combined in Benn's thinking with a view of socialism which involves extended state control, albeit with some more democratic elements in state enterprises.

As a rival or potential balance between those two positions, the trade unions maintain their influence through their position on the Labour National Executive Committee, their funding, and their sponsorship of MPs. However, this situation, the source of which can be traced to the origins of the Labour Party, means that in no real sense does the party exist as a community

---

14. See T. Benn, *Speeches by Tony Benn* (Nottingham, 1974) and *Arguments for Socialism*, edited by C. Mullen (London, 1979).

of political conviction. Internal activities tend to be strategic rather than reflective of underlying, shared convictions, just as the position of the party is articulated more toward how it can have a successful election strategy rather than toward what its convictions are.

The weakness of the Labour Party is noted by many commentators, but both parties share the same fundamental malaise, which is given by our culture generally. Obtaining power takes priority over political conviction and principle, and the ethic is one of pragmatic reaction to the historical flow of events. This is serious not only as reflected in the pattern of government, but also in the decline in grass-roots political commitment; Labour Party membership has fallen badly, and Conservative Party membership, although high, tends to be delegatory. Because no larger communities of political faith exist or are encouraged, the independent voter, who is driven and tossed by the wind like a wave of the sea, is becoming more usual. The mass lack all conviction, and the few are full of passionate intensity.

Conclusion

These are, then, some of the attitudes toward power which jostle on the British political scene. They have been sketched briefly, inadequately, and possibly inaccurately; yet this approximation suggests that specific political issues will tend to become increasingly acute problems partly because of the inconsistencies and weaknesses of these specific views. They are a recipe for long-term paralysis.

More than this, however, these attitudes toward power evidence the pervasive influence of the lie that *man* is the source of power. It is here that disorder and frustration have their origin, and it is the outworking of human rebellion that is detailed in different forms in at least part of the various responses that we have considered. A detailed Christian response to these problems cannot and need not be developed here, but the main thesis has already been stated, and I gratefully recall it:

> The rebel cannot *really* change the world. It is anchored in the creation-ordinance, the Will of the sovereign God. God maintains His Thesis. Not able to make a world in which the relations are other than they really are, rebellious man can only *attempt, in his imagination,* to live in another world that is not real. But even this, of course, can only be an unsuccessful experiment. For there is but one world, and in the world that God made *he really lives.* The only possibility open to man the rebel is to misform or *distort in his imagination the existing* powerful and firmly-anchored revelational Truth of God's Thesis.[15]

The subsequent conclusion still seems inescapably correct.

> Having seen in what way the Word of God directs our political "goings" from the beginning, and what the nature of the present political world really is, we shall have, I believe, to come to the conclusion that there is only one course for us to take: the building of a community of opinion and the forming of a Christian political party as an instrument for the accomplishing of the necessary integral reformation of our political life. The forming of such a party will itself bring an important reorganization and realignment in [British] society, the strongest kind of witnessing in the biblical sense of the word.[16]

---

15. Runner, pp. 46-47.
16.. Runner, p. 102.

PART FOUR

Natural Science

"Modern men who have committed themselves to science as the way to meaning are not able to find the meaning they are seeking. By employing scientific methods men can arrive at some under-standing of the functional relations of things, but meaning is never a matter of scientific analysis. Meaning has to do with a religiously perceived unity in order and coherence."

— H. Evan Runner, *Point Counter Point*, p. 8.

UKO ZYLSTRA

Dooyeweerd's Concept
of Classification in Biology

EVERY SYSTEM OF CLASSIFICATION, if it is a meaningful system, is based on the order and patterns present in created reality. Classification does not put order into reality; rather, it reflects the order in reality. A classification system only serves to systematize our understanding of the order within reality which makes classification as such possible. If a classification system is to be useful in providing insight into this order, then the criteria on which the system is based play a critical role. These criteria are related to an understanding of the nature and structure of reality and thus reflect the philosophical underpinnings of the systems of classification. In view of this, Herman Dooyeweerd's systematic analysis of the structures of reality can be useful in evaluating systems of classification as well as in providing a basis for classification.

Traditionally, living things have been classified into two groups or kingdoms, namely, plants and animals. Some general criteria can be used to classify readily visible organisms as plants or animals. These criteria usually reflect opposing characteristics. Plants generally have an autotrophic mode of nutrition, obtaining their food through photosynthesis; this characteristic is easily identified by the green color due to the chloroplasts involved in photosynthesis. Animals, on the other hand, are heterotrophic, obtaining their food by ingesting plants, animals, or some other form of organic material. Plant cells possess inelastic cell walls, which frequently are also rigid, thereby providing support for the plant as a whole; animals have cells which lack such walls, and they usually derive support from an exo-or endo-skeleton. Plants usually display continuous growth throughout their lifetime, whereas animals usually terminate their growth processes when they reach the adult stage. Plants are generally sessile, whereas animals are typically creatures which possess structures for motility.

Although the above criteria are fairly obvious and can be applied to most living things, difficulties persist in applying these criteria in classifying living things into kingdoms. The application of the criteria to certain types of living things yields ambiguous results. For example, the fungi, which are considered plants in a two-kingdom classification, are heterotrophic, lacking photosynthetic pigments and possessing cell walls which are distinctly different in composition from the plant cell walls. Many one-celled organisms also possess both plant-like and animal-like characteristics, making it difficult to classify these organisms as either plant or animal. These difficulties essentially result from a definition of plant and animal life derived from a select collection of characteristics which pertain to structural or functional features. The problem is that the essence of plantness or animalness is not established by the classifying characteristics used.

During the past few decades there has been a shift away from the two-kingdom classifications. Alternative systems include, on the one side, attempts to establish multi-kingdom classifications and, on the other side, an attempt to establish a single kingdom which embraces all living things. Some prominent spokesmen for multi-kingdom systems of classification are H. F. Copeland,[1] who argues for a

---

1.   H. F. Copeland, "The Kingdoms of Organisms," *Quarterly Review of*

four-kingdom system, R. H. Whittaker,[2] who more recently defends a five-kingdom system, and E. O. Dodson,[3] who supports a three-kingdom system. An articulation of the basis for a one-kingdom system which emphasizes the unity of all organisms has been presented by J. Lever.[4] It is instructive to briefly examine the basis for each of these sample systems. This analysis may provide us with further insight into the nature of various types of groups of living things.

Copeland's system includes four kingdoms: Monera, Protista, Plantae, and Animalia. These are distinguished primarily on the basis of structural features. The Kingdom Monera includes the prokaryotic organisms whose cells lack nuclei and other membranous organelles. The Kingdom Protista includes the eukaryotic unicellular organisms and multicellular organisms lacking extensive tissue differentiation. The Protista are distinguished by the absence of characteristics found in plants relegated to the Kingdom Plantae or characteristics found in animals placed in the Kingdom Animalia. The Kingdom Plantae includes those multicellular organisms which possess chloroplasts containing a specific set of pigments not found in photosynthetic protists, whereas the Kingdom Animalia includes multicellular organisms which are characterized by a certain type of nutrition and which pass through certain developmental stages (blastula and gastrula).

The system which is presently receiving wide acceptance is the five-kingdom system developed by Whittaker with perhaps some

---

Biology, 13 (1938), 383-420.

2.   R. H. Whittaker, "New Concepts of Kingdoms of Organisms," *Science,* 163 (1969), 150-60.

3.   E. O. Dodson, "The Kingdoms of Organisms," *Systematic Zoology,* 20 (1971), 265-81.

4.   J. Lever, *Geintegreerde Biologie* (Utrecht, 1973), pp. 6-27.

modification in the placing of a particular group. Whittaker's kingdoms differ from Copeland's largely in establishing a separate kingdom of fungi. The general outlines of the five kingdoms— Monera, Protista, Fungi, Plantae, and Animalia—are given in Figure 1. Whittaker combines two criteria in establishing these kingdoms: the type or level of organization and the mode of nutrition. Three levels of organization are applied: the prokaryotic, which distinguishes the Monera; the eukaryotic unicellular, which defines the Protista; the eukaryotic multicellular and multinucleate, which separates the Plantae, Fungi, and Animalia from the Protista. The latter three groups composing the eukaryotic multicellular are then distinguished on the basis of modes of nutrition: the green plants within the Kingdom Plantae are photosynthetic (autotrophic); Fungi obtain nutrients by absorption (heterotrophic); members of the Kingdom Animalia obtain food primarily by ingestion (heterotrophic). The distinction between Protista and the multicellular eukaryotes can be blurred since several phyla include both unicellular and multicellular forms. Thus it becomes difficult to place them in this scheme without splitting the phylum.

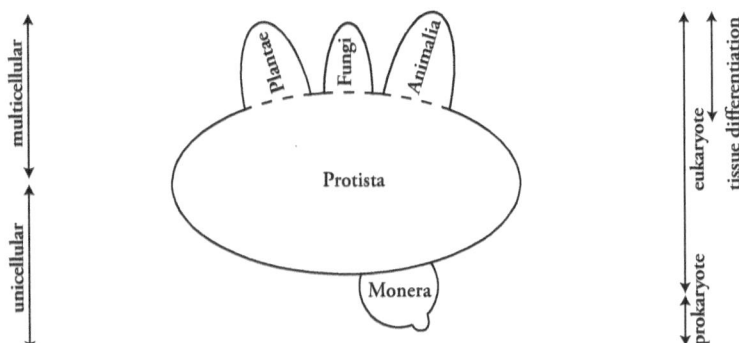

Figure 1. General outline of a five-kingdom classification (adapted from R. H. Whittaker, *Science*, 163:157, 1969).

Dodson's three-kingdom system essentially accepts the traditional plant and animal kingdoms with the removal of the prokaryotes into a separate kingdom referred to as Mycota (rather than Monera). This system is thus defined primarily on the basis of structural features in which the prokaryote/eukaryote distinction is considered to represent the greatest discontinuity among living things. Dodson considers the unicellular/ multicellular distinction to be insufficient as a basis for kingdom status since there do not exist clear distinctions among several groups of eukaryotes.

In contrast to these multi-kingdom systems, J. Lever presents an argument for a single kingdom of organisms. This viewpoint stresses the universal vital processes of living things. The basic elements of this viewpoint are as follows:

a) Recent observations reveal similarities of structure and funtion at the molecular level for all organisms. For example, all organisms possess a universal genetic language and a universal biotic energy unit (ATP).

b) There is no single criterion upon which organisms can satisfactorily be divided into two types, and thus the classical terms of plant and animal kingdoms lose their meaning.

c) Within the Kingdom of Organisms two trends are evident: a specialization in the direction of feeding, in a general sense; a specialization towards a manipulation of the environment, thus toward behavior. The former can be referred to as the vegetative trend, the latter as the animal trend.

d) These trends do not appear separate among two types of organisms; both are present in the same organism, although in different degrees of intensity.

Thus, according to Lever each organism possesses vegetative and animal elements; consequently, each organism is both plant and animal. Since there is no definitive discontinuity, a single kingdom embraces all living things.[5]

These selected theories on the classification of organisms into kingdoms certainly point out a basic problem with the traditional classification of all living things into two kingdoms, either plant or animal. One common difficulty is the classification of the diverse microorganisms. The interpretation of the diverse structural and functional features among microorganisms leads to the different theories of kingdom systems. On the one hand, the microorganisms are seen as intergrades between the extreme plant forms and animal forms. Since a basic discontinuity is absent, a single kingdom of organisms is purposed. The multi-kingdom theories, on the other hand, are largely built upon the recognition of structural discontinuities of prokaryote/eukaryote, unicellular/multicellular, and presence or absence of cell walls, chloroplasts, and neuromuscular systems. Whittaker also introduces a functional discontinuity in the mode of nutrition in order to distinguish fungi, plants, and animals.

The question that one must address in evaluating these theories of kingdoms is the appropriate basis for establishing a kingdom. In a multi-kingdom system, what actually accounts for the radical [6] nature of a kingdom as distinct from other kingdoms? Even a single-kingdom system must still give an account of the radical distinction of organisms from non-living things. If one were to pursue the type of argumentation that Lever uses, then the viruses, whose status as living things is considered dubious in spite of the possession of nucleic acids, could readily be taken as the intergrade between living

---

5.   Lever, p. 23.

6.   The term *radical* is used here and throughout the essay in the sense of fundamental. As applied to the kingdom level of organization, the term *radical* denotes that which is basic or foundational to an assembly of things embraced within a kingdom in distinction from those embraced in another kingdom.

and non-living, thus eliminating the distinction between living and non-living things. We could then simply have one kingdom which embraces all things, living and non-living. The multi-kingdom systems appear to attribute a radical character to the kingdoms on the basis of evolutionary developments and relationships. Thus the prokaryote/eukaryote discontinuity is the basis for radical distinctions because the evolution of the eukaryotic cell from a prokaryotic cell is considered to be a major step in evolution.[7] Likewise, multicellularity is considered to be another major step. Whittaker,[8] in establishing the additional three kingdoms of multicellular eukaryotes, interprets the photosynthetic ingestive and absorptive modes of nutrition as providing "evolutionary meaning" for the plant, animal, and fungi kingdoms. The radical character of the kingdoms is thus to be found in this evolutionary meaning. One consequence of this approach is that relationships among living things are essentially conceived of phylogenetically rather than simply in terms of a structural/functional order which provides for the boundaries and conditions for the existence and development of living things. Although evolutionary thought recognizes structural and functional relationships, the very existence of the order which provides for those relationships is conceived of as being produced by a hypothetical evolutionary development.[9]

Herman Dooyeweerd, in his analysis of thing structures, provides an alternate theoretical basis for establishing a classification of kingdoms.[10] At the heart of Dooyeweerd's theory is the recognition

---

7.   Whittaker, p. 151; Dodson, p. 270.

8.   Whittaker, p. 153.

9.   See, for example, E. Mayr, *Principles of Systematic Zoology* (New York), p. 78; G.G. Simpson, "The Status of the Study of Organisms," *American Scientist*, 50:36-45.

10. H. Dooyeweerd, *A New Critique of Theoretical Thought*, (Amsterdam, 1957), III, Ch. 2.

that the factual things of our experience are correlated to a law structure which sets the conditions or boundaries for the very existence of things. Apart from such a law structure, the factual things (stones, oak trees, birds, etc.) of our experience would not even exist. Nor would there be any possibility of our experiencing such things. These law structures are referred to as internal structural principles or as individuality structures.[11] The correlation that exists between the factual thing and its internal structural principle is referred respectively as the subject-side and the law-side of a thing. A thing is always subject to a law; otherwise it would not exist. A thing cannot exist in and of itself or of its own power. The subject-side is expressed in both the subjective and objective functioning of an individual whole. The internal principle (the law-side) with its coherence of modal aspects becomes individualized in a factual thing of our experience (the subject-side).

According to Dooyeweerd, the concept of individuality structures, i.e., law structures or lawful orders, provides a theoretical basis for a typology, for a logical system of classification. Every individuality structure reveals a *typical* set or group of modal functions. This typical group defines or determines the *type* of things of our experience in the sense that the functions of a thing are delimited by the thing's law structure. Each thing possesses a certain order or hierarchy of functions such that certain functions are presupposed in functions that are higher in the hierarchical scale. Thus, for example, the biotic function presupposes the physical function of a living thing. Certain things function subjectively only in a limited number of functions. In view of the hierarchy of functions, one of the functions

---

11. A good summary of Dooyeweerd's theory of individuality structures is provided in K. Ziterman's master's thesis entitled *Dooyeweerd's Theory of Individuality Structure as an Alternative to a Substantive Position, Especially that of Aristotle* (Institute for Christian Studies, Toronto, 1971), 141 pp.

serves as the highest subject function of a thing, with all the other subjective functions being presupposed by the highest subject function. The latter serves as the qualifying function of a thing; as such it determines the internal destination of the typical group of modal functions. All of the other subject functions of a thing are guided or opened up under the direction of the qualifying function. The qualifying function serves as "the ultimate point of reference for the entire internal structural coherence of the individual whole in the typical groupage of the aspects."[12] This internal destination, as determined by the qualifying function, reveals the basis or radical type of a thing within a system of classification.

As an illustration, a plant, such as a tree, functions subjectively in the numerical, spatial, kinematic, physical, and biotic aspects. A tree, according to Dooyeweerd, is biotically qualified, which means that the biotic aspect plays a central role in the unfolding process of the tree as a whole. The tree still functions in a spatial and physical way, and so forth, but the latter do not determine the nature of the tree; they do not serve as the ultimate point of reference for the tree. All the functions of the tree are thus under the leading of the qualifying function which reveals the internal destination of the tree. Of critical importance is that all of the tree's functions are irreducible. The biotic functions cannot be reduced to the physical-chemical functions of the tree; nor can the physical-chemical functions be swallowed up by the biotic. Each aspect has its own sphere of sovereignty such that, for example, the molecular interactions in a tree are always subject to physical-chemical laws. However, these molecular interactions occur within the tree as an individual whole under the guidance of the tree's qualifying function. Thus the internal destination of a tree can never be reduced to its physical-chemical functioning as attempted by mechanistic explanations. Physical-chemical in-

---

12. Dooyeweerd, p. 58.

teractions do not function in some causal, determinative way. Causality is rooted in the correlation of the law-side determining the subject-side.

This is related to typicality because the type is not found in the subject-side of a thing but rather in the law-side. A type is a structure of individuality, and as such it has the character of law.[13] We recognize typicality in things because they are expressions of the typical groupage of functions found in the internal structural principles. The most fundamental types for Dooyeweerd are the radical types, which are determined by the modality of the leading or qualifying function in the typical groupage of functions. The radical types are the ultimate types of individuality structures which encompass the various realms of things which we call kingdoms. Dooyeweerd distinguishes three kingdoms: physical things, plants, and animals, which are qualified by the physical, biotic, and psychic (sensitive) modal functions respectively. Within the radical types or kingdoms there exists a descending order of genotypes[14] which corresponds to the various taxa of classification: the phyla, classes, order, families, genera, and species. These various genotypes represent inner articulations of the primary, radical type, and thus they all express an internal destination determined by the qualifying function of the radical type to which they belong.

Thus, according to Dooyeweerd's analysis, a system of kingdom classification is based upon the typical groupage of modal aspects of the structural wholes of naive or everyday experience. Since naive experience is essentially confronted only with the things of the "macro-world," Dooyeweerd concludes that there are only two kingdoms of living things—plants and animals—in addition

---

13. Dooyeweerd, p. 97.

14. The term *genotype* as used here is distinct from the term as used in genetics, where it refers to a particular combination of genes.

to the kingdom of non-living things. Humans are not encompassed in a kingdom since they have no typical qualification.[15] With regard to microorganisms, Dooyeweerd does not think that they affect the three kingdoms. He believes that the criteria used to distinguish the plants and animals of the macro-world are applicable to microorganisms, border cases notwithstanding.

I think that here Dooyeweerd runs into a problem in his analysis of the data of native experience, which also affects his general theory of modal spheres. By excluding microorganisms from naive experience, Dooyeweerd has failed to recognize a radical distinction between microorganisms on the one hand and plants and animals on the other. First of all, I think it can be argued that to some degree the micro-world is accessible to naive experience. Colonies of microorganisms are often directly visible. Furthermore, the aid of a microscope does not make our experience of things necessarily theoretical but can simply serve to expand that which is accessible to naive experience.

An examination of the things belonging to the micro-world of naive experience soon reveals that the application of the specific criteria used to distinguish plants and animals in the micro-world of naive experience simply breaks down. Our concepts of plantness and animalness are forced to become modified when they are applied to microorganisms. The criteria which assume great significance are the presence or absence of cell walls and/or chlorophyll pigments. The criterion of the presence of cell walls is not even directly apparent in our naive experience. This is also true for many of the other criteria which are typically used for distinguishing plants and animals. This is the basic reason for many of the difficulties encountered in trying to determine the radical type of the microorganisms.

---

15. The reason for this, according to Dooyeweerd, is that human existence is not restricted to this world of temporal experience and does not find its ultimate destination in this world (pp. 87-89).

This attempt to apply criteria of plantness or animalness in distinguishing microorganisms has tended to obscure a more fundamental distinguishing characteristic of microorganisms, namely, the lack of differentiation resulting from growth and development. Microorganisms are typically one-celled; when the cells divide, generally two distinct organisms are formed. The cells do not stick together to form or differentiate into tissues of a larger whole organism as is the case for the plants and animals of our naive experience. Plants and animals undergo a morphogenetic type of differentiation, which is distinct from the type of differentiation present among unicellular living things. The latter display a differentiation in cell structure but not a differentiation into tissues and organs, which is typical for multicellular organisms. This distinction is not simply that of unicellular versus multicellular but rather a distinction involving morphogenesis. Several forms of microorganisms will form aggregates of cells and are therefore considered to be multicellular; however, the cells making up these aggregates lack differentiation of cell types and thus do not display a morphogenetic aspect.

We are here confronted, in my opinion, with a third fundamental, radical distinction among living things. This distinction is based upon a modal aspect which is displayed in plants and animals but lacking among microorganisms. I shall refer to this aspect as the *morphogenetic* aspect. This morphogenetic aspect obviously presupposes the biotic aspect and the other "lower" aspects (the numerical, spatial, kinematic, and physical aspects) as foundational to it. The morphogenetic aspect has its place between the biotic and psychical aspects in the hierarchy of modal functions. The psychical or sensitive aspect presupposes the differentiation of tissues in the development of an integrative system of tissues which enables the whole organism to coordinate responses to sensory phenomena. The introduction of a morphogenetic aspect requires a slightly modified meaning of the biotic aspect, but it is not of essential significance. Dooyeweerd's defining of the biotic focuses primarily upon cellular functioning. Occasionally he substituted the term *vegetative* for the biotic, but it is generally used in the sense of growth or increase rather than differentiation of form. Even though he often made use of a linden tree as an example of a biotically qualified thing, the focus is on those functions which are typically cellular. This also points to Dooyeweerd's shortcoming in his analysis of the plant kingdom: he really fails to adequately define plantness in defining plants as biotically qualified.

The recognition of the morphogenetic aspect as distinct from the biotic and psychical aspects makes possible a modification of the two-kingdom system of classification which Dooyeweerd maintained. In line with Dooyeweerd's concept of kingdoms as being radical types which are distinguished by a typical qualification, I propose three kingdoms of living things: Protista, Plantae, and Animalia. The protists are distinguished from non-living things in their biotic qualification, which is displayed in various types of metabolic activities: cell division and reproduction, cell motility (in many, but not necessarily all, protists), intra-cellular movement of particles and organelles, systems for control of cellular phenomena, and hereditary systems. J. G. Miller has aptly summarized the diverse forms of biotic functioning as the processing of matter-energy and the processing of information.[16] The particular expression of these general forms of processing is then determined by the structural principle of the particular living thing in question.

Plants also display a biotic aspect, but the biotic functions are opened up under the guidance of the morphogenetic aspect, which is the highest subjective function of plants. Thus plants are distinguished from other living things in being qualified by the morphogenetic aspect. This aspect is displayed in tissue differentiation and interaction which gives expression to the form which is typical for that

---

16. J. G. Miller, *Living Systems* (New York, 1978), p. 3.

particular living thing. This tissue interaction implies that the individual cells are not completely autonomous since the cells exert some degree of influence on each other. This influence can be mediated by intercellular pathways or even by cytoplasmic connections (plasmodesmata) which are very common in plants.

Dooyeweerd's criteria for distinguishing the animal kingdom remains essentially unchanged in this modification of kingdom systems. Animals are sensitively qualified. However, since all foundational functions have an important determining role with regard to establishing structural types, the inclusion of a morphogenetic aspect as one of the foundational functions in the radical structural type animal alters the criteria in the consideration of whether certain living things are indeed animals. Dooyeweerd considered the protozoa to be animals because he thought that they displayed a sensitive aspect. But protozoa are unicellular and lack a morphogenetic aspect as defined above. Thus protozoa are classified as protists rather than as animals in this modified system of classification.

Functions are what things do, and thus there is always a correlation between the function and the structure of a thing. If we recognize that living things can be distinguished into radical types or kingdoms on the basis of the thing's qualifying function, can we also recognize correlating structures to such functions?

J. G. Miller, in his treatise entitled *Living Systems*,[17] presents a rather thorough analysis of the subsystems of living things. The subsystems can be categorized, in a summary way, on the basis of whether they process matter-energy and information at the various levels of organization. At the cellular level, the processing of matter and energy is carried out by several structures, including the plasma membrane, mitochondria, chloroplasts, ribosomes, endoplasmic reticu-

---

17. Miller, Chapter 6 provides an in depth analysis of the subsystems of the cell.

lum, Golgi bodies, and lysosomes, as well as the hyaloplasm. The processing of information is a primary function of the nucleus with its chromatin and nucleic acids in and outside of the nucleus; in addition, processing information is also a function of the plasma membrane, endoplasmic reticulum, ribosomes, spindle, and centrioles, just to mention the prominent structures. In prokaryotic organisms, the processing activities, of course, are much more simplified in terms of the structure which performs the functioning. The plasma membrane, the nucleoid, and ribosomes are the primary centers of such activity.

Multicellular, differentiated living systems also display a cellular level of organization. However, as Cox, et al.,[18] suggest, the functional unit of multicellular organisms may well be the interconnected cell systems rather than individual cells. Analysis of developmental systems clearly leads to the conclusion that cell interaction is a cardinal principle of development.[19] This is also supported by Bullough's observations in his treatment of the evolution of differentiation. He points out that whereas "differentiation in unicellular organisms depends on chemical messengers that operate within the cell, differentiation in multicellular organisms depends on chemical messengers that pass from cell to cell."[20] Thus differentiation and development of tissues apparently requires some form of inter-cellular communication which serves to integrate individual cells into a functional multicellular whole. Inter-cellular communication can be achieved indirectly via transport of molecules or ions from one cell to another cell,

18. R. P. Cox, M. R. Krauss, M. E. Balis, and J. Dancis, "Metabolic Cooperation in Cell Culture: A Model for Cell-to-Cell Communication," *Cell Communication*, edited by R. P. Cox (New York, 1974), pp. 67-96.

19. J. D. Ebert and I. M. Sussex, *Interacting Systems in Development* (New York, 1970), p. 49.

20. W. S. Bullough, *The Evolution of Differentiation* (New York, 1967), p. 174.

directly by means of specialized cell junctions or by cell contact at their surfaces.

In plants these cell junctions take the form of cytoplasmic continuities which actually penetrate the cell walls. These continuities, referred to as plasmodesmata, appear to be a feature of all living cells of (multicellular) plants.[21] Various types of cell junctions occur between cells of animal tissues.[22] Gap junctions and possibly septate junctions appear to provide a pathway of low electrical and molecular transport resistance between adjacent cells. These low resistance pathways make possible ionic and metabolic coupling between cells. Tight junctions, desmosomes, and septate junctions appear to function primarily for adhesions of adjacent cells and as permeability barriers in epithelial tissues. Cells which have lost the ability to form intercellular adhesions and to maintain cell contact seem to have lost control over cell division processes and subsequently over differentiation.

Cell interactions are also important in the formation of tissues in animals. This interaction involves some system of recognition between cells which may lead to enhanced association and/or contact between certain cell types during developmental and differentiative processes. The basis for this recognition appears to be the glycoproteins and glycolipids which are constituents of the plasma membrane. Evidence indicates that these molecules are oriented in such a way that the lipid or protein moiety is largely embedded in the membrane, with the carbohydrate portion extending outward from the membrane surface. These molecules can then serve as binding sites for other molecules which are present in the extracellular environ-

---

21. B. E. S. Gunning and M. W. Steer, *Ultrastructure and the Biology of Plant Cells* (London, 1975), pp. 26-30.

22. N. B. Gilula, "Junctions Between Cells," *Cell Communication*, edited by R. P. Cox (New York, 1974), pp. 1-29.

ment. Interaction at these acceptor or binding sites may trigger a particular response within the cell. Thus the plasma membrane is a structure which is rich in information in terms of the types and location of molecules present on its surfaces. This information has a structural dimension to it, even though it is in constant flux in view of the dynamic interactions with the internal cytoplasm and external environment. Although all cells possess some degree of structural information of the plasma membrane, it appears that some particular set of structural membrane information is necessary for tissue interaction and differentiation. This is exemplified in the development of tumor cells, which is associated with structural changes in the plasma membrane. These structural changes are believed to be related to the loss of integrative interaction between cells.

Animals are distinguished from plants not only in their mode of differentiation but also in being qualified by a sensitive function. The structural basis for such a function lies in the possession of sensory neurons which are integrated into the neuronal system. This neuronal system is itself integrated with the body tissue and organ systems via the neuro-endocrine systems. Such integrative systems provide for the behavioral expressions of the whole organism.

This discussion of radical types as a basis for defining kingdoms certainly does not clear up all the problems in classifying all organisms. There are intergrades between the three proposed kingdoms which require clarification. This clarification may well require greater information and insight into the structural principles of each of the radical types. A couple of examples may be illustrative of these difficulties in classification. Some forms of green algae are multicellular but lack a high degree of tissue differentiation. An example is *Volvox*, which displays a certain type of colonial morphology. This is evidence of a certain degree of cell interaction. However, the cells in the colony apparently behave as essentially independent individuals, and not as members of a well-integrated system.[23] Thus *Volvox* and probably many forms of multicellular algae appear to lack a morphogenetic qualifying function and should be classified as protists. Similar problems are encountered with certain protozoa which possess a degree of motility and irritability. Although all organisms appear to possess some element of responsiveness to their environments, irritability indicates a particular mode of responsiveness leading to motility. This resembles a form of sensitivity displayed by animals. But such responsiveness is even displayed in a certain measure by plants such as *Mimosa* and by sperm cells of various plant forms. Perhaps this irritability displayed by such forms is simply anticipatory of the feeling-sensitivity aspect of animal forms of living things. This problem may be analogous to the consideration of the so-called "social life" of certain types of animals,[24] such as revealed, for example, in a beehive. But such an interaction is an expression of instinct under the guidance of the sensitive qualifying function of such organisms. This type of "social" behavior is not a response to the normative structural principles for social interaction evident in human life.

These problematic examples, however, do not necessarily destroy a system of classification. On the contrary, the structural principles for the radical types provide for a diversity of forms, some of which approach the limiting boundary of the radical type. The latter are then easily perceived as intergrades between radical types, even though they belong to one of the radical types. Such cases simply point to the need for further research which will enable us to define more precisely the structural principles which provide for the typical groupage of the radical types. I believe that Dooyeweerd's systematics

---

23. G. Kochert, "Colony Differentiation in Green Algae," *Developmental Regulation: Aspects of Cell Differentiation* (New York, 1973), pp. 155-68.

24. A. Portmann, *Animals as Social Beings* (New York, 1961), p. 246.

can serve as a basis for such ongoing research. One very positive feature of such an analysis is that it provides an alternative to an evolutionary explanation which is forced to explain biological principles of structure and function in terms of emergent properties of molecular interactions and organization. Such immanent thinking fails to give an adequate account of the existence of biological principles because it ignores or refuses to acknowledge the createdness of reality with its implications for the order and lawfulness through which God sustains the created world order.

ARIE LEEGWATER

Creation: Does It Matter?

ALL IS NOT WELL in the house of science and technology:

> Stinking rivers, filth in the air we breathe, omnipresent
> noise, the plunder of raw materials, weapons of devilish
> savagery—all these bear witness to the dark face of science
> and technology. Despite attempts by the experts to per-
> suade us that such horrors are merely temporary problems
> thrown up in the course of progress, people have recently
> begun to rebel. The products and processes of science and
> technology are under sustained attack. Yet, seen on a
> broader canvas, there are even more serious allegations
> against science on a different level altogether. The crucial
> criticism—all the more potent because we are seldom con-
> sciously aware of the case that supports it—is of the extent
> to which science dominates our lives, our "world-view,"
> habits of thought, human relationships, and values—our
> entire cradle-to-grave existence.[1]

Within modern humanism a schizophrenic attitude towards science
is becoming increasingly manifest. A perpetual oscillation between a
religion (faith) of science and a religion of anti-science, between a
trust in rationality and irrational myths, between objective and subjective views of science, seems inescapable. Witness the difference in

---

1.   B. Dixon, *What Is Science For?* (New York, 1974), p. 165.

points of view between Philip Handler, President of the National Academy of Science, and Paul Feyerabend, philosopher of science. In a recent essay entitled "*In Praise of Science,*" Handler states:

Our current malaise stems from a few bad experiences—from time-delay in meeting the high hopes and expectations raised in the minds of those who appreciate the great power of science, the force of technology. Those expectations have taken on a new light as science has also revealed *the true condition of man on earth...*I retain my faith that the science that has revealed the most awesome and profound beauties we have yet beheld is also the principal tool that our civilization has developed to mitigate the condition of man.[2]

Paul Feyerabend, by contrast, asserts:

Given science, reason cannot be universal and unreason cannot be excluded. This peculiar feature of the development of science strongly supports an anarchistic epistemology. But science is not sacrosanct. The restrictions it imposes (and there are many such restrictions though it is not easy to spell them out) are not necessary in order to have general coherent and successful views about the world. There are myths, there are the dogmas of theology, there is metaphysics, and there are many other ways of constructing a world-view. It is clear that a fruitful exchange between science and such "non-scientific" world-views will be in even greater need of anarchism than science itself. Thus anarchism is not only *possible*, it is *necessary* both for the internal progress of science and for the development of our culture as a whole. And, Reason, at last, joins all those other abstract monsters such as Obligation, Duty, Morality, Truth and their more

---

2.   P. Handler, "Edison Electric Institute Symposium" (supplement to *New York Review of Books*, Sept. 27, 1979), p. 15—italics mine.

concrete predecessors, the gods, which were once used to intimidate man and restrict his free and happy development: it withers away....[3]

Such divergent opinions about the role of science in our lives and its proper methods may set us to thinking. Must we choose between these two points of view? *How* do we choose? In the light of which norm or principle? Should we choose a middle way (a *via media*)? Should we encourage efforts to humanize science, to establish a science with a human face?

The Christian scientist faces an even more pressing question—the question of Christian scholarship. It is said the sciences are in search of truth or truths; yet at the same time one knows that one is in the grip of the one who said: "I am the Way, the Truth, and the Life." I am thinking of that tremendous revelation of Jesus in John 8, "If you continue in my Word, you are truly my disciples, and you will know the Truth and the Truth will make you free." And so you seem to land in another dilemma. Need we choose between the claims of science and the claims of Christ? May we give to science with our left hand and to Christ with our right (as long as we know what we are giving)? Must we choose a middle way?

My thesis, in short, is this: Stating the problem as a choice between the truth or (truths) of science and the Truth Christ imparts is improper and distorts the issue since it assumes a position or stance which (1) is insufficiently critical of the nature and fabric of science and (2) does not do justice to the Scriptural meaning of creation. I intend to develop this thesis by examining the topic of subjectivity and objectivity in science. Such an approach may seem indirect, but it will lead to the heart of the matter: Does Creation Matter?

3.　P. Feyerabend, *Against Method* (London, 1978), p. 180.

A distinguishing mark of our culture has been its "devotion to the objectivity of true knowledge." We are said to live in a scientific age in which science is the approved form of objective knowing and research the best way of discovering the nature of the (supposed) independently existing world. Consequently, control of this world (nature) is most effective if we apply the methods and discoveries of science. Frederick Wagner expresses it eloquently:

> The faith in progress, having become a faith in scientific in-vestigation (research), undergirds that religion of science which today rules the world and everywhere awakens hopes and expectations. This religion of science is no religious sub-stitute, as the enthusiasm for sports is, but a substitute reli-gion, that is, a binding and determining force in life…This science took over the mission ideal, indeed, the idea of sal-vation of Christianity, whose ecclesiastical ties and truth of revelation she eliminated, until she herself finally appeared as Revelation.[4]

Our initial reaction could be that indeed scientism—a religion of science—in any form, whether it be an unquestioned confidence in method or an abiding trust in scientific results, is to be dis-couraged and declared historically out-of-date. We have learned from our "mistakes," and the history of science has been our teacher. But what of the idea that science presents us with *objec-tive* knowledge? How one applies scientific discoveries or how one interprets various facts may differ, but science *qua* science rests on hard, "brute" facts, and thus our knowledge is well grounded—grounded objectively.

---

4.   F. Wagner, *Die Wissenschaft und die gefährdete Welt*, second edition (Munich, 1969), p. 56—translation mine.

Objective View of Science: "Newtonian" Methodology

To a large extent, eighteenth-century thought was dominated by the concept of the "Newtonian" world-machine. God, the master clockmaker, had designed a universe so perfect that it could run almost indefinitely without any need for external adjustment and fine-tuning. An examination of Newton's own writings will show that he was actually opposed to this concept, which had been popularized by earlier writers such as René Descartes and Robert Boyle. Newton had at least two objections. The first objection rested on physical grounds: the existence of irreversible processes and gravitational perturbations requires a God who is actively involved with his handiwork. The second appealed to theological arguments: any move to restrict God to the creation and design of the world while denying his continual supervision was a step on the road to atheism.

The development of a seemingly objective science drew its impetus in large measure from Newton's methodological writings and his emphasis on the "certainty" of mathematics. Despite Newton's reservations and protestations, other eighteenth-century theorists pressed his mathematical principles of natural philosophy into the far corners of physical science. Decisive results in planetary and lunar astronomy, elasticity, fluid dynamics, electrostatics, and so forth increased the commonly shared confidence in the mechanistic world view. At one point Lagrange described *Principia* of Newton as the greatest production of the human mind. Indeed, Newton was most fortunate, "for there is but one universe, and it can happen to but one man in world's history to be interpreter of its laws."

Permit me to give one example. When Newton (and the Newtonians of the eighteenth-century) objected to Descartes' use of hypotheses and the physical content of Descartes' physics, they usually emphasize what they perceive as weaknesses in methodology. Newton's "mathematical" method of analysis provided a more certain way than those who use a method of "confutation of contrary suppositions."

> "If without deriving the properties of things from Phaenomena you feign Hypotheses and think by them to explain all nature, you may make a plausible systeme of Philosophy for getting yourself a name, but your systeme will be little better than a Romance. To explain all nature is too difficult a task for any one man or even for any one age...Tis much better to do a little with certainty & leave the rest for others that come after you than to explain all things by conjecture without making sure of any thing."[5]

Newton's method of analysis, as he himself indicates, created the possibility of breaking down (resolving) the complex texture of physical phenomena into several isolated problem areas. One could definitely proceed in a step-by-step fashion.

In the structure of the *Principia*, it is easy to spot this emphasis on piecemeal and limited inquiry. In examining "the system of the world," Newton deliberately isolated certain factors and neatly side-stepped others of which he was ignorant. Newton actually had little more insight into the mechanism or nature of operation of gravitation than did Descartes. But unlike Descartes, he forced himself to refrain from making hypotheses and restricted his attention to "exploiting" the mathematical aspects of what he perceived to be the relevant factors, such as the idea of central forces operating between celestial bodies. Even the mathematical description begins in a most abstract and limited way and then is later extended to more complicated situations. Newton, for example, begins with an immutable central attracting body and a planet (idealized as a mass-point) orbiting in a

---

5. I. Newton, Cambridge University Library, MS. Add 3970 (5), as quoted by H. Guerlac, *Essays and Papers in the History of Modern Science* (Baltimore, 1977), p. 206.

plane; extends this picture to two bodies attracting each other with each free to move about the center of gravity of the system; introduces a third perturbing body; treats the moving objects not as mass-points but as homogeneous spheres; and finally treats them as having some non-spheroidal character.

The emphasis by Newton on the *Mathematical* Principles *of Natural Philosophy* (rather than the *Principles of Philosophy*) did not force him to draw the conclusion that the heliocentric system was a calculating device in the manner common to previous astronomical hypotheses; for him it was indeed the "true system of the world" because he regarded Kepler's laws as being deduced from the phenomena and made general by induction. This particular method of analysis and synthesis, although moderated and held in check by Newton's insistence on a God who acts, soon knew no barriers.

The scientifically knowable world was increasingly conceived as an extended aggregation of material (or mass) points which moved in the spatial "field" in accordance with fixed laws. The trajectories of these points were fixed, determined by forces dependent solely upon their position and mass. Accordingly, the objective world was a vast machine thoroughly characterized by primary spatial and mechanical properties.

Although this mechanical world was the object (*par excellence*) of scientific knowledge, it was conceived as being altogether alien to, and mutually exclusive of, the knowing subject. Yet somehow the mind had to become aware of its presence and nature. The relationship between them was therefore represented as one of transmission of representative "ideas." These "ideas" were often simplified to sensations, which provided the primary channel of communication between the external material world and the mind of the scientist.

The objectivity of science, therefore, rested not only on its mathematical reasoning with its inherent certainty but also upon its reference to empirically perceived data. These indubitable pillars would guarantee the construction of an edifice of "value-free" scientific knowledge. Interpretation and valuation were essentially external to scientific knowledge.

Marjorie Grene, in her telling criticism of "the faith of Darwinism," makes a similar point, although it is expressed more elegantly. She asks why the neo-Darwinian (read: synthetic) theory of evolution has such staying power. Her answer:

> Because neo-Darwinism is not only a scientific theory, and a comprehensive, seemingly self-confirming theory, but a theory deeply embedded in a metaphysical faith; in the faith that science can and must explain all the phenomena of nature in terms of one hypothesis, and that an hypothesis of maximum simplicity, of maximum impersonality and objectivity. Relatively speaking, neo-Darwinism is logically simple: there are just two things happening, chance variations, and the elimination of the worst ones among them; and both these happenings are just plain facts, things that *do* or *don't* happen, *yes* or *no*. Nature is like a vast computing machine set up in binary digits; no mystery there. And —what man has not yet achieved—the machine is self-programmed: it began by chance, it continues automatically, its master plan itself creeping up on itself, so to speak, by means of its own automatism. Again, no mystery there; man seems at home in a simply rational world.[6]

This vaunted objectivity of science—*the myth of the objective consciousness*, as Theodore Roszak calls it—has come under increasing attack, both from *within* the scientific community and from *without*.

---

6. M. Grene, *The Knower and the Known* (Berkeley, 1974), pp. 199-200.

Attack from Within

During much of the nineteenth-century, physical scientists were thought to be studying an objective physical world, a physical reality independent of the mind of the investigator. At the same time, however, there was a slow transition from this "realistic" position to one in which the knowing subject plays a more central, determinative, and active role. Immanuel Kant had already formulated its manifesto in the preface to the second edition of the *Critique of Pure Reason*:

> "When Galileo let his balls run down an inclined plane with a gravity which he had chosen himself; when Torricelli caused the air to sustain a weight which he had calculated beforehand to be equal to that of a column of water of known height;…then a light dawned upon all natural philosophers. They learnt that our reason can understand only what it creates according to its own design; that we must compel Nature to answer our questions, rather than cling to Nature's apron strings and allow her to guide us."[7]

In the course of this development, natural things became increasingly "denatured." Descartes and Newton would still maintain that physical entities had an independent existence determined by their spatial extension. For Kant, however, they became *Dinge an sich* (things in themselves, in principle unknowable). In nineteenth century positivism they became reduced to mere appearances. Natural laws suffered a similar fate and were perceived in turn as *a priori* and transcendental by Kant, as general facts by Comte, as merely economical by Mach, and as conventional by Poincaré.

An investigation of nineteenth-century physical science, especially the atomic debates, reveals the tensions and struggles concern-

---

7. For this specific translation, see K. Popper, *Conjectures and Refutations* (New York, 1968), p. 189.

ing the proper "aim and structure" of physical theory.[8] Are atomic theories to assume "objective" mechanical foundations which presuppose the existence of interacting quantities of matter (atoms with mass), or must theories be indifferent to the ontic existence of atoms since they are not directly observed? The latter course was pursued by Mach and Ostwald, who sought to establish physical laws on energetic (thermodynamic) foundations, and by many positivistically inspired chemists who preferred to describe chemical transformations in terms of equivalents and volumes of reagents rather than atomic weights.

One brief contemporary illustration of this shift in focus and its repercussions will have to suffice. A subjectivist interpretation of science comes to vivid expression in textbooks which incorporate an operational viewpoint when introducing physical concepts. What stands central and unassailable is the observer and his operations. Symbols, such as the electric field strength E, or concepts such as length, only have physical meaning if a method of measuring them is defined by a set of laboratory procedures. The purpose of measurement is therefore to assign meanings. Accordingly, physical laws, which are relationships among these operationally defined quantities, reflect our subjective knowledge rather than some objective structure of the external world. This subjectivist position, particularly enshrined in some interpretations of quantum mechanics, has come under recent attack by critical realists such as Mario Bunge and Karl Popper.[9]

---

8.   See *The Atomic Debates: Brodie and the Rejection of the Atomic Theory*, edited by W. H. Brock (Leicester, 1967), and M. J. Nye, "The Nineteenth-Century Atomic Debates and the Dilemma of an Indifferent Hypothesis," *Studies in History and Philosophy of Science*, 7 (1976), pp. 245-68.

9.   See *Quantum Theory and Reality*, edited by Mario Bunge (New York, 1967) and Mario Bunge, *Philosophy of Physics* (Dordrecht, 1973). For a recent analysis of operationalism in general physics textbooks from a dialectical materialist viewpoint, see, for example, E. Marquit,

Attack from Without

The objectivity of science has also come under attack from outside the scientific community, particularly by historians and philosophers of science. Many of these critics were at one time physicists, such as Thomas S. Kuhn, Karl Popper, and Paul Feyerabend, or engineers, such as Ludwig Wittgenstein. There has been a deliberate turn to the history of science and to specific case studies. An appeal to history is not very popular with most practicing scientists. It tends to call into question and destroy prevalent professional self-interests and the public image of science as moving ever rationally and methodically from one truth to another. This image is well described by C. Kittel et al. in *The Berkeley Physics Course*:

> Through experimental science we have been able to learn all these facts about the natural world, triumphing over darkness and ignorance to classify the stars and to estimate their masses, composition, distances, and velocities; to classify living species and unravel their genetic relations...These great accomplishments of experimental science were achieved by men of many types...Most of these men had in common only a few things: they were honest and actually made the observations they recorded, and they published the results of their work in a form permitting others to duplicate the experiment or observation.[10]

Thomas Kuhn has argued convincingly that the textbook presentation of science and its development is skewed. The development of science is not unilinear, or cumulative, or the result of a process of accretion, but is rather the result of the struggle and clash between

"Philosophy of Physics in General Physics Courses," *American Journal of Physics*, 46 (1978), No. **8**, pp. **784-89**.

10. C. Kittel, W. D. Knight, M. A. Ruderman, *The Berkeley Physics Course*, Vol. 1: *Mechanics* (New York, 1962), p. 4.

conflicting paradigms or disciplinary matrices. These paradigms are historically modifiable presuppositions about Nature which enter into the very scientific activity itself. Furthermore, this subjective, arbitrary element cannot be logically parsed. In short, Kuhn stresses the subjective side to scientific work at the expense of objectivity.

As a result of this questioning, scientific certainty appears to be an unattainable goal, and a literal description of nature has become a naive hope. Scientific knowledge does not grow in a cumulative manner, nor can it be unified into a complete and consistent axiomatic system. The norms of mathematical rationality and empirical testability—which were assumed to undergird classical mechanics and guarantee its objectivity—are rather imposed on science and found to be wanting.[11] This recent approach views science as a creative human activity requiring a wide variety of techniques and interpretative skills. Science cannot be reduced to a foundationalist autonomy, but is dependent on a wider context of meaning and ideas. The newness of this approach does not reside in the discovery of a history of science, important as that may be, but rather in the questioning of the assumed objectivity of rationality as it operates in the natural sciences.

Some would argue that this recent development offers new possibilities for the coexistence and mutual concern of science and the Christian faith. The arguments proffered are often these: (1) The inability of science to attain *certainty* (true objectivity) supports the Christian view of man's *finiteness*. (2) The recognition of other than *intellectual* (read: rational) factors in the development of science supports a positive role for *faith*.

---

11. The development of classical chemistry, for example, clearly reveals the debilitating effects of these norms. For a discussion of eighteenth- and early nineteenth-century chemistry, see A. Thackeray, *Atoms and Powers: An Essay on Newtonian Matter-Theory and the Development of Chemistry* (Cambridge, Massachusetts, 1970).

The assertion that science is riddled with uncertainties and is therefore deficient and in need of a higher certainty (a certainty from above?) can be easily answered by a modern humanist. Granted we may need a measure of certainty, but why look for it outside the arena of science? The uncertainties of life and even those in science itself need not be cause for *Angst*. One merely has to shift one's allegiance away from ever-changing scientific results to scientific methodology. Uncertainty can play a positive role if we appropriate the method of science. Uncertainty becomes the arbitrary element which prevents scientific theories from becoming ossified. How else would scientific change be possible?

Recall John Dewey's famous statement on scientific method in his book *A Common Faith*:

> There is but one sure road of access to truth—the road of patient, cooperative inquiry operating by means of observation, experiment, record and controlled reflection.[12]

This scientific method has become a source of *revelation*. It is seen as:
the *only* method in pursuit of truth(s)
the method *common* to all men
the method applicable to all problem-*situations*
the method is a *process* (truth is in the making, it is dynamic.
We never possess it as immutable, absolute or
    (*a priori*)
the method is *self-corrective*
the method is *open* and *public*.

Science is therefore never a finished (static) body of knowledge, a dogma with specific doctrines, but rather a *way-of-knowing*, an open-ended process of inquiry, a question of know-how (technique).

And what about those "other" factors in this recent effort to humanize science and tell it "like it really is within the scientific com-

---

12. J. Dewey, *A Common Faith* (New Haven, 1969), p. 32.

munity"? Granted, this (new) historical perspective allows more factors—sociological, political, religious beliefs, cultural *Zeitgeister*,
etc.—to play a role in the development of science. But does this turn
to the concrete person (or social group) in real life situations add
anything substantive to our discussion? Is it indeed a plus point
that religious opinions and commitments may be allowed to play
a role as factors and add their own peculiar language to the scientific enterprise? If it becomes a question of many factors (truths)—
Christian and scientific, the partial truths of theology and the partial
truths of science, irrational and rational, etc.—all of these may appear to be disparate elements. But shouldn't these elements or factors
form a coherence, and are they not experienced as such? In other
words, we are persistently driven back to the ordering principle of all
of these factors.[13]

Restatement

Are we forced to choose between a *subjective* view of science and an
objective view of science, between a point of view that recognizes
many factors which find their point of integration in the subject and
one that speaks of objective reality—physical reality, if you will? Is
there a third way which somehow harmonizes these divergent points
of view? Expressing the problem as a choice between a subjective and
an objective point of view presupposes the legitimacy of placing the
following in opposition: fact/interpretation; fact/value; explanation/
meaning; objective given/subjective commitment; scientific result/
non-scientific extra; object/subject. As long as the problem is posed
in this manner, we will never, in my opinion, escape the dialectical

---

13. For a recent discussion of these various factors and an appeal to the
concept of *Kulturwissenschaft* as a means of integrating these aspects,
see M. J. S. Rudwick, "The History of the Natural Sciences as Cultural
History" (Amsterdam: Vrije Universiteit Inaugureele Rede, May
23, 1975).

movements between a subjective and objective point of view, despite our best efforts at harmonization. On the one hand we will remain uncomfortable with the view of a totally objective science—with a view, that is, of scientific knowledge as a cumulative march towards the truth. And on the other hand we will continue to deplore the emphasis on the relativism and anarchism seen in many recent analyses of science (see the work of Kuhn and Feyerabend).

Both of these positions assume, in one way or another, the power and self-assured status of the knowing subject and man's ability to understand Nature, which is conceived of as an independent, self-contained "intelligible" reality. The quarrel is a battle within a humanistic interpretation of science. It is a battle we should understand, but refuse to take sides in.

Is there a solution to this impasse? As I already mentioned, we are in need of an ordering principle, a point of coherence, in which and through which all the various factors derive their meaning. Our scientific activity and our everyday life should be of one piece. We wish to experience wholehearted lives, undivided in our commitments. Such efforts at integration do not stand on their own, but are rather nourished by a deeper unity—an order which comes to us as revelation from God's good hand. And so I wish to appeal to the Biblical view of creation, that is, to creation which reveals God's normative good order and will for our lives from the beginning.

This emphasis on creation is not an extra factor, one among many, but is rather an expression of our human condition. Man stands in Covenant with God and responds in one way or another to God's revelation in creation. Creation is both norm and condition for man. It is norm in the sense that it is a good order, God's will for life, for Shalom. We indeed live in a God-ordered world. That revelation is as bright as the sun, as near to us as the falling rain, and as down-to-earth as the farmer's agricultural practices mentioned in Isaiah 28:23-29.

God, in the beginning, ordered how everything should be, down to the minutest detail. The laws and ordinances—the ways things function and develop—all these originate and are faithfully maintained by Yahweh, the Faithful One, the God of Abraham, Isaac, and Jacob. God's *provide*-ence is sure; it can be counted on from every sunrise to sunset. It takes the Bible to tell us the Truth about the sun, i.e., that it is a servant of the Lord (Psalm 19). The sun is not so much a matter of fact—an astronomical object with certain spatial dimensions, a particular angular momentum, luminosity, or elemental composition—but is a minister for our good. The Bible does not give us some extra information, an additional truth about the sun which we can store or file away for future use. Rather, it reveals to us the Truth—Truth which calls for response and leaves us without excuse (Romans 1).

The way of sowing caraway seeds, the proper method of harvesting wheat, the orbital path of the sun, the erosion of rocks—all of these natural creaturely things are not isolated facts waiting for some supernatural heavenly meaning. Meaning and facts simply do not stand next to each other as complements, but are given together. Meaning and factuality are of one piece. The God who puts his Law to the creation and called it into existence is faithful to his Law. Sin does not abrogate God's good intentions for his creation. Christ, by whom and for whom all things were created and "in whom all the treasures of knowledge and wisdom are hid," has come to redeem the creation, to restore it to its proper end, that is, to its full and manifest disclosure of meaning. That path of disclosure goes by the way of suffering and even death, but it anticipates triumph—a new heaven and a new earth.

The centrality of creation revelation for our work in the sciences has received too little attention. Yet it is fundamental to any Christian scientific enterprise or any responsible analysis of the history of science. Certainly more can and should be said than that this revelation is not in conflict with God's revelation in the Scriptures. Adjectives such as *non-deceptive* and *non-contradictory* are far too limited. Besides, such arguments are very old and carry the stains of a medieval scholastic discussion. Galileo, for example, made ample use of them in his famous letter to the Grand Duchess Christina of Tuscany in 1615. I would like to list some positive themes which flow from a Biblical view of creation.

(1) The whole of reality, including man, is the creation of the sovereign Lord. Basic to any understanding of reality is a recognition of its created, temporal, dependent character. Nothing in reality is self-contained or self-sufficient. Nature, in the Biblical sense, does not denote some material substance(s) or, in the sense of Mother Nature, but "is an order established by God within which all his works are enacted" (Diemer). Nature is as extensive as created reality. This emphasis undercuts all sacred/secular distinctions and approaches to reality. There is not a normal *natural* course of events (deterministically or indeterministically conceived) which God has to occasionally interrupt or break through in special *spiritual* acts of Grace. Grace renews Nature; it does not abrogate or annul Nature.

(2) Creation is an integral whole. It is not a chaos or a void, but a place to be inhabited (Isaiah 45). Man is the crown of creation, and all creatures, great and small, are interrelated and interdependent. Man is at home in the creation, which he is called to develop, cultivate, and preserve. This coherence and unity are reflected, for example, in the interdependence of physical theories and in the relationships between sound scientific insights and an appropriate technology.

(3) Laws, principles, ordinances are in the first instance God's Will or Word for his creation. They hold for reality and undergird it, but are not coincident with it. When we speak of a physical law such as the law of gravity, we are usually referring to our formulation, our response to God's revelation for the structured interaction of physical

subjects. Our responses and formulations are more or less accurate, more or less correct, and do in fact change in time. This approach relativizes our work in the sciences without causing us to fall prey to historical relativism; that is, it accounts for the provisional character of science without succumbing to a viewpoint which denies all structural features or holds that any discussion of structural matters can at best be heuristic or pragmatically useful. This is also a liberating perspective. We work in the sure confidence that God is faithful to what he has made, and thus we do not have to dogmatically retain our theories at all costs. Change in our theories is not at bottom a conflict between different scientific paradigms, but a result of man's changing response to God's impinging revelation.

(4) Human response to God's (general) revelation in creation is directed to God or some idol substitute. The antithesis, which cuts through all our lives, also divides our scientific practice. But I can almost hear you ask: Don't all men, Christian and non-Christian alike, live in the same created reality, and isn't there a measure of agreement on many matters of detail, particularly in mathematics and the physical sciences? Doesn't two times two equal four for everyone? Surely we can agree on the facts; it is just a matter of differing interpretations. The Christian simply knows something extra that the non-Christian does not, namely, that the facts are God-created and God-interpretable. Aren't scientific and theological descriptions of reality complementary?

A proper view of creation, I think, undermines this line of argument. The apparent commonness and agreement in matters of technical detail are not attributable to *our* excellent insight into reality, but are rather an indication of the overpowering nature of God's revelation. Nor does the commonness preclude deep religious and philosophical conflicts which extend to matters of definition, to questions of proper methodology, and even to what the facts are. Witness the struggles during the transition from medieval mechanics to Galilean mechanics, the differences concerning the ontic status of atoms in the nineteenth-century, the questions surrounding the wave/particle duality in quantum physics, or the sociobiology debates of the last few years.

These few positive points should be handled with care. Indeed, if you are looking for handy formulas or recipes for practicing science Christianly, or if you somehow believe that a set of rules can be drawn up which will insure a Christian science, you have missed the thrust of my remarks. The heart of the Christian scientific enterprise is first of all not science and its (tentative) results, but rather the Truth (the Revelation) by which science is to be practiced. That Truth cannot be objectified, pointed to, or put down on paper. Rather, it is the source of renewal and the horizon of our life in all its multiplicity of actions.

Appendix

ALL CHRISTOCENTRIC AND CHRISTOLOGICAL interpretations of the Old Testament deserve mention and scrutiny in this context. However, some also deserve an equally careful affirmation since there remains without dispute the unavoidable fact of the overarching Christic perspective on all things that is introduced into the canon by the inclusion of the New Testament. (Though this may mean that the *means* of all true knowledge of God is Scripture and Jesus Christ, the *rex et dominus scripturae*, this does not mean that Jesus Christ is the sole *content* of scriptural revelation. As Calvin well knew, the unity of revelation is to be found in God in the establishment of his covenant with us and his kingdom among us.) Exactly how the Christic perspective should be related to the Old Testament (whether through the model of promise in the Old and fulfillment in the New, or whatever) is, of course, a matter of dispute. However, with van Ruler I think it safe to say that it is better to proceed with caution and reserve than to dash into the Old with the effort to squeeze it all through the bottleneck of Christology.

Van Ruler cites at least four Christological theories which merit his opposition to one degree or another. He mentions the dominant Catholic view that "the Old Testament [is]…a providential preparation in earthly history for the supernatural Christian salvation first disclosed in Christ and his church." In addition he mentions typological interpretation that sees in Old Testament figures and events an anticipatory proclamation of the things of Christ. (I am personally not convinced—as some van Ruler readers seem to be (Vriezen,

Essays, p. 212)—that van Ruler is closed to any and every typological kind of Old Testament interpretation.) Furthermore, allegorization is criticized severely as a negation of the theological meaningfulness of historical and earthly reality. Finally, van Ruler expresses reservations about the salvation-historical perspective that views the Old Testament as concealing what the New progressively reveals to fullness and clarity (*The Christian Church and the Old Testament*, Grand Rapids, 1970, pp. 12-13).

In the body of this essay I have chosen to deal only with Barth because his work has been so influential and because his universal Christic perspective, though a colossal accomplishment, is based upon the—in my judgment—false assumption that the existence of the world and the Old Testament vision of life can be centered directly on God in every area it must be seen as having its foundation in a divine orientation toward redemption. In brief, Barth has done more than any other modern theologian to flesh out the implications of a universal Christic perspective that presupposes the logical as well as ontological priority of redemption over creation. Besides the argument I present with respect to this in the body of the paper, for a textual example from Barth of the assertion of creation's logical and ontological non-independence in relation to redemption, see *Church Dogmatics*, III/1 (Edinburgh, 1966), pp. 228-329.

Index of Names

Contributors

1. John H. Gerstner:

Formerly, until his retirement, Professor of Church History, Pittsburgh Theological Seminary. Presently, Professor at large for Ligonier Valley Study Center, Visiting Professor at Trinity Evangelical Divinity School, and Lecturer in Bible at Geneva College. He recently has authored *Jonathan Edwards on Heaven and Hell* (Baker, 1980). He holds the Ph.D. from Harvard University.

2. Robert D. Knudsen:

Presently, Associate Professor of Apologetics, Westminster Theological Seminary. He has recently authored *History: The Encounter of Christianity with Secular Science* (Mack Publishing Co., 1976). He is also presently Editor-in-Chief for *The Collected Works of Herman Dooyeweerd*. He holds the Th.D. from the Free University of Amsterdam and the Th.B. and Th.M. from Westminster Seminary.

3. Arie Leegwater:

Presently, Associate Professor of Chemistry, Calvin College; formerly, Assistant Professor of Chemistry, Trinity College, Palos Heights, Illinois. He holds the Ph.D. from Ohio State University.

4. Richard J. Mouw:

Presently, Professor of Philosophy, Calvin College and visiting lecturer, Juniata College. He has authored *Political Evangelism* (Eerdmans, 1976). *Politics and the Biblical Drama* (Eerdmans, 1976), and *Called to Holy Worldliness* (Fortress, 1980). He holds the Ph.D. from the University of Chicago.

5. Theodore Plantinga:

Presently, Assistant Professor of Philosophy, Calvin College; formerly, Editor, Paideia Press, St. Catharines, Ontario. He has authored *Historical Understanding in the Thought of Wilhelm Dilthey* (University of Toronto Press, 1980), *Rationale for a Christian College* (Paideia Press, 1980), and *Reading the Bible as History* (Welch, 1980). He holds the Ph.D. from the University of Toronto.

6. M. Howard Rienstra:

Presently, Professor of History, Calvin College and Commissioner of the City of Grand Rapids. Recently he has authored "Christianity and History: A Bibliographical Essay," in *A Christian View of History* (Eerdmans, 1975) and "History, Objectivity, and the Christian Scholar," *Fides et Historia* X (Fall, 1977). He holds the Ph.D. from the University of Michigan.

7. Peter A. Schouls:

Presently, Professor of Philosophy, University of Alberta. He has authored *Insight, Authority, and Power: A Biblical Appraisal* (Wedge, 1972) and more recently *The Imposition of Method, A Study of Descartes and Locke* (Oxford University Press, 1980). He holds the Ph.D. from the University of Toronto.

8. James W. Skillen:

Presently, Associate Professor of Political Science, Dordt College and Research Director of the Association for Public Justice (APJ). He has authored *Christians Organizing for Political Service* (APJ, 1980) and *International Politics and the Demand for Global Justice* (Dordt College Press, 1981). He holds the M.Div. from Westminster Seminary and the Ph.D. from Duke University.

9. Gordon J. Spykman:

Presently, Professor of Religion and Theology, Calvin College. He has authored *Christian Faith in Focus* (Baker, 1970), and a study of

Albertus Van Raalte entitled *Pioneer Preacher* (CRC, 1976). He holds the B.D. from Calvin Theological Seminary and the Th.D. from the Free University of Amsterdam.

10. Alan Storkey:

Presently, Visiting Fellow, Calvin Center for Christian Scholarship, Calvin College. Formerly of Workshop College, England, and Director of the Shaftesbury Project. He has authored *A Christian Social Perspective* (I.V.P., 1979). He holds the M.A. and Dip.Ed. from the London School of Economics.

11. Henry Vander Goot:

Presently, Associate Professor of Religion and Theology, Calvin College. He has authored "Religion and Culture in the Early Schleiermacher," in *Hearing and Doing* (Wedge, 1979), edited *Creation and Gospel* (Edwin Mellen, 1979) and *Creation and Method* (University Press of America, 1981). He holds the M.Div. from Princeton Theological Seminary and the Ph.D. from St. Michael's College of the University of Toronto.

12. Johan van der Hoeven:

Presently, Professor of Philosophy, the Free University of Amsterdam. He has authored *Heidegger en de geschiedenis der wijsbegeerte* (Buijten en Schipperheijn, 1963), *Karl Marx: The Roots of his Thought* (Wedge, 1976), and *Christelijk Perspectief, 27* (Buijten en Schipperheijn, 1980). He holds the Ph.D. from the University of Leiden.

13. Cornelis Veenhof:

Until 1946, a well-known pastor in the Gereformeerde Kerk of the Netherlands. In 1946 he became Professor of Practical Theology at Kampen (Vrijgemaakte Kerk). Presently he is retired from that post and is a member of the Nederlandse Gereformeerde Kerk (Buiten Verband). He has authored *Om de 'unica catholica'* (Oosterbaan en Le

Cointre, 1949), *Prediking en Uitverkiezing* (Kok, 1959), *Volk van God* (Buijten en Schipperheijn, 1969), and *Kerkgemeenschap en Kerkorde* (Buijten en Schipperheijn, 1974).

14. Albert M. Wolters:

Presently, Senior Fellow in Philosophy, Institute for Christian Studies, Toronto. He has authored *Our Place in the Philosophical Tradition* (1977) and holds the Ph.D. from the Free University of Amsterdam.

15. Bernard Zylstra:

Presently, Principal of the Institute for Christian Studies in Toronto. He has authored *From Pluralism to Collectivism: The Development of Harold Laski's Political Thought* (1968) and edited *Contours of a Christian Philosophy: An Introduction to Herman Dooyeweerd's Thought* (Wedge, 1975), and *Roots of Western Culture: Pagan, Secular, and Christian Options* (Wedge, 1979). He holds a B.D. from Calvin Theological Seminary, LL.B. from the University of Michigan Law School, and the S.J.D. from the Free University of Amsterdam.

16. Uko Zylstra:

Presently, Associate Professor of Biology, Calvin College. He has authored "Ecological Aspects of Food Production: Biblical Directives for Agriculture," in proceedings, *AuSable Forum*—1980, and "Ultrastructure, Histology, and Innervation of the Mantle Edge of the Freshwater Pulmonate Snails *Lumnaea stagnalis* and *Biomphalaria pfeifferi,*" *Calcified Tissue Research* 26, (1978). He holds the Ph.D. from the Free University of Amsterdam.

ABOUT THE CÁNTARO INSTITUTE

Inheriting, Informing, Inspiring

Cántaro Institute is a reformed evangelical organization committed to advancing the Christian worldview for the reformation and renewal of the church and culture.

We believe that as the Christian church returns to the fount of the Scriptures as its ultimate authority for all knowledge and life, and wisely applies God's truth to every aspect of life, its missiological activity will result not only in the renewal of the human person but also in the reformation of culture—an inevitable outcome when the true scope and nature of the gospel are made known and applied.